W9-CSA-795

To Beverly,
May your dreams come true

Randal Cherevbl

"In *Become the Dream* Randal Churchill provides innovative approaches to combining hypnosis and dreamwork in support of therapeutic goals, which simultaneously encourages integration of conscious and unconscious processes in service of honoring the whole person. The generous inclusion of verbatim case history transcripts vividly underscores the significance of the client/therapist relationship in any counseling situation. The dialogues are particularly interesting and valuable in illustrating how much the client (and the client's unconscious resources) contributes to the therapeutic process."

Joseph P. Reel, Ph.D., Dir., Hypnosis Career Institute, Albuquerque, N.M.

"Randal Churchill's caring style and humor provide an added dimension to this inspiring and pioneering work. *Become the Dream* illuminates the personal and existential relationship of the dream to the dreamer. Unlike interpretive dreamwork, the dream is re-experienced on a heart and soul level, where the subconscious mind reveals real dramas being played out in life. Connecting with the dreamer's own innate wisdom, Randal skillfully combines an eclectic array of techniques with gifted intuition to lead the dreamer to profound insights and personal transformation. It is truly a pleasure to read this innovative and non-analytical approach to dreamwork."

Cheryl Canfield, CHT, author of *Peace Pilgrim's Wisdom*

"*Become the Dream* is a clear and comprehensive guide to integrating hypnotherapy and Gestalt dreamwork. The book is filled with information on the best methods and techniques for working with dreams, hypnosis, regression and the subconscious mind. The detailed client stories, where actual dreams are explored in depth, make the book entertaining as well as enlightening."

Jim Dreaver, D.C., author of *The Ultimate Cure*

"Randal Churchill provides a crucial service for dreamworkers, hypnotherapists, and other professionals by writing an up-close and personal account of processing dreams, using the gentle yet potent combination of hypnotherapy and Gestalt dreamwork. In *Become the Dream* he presents his 25 years of pioneering work in a manner that makes the elusive and magical transformative process both believably real and reassuringly approachable. I highly recommend this book for anyone who offers process work professionally or for anyone curious as to whether their own dreams may be worth exploring."

Jill Gregory, Director, Dream Library & Archives, Novato, CA

About the Author

Randal Churchill is known as "Teacher of the Teachers,"™ having trained many of the state-approved hypnotherapy instructors in the United States. He is founder, director and instructor of the Hypnotherapy Training Institute in Corte Madera, near San Francisco, California. One of the oldest and largest state licensed hypnotherapy schools in the United States, HTI has drawn over 2000 students from around the world. The school is licensed by the Council for Private Postsecondary and Vocational Education of the California Board of Education, and approved by the Board of Registered Nursing and other state boards for Continuing Education Units. HTI is approved by the California Board of Behavioral Science Examiners, the Department of Vocational Rehabilitation and many other agencies.

A clinical hypnotherapist since 1969, Randal Churchill has logged over 25,000 hours of hypnotherapy sessions. He is a graduate of Sonoma State University, receiving his degree in psychology with honors. Randal holds a Teacher's Credential and is a former instructor of Santa Rosa Junior College. He is on the Advisory Board of the American Council of Hypnotist Examiners, on the Board of Directors of the Hypnotist Examining Council of California, and on the Professional Affairs and Ethics Committee of the Association for Humanistic Psychology.

Randal Churchill has received international acclaim for his skill, creativity, sensitivity and comprehensive approach to a wide range of challenging issues. An intuitive and supportive therapist, he is a specialist in dreamwork, regression, advanced ideomotor methods and the assimilation of Gestalt and other modalities with hypnotherapy. He has taught hypnotherapy to psychiatrists at Napa State Hospital and has taught at various other institutions. He has also been a featured speaker and workshop leader at many International Hypnotherapy Conferences.

Randal Churchill is the author of numerous published works on hypnotherapy, including *Regression Hypnotherapy* and *Churchill's Law*. He has been the subject of various television news documentaries and has been interviewed on many radio talk shows.

Become the Dream

Become the Dream

The Transforming Power
of Hypnotic Dreamwork

Randal Churchill

P.O.Box 9369
Santa Rosa, CA 95405

BECOME THE DREAM: The Transforming Power of Hypnotic Dreamwork
is printed on acid free, natural recycled paper with soy-based ink.

Transforming Press
P.O. Box 9369
Santa Rosa, CA 95405
Ph: 707-538-9669 Fax: 707-537-9547
email: TransformP@aol.com

ISBN 0-9656218-0-4

Library of Congress Catalog Card Number 97-60102

FIRST EDITION. Printed in the United States of America

10 9 8 7 6 5 4 3 2 1

To Paul Hawken
whose book, *The Ecology of Commerce*,
does so much to strengthen the dream
of restoring our Earth
and our future

Contents

Acknowledgments

My gratitude goes to the many people whose support has led to the publication of this book; what I give here is only a partial synopsis. First, there are no words to express my profound appreciation to my parents, Winston and Vera Churchill, who have given so much to me.

I am most grateful for the wonderful initial trainings and encouragement I received in hypnotherapy from Gil Boyne and in encounter groups and Gestalt dreamwork with Ann and Gil Boyne in the late sixties. I also appreciate Gil Boyne's frequent support and insights since, and all the leadership and contributions he has given to the profession of hypnotherapy.

I deeply appreciate the tremendous dedication Marleen Mulder has shown for many years as co-director of the Hypnotherapy Training Institute. Also, specifically, I thank her for being in charge of most of the videotaping that led to this book's transcripts.

I am grateful for all of my students and clients. In particular, the volunteers for therapy in class who, in baring their souls, have given so much to the classes through their trust and courage.

I wish to thank Pat Stone, Gary Beckwith, Debra Newlen and Tom Casey for their contributions to this book. I also appreciate the proofreading, ideas and enthusiasm of many hypnotherapists in the HTI Winter 1996-97 graduate programs.

I thank Jeff Blom and Richard Polese for donating their expertise so generously to this book. My gratitude also goes to Jan Shade and Carol Morse for their book production work, Brian Mouka for the cover design and David Cavagnaro for his butterfly slides and inspiring prolific work for the Earth. I am grateful for each of the endorsements, and give special thanks to Ormond McGill for his Foreword.

I cannot give enough appreciation for the enormous amount of excellent work done on all phases of this book by my editor, Cheryl Canfield. From her initial transcriptions to her organizational work, editing, book production and fine-tuning of the galley, her beneficial influence is found from cover to cover.

Foreword

Randal Churchill, originator of Hypnotic Dreamwork™, is a master clinician and instructor of this superlative form of therapy. In *Become the Dream: The Transforming Power of Hypnotic Dreamwork*, he draws from the non-analytical Gestalt perspective. Rather than interpret, Gestalt is based on experientially "becoming" aspects of the dream, acting out different parts, and then having various characters engage in dialogue.

What makes Randal Churchill's approach and this book unique and revolutionary in the field of dreamwork, is that he has combined Gestalt dreamwork with hypnotherapy, taking it to exciting new levels.

According to Gestalt dreamwork theory, every part of a dream (no matter what else it might be) is considered to be a projected part of the dreamer. For some, this aspect of Gestalt may at first require a leap of faith. Yet as the actual dreamwork transcripts reveal, even when it is initially difficult for the dreamer to act out a negative or unappealing character, encouraging continuation of the process can lead to insights in which a certain energy or strength of that character can be integrated in a positive way to empower the dreamer. Skillful use of Gestalt dialogue between dream characters are consistently discovered to be dialogues between parts of the individual regarding significant issues. In an eclectic approach, Randal Churchill weaves hypnotic deepening, suggestion and other hypnotic techniques into the dreamwork to further ground and integrate insights derived from Gestalt methods.

Trusting our own inner wisdom isn't always easy, but as the client is led through these processes it becomes clear that an important source of guidance can be found in dreams. Shamans, the earliest known dreamworkers, often obtained knowledge from what was called guiding spirits. Many natives still believe that power and knowledge is imparted by spirits in dreamtime. In *Become the Dream*, hypnotic methods are used to empower the dreamer by leading him or her into direct communication with his or her inner guidance to discover and uproot limiting personal myths or misconceptions.

Psychotherapist Rollo May said of dreams, "We can often get a more accurate and meaningful picture of the significant changes in the patient's life from the symbols and myths he creates and then molds and recreates in his dream existence than we can from what he says." Throughout these transcripts, Randal Churchill's supportive style and humor encourages trust and openness, assisting the dreamer to reach those deep inner resources.

Become the Dream integrates the fields of Gestalt dreamwork and hypnotherapy, based on original work the author has been developing since 1970. With the use of various hypnotic processes, the dreamwork evolves according to what emerges - at times spontaneously progressing, for example, from a Gestalt dialogue directly into a regression to help release the effects of an initial trauma that is relevant to a current life issue.

This is not a how-to book in the usual sense, as it is written from the perspective of an educator. Using his years of personal practice, as well as being Director and instructor of the Hypnotherapy Training Institute, Randal Churchill teaches hypnotherapists and professionals in the many health and counseling fields to enrich their own practices, making them even more effective.

The first two chapters of the book provide a foundation for understanding the potential value of hypnosis, hypnotherapy, Gestalt dreamwork, and the integration of these forms of therapy. Intriguing perspectives of the significance of direct contact with the subconscious mind are developed. The third chapter gives many insights regarding developing dream recall and lucid dream skills. From there the book focuses primarily on a superb collection of verbatim transcripts of actual sessions demonstrated within an audience of therapists and hypnotherapy students. A later chapter emphasizes the author's signature processes of elicited and guided hypnodreams. Care is given to help the reader toward a deeper understanding of these sessions through commentary by the author, selected questions and answers, and follow-up reflections from some of the dreamers.

Even the nonprofessional reader interested in personal growth through understanding the mystery of "the language of the night" can gain much from reading this very approachable book. Beyond techniques, the author's sensitive guidance and attention in the actual transcripts make for inspiring reading, sparking an awareness of the creative and healing potential in all of us. Through understanding gleaned as a result of Hypnotic Dreamwork, truth will out!

Randal Churchill is one of the most insightful and innovative practitioners in the field of hypnotherapy today. His integration of approaches to beneficially influence the subconscious mind is so clearly and compassionately demonstrated that this fascinating book is an important addition to the fields of dream therapy, hypnotism, Gestalt therapy and psychology. *Become the Dream* is a major breakthrough, a text of university and universal level, worthy of worldwide acclaim.

–Ormond McGill
Palo Alto, CA 1997

Ormond McGill is the author of 19 books, including *Hypnotism and Meditation*. In the field since 1927, he is known as "The Dean of American Hypnotists."

Author's Preface

Become the Dream is primarily designed as a teaching text for the use of Hypnotic Dreamwork™ in therapy. While it provides a basic introduction to hypnotherapy, the professional without previous hypnosis education is urged to get qualified training from a state licensed school before using certain hypnotic interventions in this book as an adjunctive therapeutic modality.

Even though it is a teaching text, this book is also designed to be "user friendly" and selectively applied as an effective personal growth tool. Gestalt dreamwork methods and many basic self-hypnosis techniques (found in those books oriented toward self-hypnosis which are listed in the bibliography) can be learned by aware, emotionally stable individuals and utilized in self-hypnosis. However, it is not recommended for professionals or nonprofessionals to attempt hypnotic regression work to a traumatic experience alone in self-hypnosis. It is important to have the support of a well-trained and skilled professional under such circumstances.

The dreamwork sessions in this book are of actual demonstrations during my Hypnotherapy Training classes and Hypnotic Dreamwork seminars, transcribed from videotape (in most cases) or audiotape. Selected questions and answers from the transcripts have been retained as one of the forms of commentary. There are potential advantages to the client inherent in such demonstrational therapy in contrast to private session work. This includes occasional feedback from class members during some sessions, and the intrinsic value of a supportive group presence that is hard to quantify, but for which the dreamer and I can be most grateful.

Become the Dream

CHAPTER 1

The Transformational Nature of Hypnotherapy

The Subconscious is the Key

To get powerful, lasting and fairly rapid results in therapy, it is essential that the methods employed reach and affect the subconscious mind. The subconscious houses the emotions, imagination, memory, habits, intuition, and is the pathway to the superconscious. It also regulates our autonomic body functions. It is the very core or essence of how we experience ourselves and the world. Meaningful personal transformation, whether in or out of therapy, results from a shift in the subconscious mind.

Through hypnosis, we have access to the subconscious. In fact, during waking states, the only way to reach and change major set beliefs and emotional responses of the subconscious mind is during experiences that are hypnotic. Hypnosis is an altered state beyond ordinary consciousness, but a natural state that can occur spontaneously. In addition, there are many ways hypnosis can be induced and deepened. Once in hypnosis during therapy, there is a vast range of therapeutic possibilities to harness and transform the subconscious. Hypnotherapists are taught to use a variety of methods to bring a person into a state of hypnosis, deepen and lighten the state, direct various processes and return the subject back to normal awareness.

Eclectic training in the uses of hypnotherapy can substantially enhance the skills of any health, counseling or teaching professional. Examples include psychologists, physicians, dentists, chiropractors, social workers, marriage counselors, physical therapists, optometrists, ministerial professionals, nurses, massage practitioners, coaches and electrologists. Hypnosis, while often unrecognized as such, weaves a common thread through the healing arts and sciences. Effective therapists often use hypnotic methods whether they use or understand that semantic or not. As understanding of the field spreads, the deliberate use of hypnotic processes is currently making a major impact in the health professions and truly revolutionizing the field of counseling. While it won't work for everything or for everybody all the time, it is often a powerful therapy that is as much an art as a science.

Within the field of hypnotherapy, there are a great variety of ways to harness the power of the subconscious mind to affect change. Hypnosis is used in areas such as chronic and acute pain control, to change the pain threshold or affect the psychological associations of pain. It can be effective to improve confidence, concentration, recall, motivation, achievement, focus, health and stress management. Hypnosis can help overcome addictions, habits, eating disorders, insomnia, fears, phobias, and negative thought, emotional and behavior patterns. It can also tap people into the utilization of their full potential in endeavors like work, sports, art or creative expression.

Hypnotic Phenomena

Within a therapeutic setting, hypnosis is often induced through various methods of relaxation. As a result of this process the critical factor of the conscious mind is bypassed, giving the hypnotherapist and subject direct access to the deeper mind, the subconscious, which has been called "the other 90% of the mind."

Generally, the most well known characteristic of hypnosis is increased suggestibility. Though there are varying degrees of this heightened responsiveness to suggestion, the potential power of this direct access to the subconscious should not be underestimated.

For example, I worked with a man named Gino who had been a three-pack a day smoker for over 20 years. He had never been able to quit for even a day since his early years as a smoker. After his first hypnosis session, he called his wife from work later that day. "I can't believe how easy it is. It's like I never smoked," he exclaimed. "I can remember smoking, of course, but there's no desire at all!" While I cautioned him during our follow-up session not to be overconfident, he continued to do fine, including no negative side effects. To the contrary, he was constructively redirecting his energy, and had dramatically increased confidence and vitality.

I remember Gino vividly because after referring many of his friends and acquaintances to me for hypnotherapy, he came back a few years later to take my training to become a hypnotherapist. He introduced himself to the class with a twinkle in his eye, saying, "Randal helped me quit smoking, but I've never been hypnotized." In spite of his results, he had a hard time accepting that he had entered hypnosis, even though he knew he must have, because his hypnotic experiences were so subtle to him. Initial doubts about the hypnotic state are not unusual, and more about the subjective experience of hypnosis will be discussed later in this chapter. What was unusual was the immediate ease of his results, although such a response is not rare in the practice of an attentive, skilled hypnotherapist.

While varying degrees of initial struggle are the norm for addiction or habit cessation through hypnosis sessions, my experience has been that more than ten percent of such clients will achieve the desired results and more, with astonishing ease from the beginning. It is not rare for a skilled hypnotherapist in rapport with a motivated client to produce such profound suggestibility that it can have the effect of an imprint. An imprint is a powerful, emotional, single impact learning experience that can affect a person (or an animal) in many cases for a lifetime. But even when results are not exceptional, responsiveness to suggestion is routinely greatly heightened during hypnosis.

As important as increased suggestibility can be, it is only one of many kinds of value that can result from access to the subconscious. Concentration typically increases dramatically during hypnosis. There are many benefits from this. For example, many indigenous cultures have kept oral records for centuries or millennia. Successive generations of historians would enter hypnotic trances and recite detailed, prolonged ancestral records. A famous example involves Alex Haley's attempt to find possible validation for the childhood legends about his apparent African ancestor, Kunta Kinte, which was the basis of his book, *Roots*. His search led him to an

African village historian who, a few hours into a trance recitation, came to a verse about the disappearance of Haley's ancestor.

Within the context of therapy, heightened hypnotic concentration has value as an inherent aspect of trance and is a partial explanation of the effectiveness of hypnotic suggestion. In addition, specific issues such as improved study habits and various achievement goals ranging from public speaking to improved sports performance, are addressed directly by this hypnotic phenomenon. The subject can actually re-enter a state of self-hypnosis later while studying or performing, to gain further value from the concentration inherent to the hypnotic state.

While sometimes directly associated with concentration (as in some of the above examples), heightened recall during hypnosis has many functions. Revivification of significant events, whether or not they were previously repressed, can be combined with many therapeutic modalities. Also, many persons have used hypnotic access to buried memories to find missing objects of value. Although the use of hypnosis for solving crimes has been restricted in recent years by the courts, hundreds of crimes have been solved by the use of forensic hypnosis, such as when Ed Ray's hypnotic recall of the license plate after the Chowchilla kidnapping led investigators to the kidnappers. Victims and witnesses to crimes have hypnotically recalled crucial memories, whether buried because of detail or time or trauma.

A person can be taught to re-enter hypnosis to access stored memories while taking examinations or, in certain situations, to improve job effectiveness. Therefore, persons developing memory recall skills are supported by the value of increased suggestibility during the initial hypnosis sessions, as well as by the later heightened concentration and recall natural to the state of self-hypnosis. (Other values of hypnosis will also apply to improved recall, such as various uses of therapy for test anxiety.)

The pain threshold changes dramatically during hypnosis or self-hypnosis. Hypnosis can provide great relief for chronic pain sufferers referred by their physicians for such complaints as back pain, arthritis, headaches or recovery from injury. As with any issue, the good hypnotherapist will work comprehensively and holistically toward lasting results, dealing with life-style, stress, emotions and personality factors, as well as possible secondary gains.

Pain alleviation during and in hours following a daily practice of self-hypnosis can often provide some immediate benefit, while any underlying emotional and life-style issues are addressed during hypnotherapy sessions.

In deeper levels of hypnosis major surgery can, in many cases, be painlessly performed with no other anesthetic agent. In addition, physiological functions normally controlled by the subconscious can be effected, such as by suggestions from a dentist to a hypnotically anesthetized patient to control salivation and bleeding.

Increased access to the emotions during hypnosis has many uses. Often hypnotized persons later report having experienced feelings of bliss, joy or euphoria, sometimes spontaneously and other times as a response to post-hypnotic suggestions or therapeutic methods. Such feelings can be very meaningful and have substantial therapeutic value. When a person has been struggling with feelings such as fear, grief or anger, there are various therapeutic methods during hypnosis to help him or her access those feelings when appropriate and express, release or transform them.

Facts and Fallacies

Misconceptions about hypnosis are still fairly prevalent but gradually diminishing with time. The fear of loss of control is a result, in part, of stage hypnosis demonstrations. Volunteers may seem to be "under the spell" of the stage hypnotist. Some develop the notion that the participants will do whatever the hypnotist suggests. Actually, some operators have been known to survey the audience and express disappointment if, say, five volunteers are needed and there are only 60 people in the audience. Most people will not respond well to stage hypnosis and those that do, will do so only under the right circumstances.

Stage hypnosis is a chance for a person with some extrovert tendencies to perform, have fun, and be a star. It is no coincidence that the longest running series of stage hypnosis shows in history, with Pat Collins, was in Hollywood. A large percentage of volunteers for her shows were striving to become actors and actresses. Volunteers of any stage show know they will be expected to do silly things in front of an audience, and find that appealing. The ones who show timid or self-conscious responses are asked early on to go back to the audience. The participants who are receptive to hypnosis will have, to some extent, a loss of inhibition. However, the volunteer would not do anything against his or her moral beliefs. For example, if handed an imaginary glass of champagne, a non-drinker will refuse to pretend to drink. Also, some otherwise responsive persons will back off to a specific suggestion (e.g., to sing) because of a lack of self-confidence in that area. Even during stage hypnosis, individuals retain control in areas of principle or in which there is major subconscious resistance.

During a hypnotherapy session you know you may be open to suggestion. Rather than losing control, a comprehensive series of sessions can help a person to gain control. If during the initial consultation I am not convinced of my new client's firm commitment toward a proclaimed goal, I will not continue with the person. In spite of the increased suggestibility inherent with hypnosis, genuine motivation is necessary for a person to achieve meaningful results in therapy. Clients become more motivated toward their goals if significant underlying resistance issues get properly addressed and there is some degree of rapport with the therapist.

Many persons who have not previously experienced a formal hypnotic induction expect the experience of the state of hypnosis to be far different, and often more extreme, than what it is. Even after attempts prior to the induction to alleviate such misconceptions, a classic response after a first hypnosis is, "I know I wasn't hypnotized. I heard every word you said." Ironically, the same person, when asked what this "non-hypnosis" experience was like, may give a dramatic response, such as, "Well, I haven't relaxed so much in twenty years." (The initial subjective experience of the state is often disappointing to some extent, but the results, as with Gino, can nevertheless be profound.) Some will doubt in early sessions whether they went into hypnosis at all. Others who achieve significant depth may believe only light hypnosis was achieved. With continuing experience, people tend to go deeper and also begin to recognize the signs that for them are associated with hypnosis.

Rather than losing consciousness during hypnosis, there is typically heightened consciousness. Awareness is much greater than normal, which is related to the increased focus previously described.

When somnambulism (a deep state of hypnosis) is reached, however, the shift back to normal consciousness is so great that the ᵊmory of the experience may stay buried in the subconscious after ₚerson comes out of hypnosis. This can be similar to the experience of someone who has been asleep and dreaming, and upon awakening remembers the dream at first, only to be unable to recall it a few minutes later. The memory of the dream or of the hypnotic experience is still there in the subconscious, even when conscious recall fades. Though the somnambulistic state is the exception, it has led to the still somewhat common misconception that a person in hypnosis will automatically experience amnesia. Hypnosis actually leads to increased awareness, and one result of this is that distant or previously unconscious memories may be recalled in vivid detail.

Hypnosis is a natural state of mind that is entered spontaneously every day. Examples include states of narrow focus, such as you might experience when watching television or absorbed in a good book. Highway hypnosis can occur when driving on the freeway and suddenly realizing you have no conscious memory of the past several miles traveled. A form of hypnosis, the hypnogogic state, is entered just prior to falling asleep, and the heightened suggestibility of the hypnopompic state occurs when first waking up. Even daydreaming is considered by many experts to be a form of light hypnosis, or a borderline (hypnoidal) state. The conscious mind begins to recede and the subconscious mind comes to the foreground, giving you greater access to the imagination, memories and feelings.

Beginning around the age of five, the overwhelming majority of the population is hypnotizable in the formal sense. Exceptions include some psychotic individuals who don't have the necessary trust to be open and receptive, and some retarded persons and those with advanced Alzheimer's, who don't have the necessary concentration or imagination. However, I have used hypnosis with the developmentally disabled through the Sonoma County Mental Health Department and found that some of the higher functioning individuals were able to respond rather well.

During most of our daily lives we are in touch with our conscious minds, while subconscious activities below the surface regulate physical functions such as the autonomic nervous system and circulatory system. The subconscious can leap into action during emergencies, but it is in part that portion of the mind that is on "automatic pilot" while we are awake or asleep.

People who enter hypnosis deliberately in session or during self-hypnosis know they are suggestible. The most common danger with hypnosis lies primarily outside of the therapeutic context, in situations in which people are not aware that they are in suggestible states. For example, we can be influenced by an authority figure, such as a doctor or other professional, or a political or parental figure. When a person is unduly influenced by an authority, a spontaneous hypnosis can develop and the person may become extremely suggestible.

To give another example, double-blind suggestibility studies have documented that most persons will respond well to placebos, even when used in place of morphine for severe pain. That gives us a glimpse at the enormous power of the subconscious mind. A person who deliberately uses hypnotic states to control his or her subconscious mind can create extreme physiological changes and other exceptional achievements without needing to project power onto a pill or an authority figure.

Additionally, our consumer culture bombards us with various forms of advertising that can have a hypnotic affect. Advertisers may even pay a premium for broadcasting late at night or early in the morning when people are more likely to be highly suggestible. Learning about hypnosis and suggestibility helps us recognize times when we may be more open or vulnerable so that we can retain awareness and have more control.

There are many therapy or healing practices that include forms of hypnosis. Biofeedback techniques, for instance, are used in conjunction with hypnosis. Jose Silva, in developing Silva Mind Control methods, borrowed liberally from Dave Elman's hypnotic inductions. Christian Scientists use hypnotic methods for pain control. Guided imagery, guided fantasy, visualization, selective awareness, autogenic training, progressive relaxation and relaxology are examples of hypnotic methods. Sometimes the practitioner, teacher, nurse, psychotherapist, etc., who uses such methods will not associate the methods with hypnosis. If these methods are recognized as hypnotic and that is communicated to the client, time needs to be taken to alleviate possible misconceptions. Any practitioner who sometimes uses hypnotic methods but has not previously recognized them as such, would find hypnotic skills magnified tremendously by a thorough training in hypnosis.

The various forms of meditation (Zen, Vipassana, TM, etc.) are also forms of hypnosis. A group at U.C.L.A. in 1969 set out to prove that their particular form of meditation was different from hypnosis. Their study compared the meditation experience of persons who had been practicing meditation every day for many months and getting excellent results, with the initial hypnosis experience of persons that had never practiced hypnosis or meditation. The hypnotist was a member of the meditation group. The two groups naturally had different results and a claim was then made that this meditation practice causes more profound physiological differences than hypnosis. But just as with meditation, increased hypnotic depth (and the dramatically different physiological changes that entails) is a skill that develops with practice.

The therapeutic value of hypnosis is gradually becoming much more widely recognized. As the myths and misconceptions are exposed and word continues to spread about the values of hypnosis, growing acceptance and interest has increased in academic and scientific communities as well. Many doctors and other professionals are being trained themselves or referring patients to hypnotherapists for work in conjunction with conventional treatments. While there is still residual misunderstanding in some people's minds, the misconceptions of many have lessened over the years.

The Experience of Hypnosis

Following a preliminary discussion and alleviation of any misconceptions, three things are needed for hypnosis in a therapeutic setting: concentration, imagination, and a motivation to be hypnotized. Hetero-hypnosis, in which a therapist works with an individual or a group, is in a sense self-hypnosis because each individual goes into hypnosis by choice. If a person doesn't feel rapport with the operator or doesn't desire to, that person will resist entering hypnosis.

The more you practice hypnosis the deeper you tend to go, but it isn't necessary to reach deep levels to be therapeutic. Excellent results in therapy can be achieved in light and medium states. Practicing hypnotherapists can train many of their clients in self-hypnosis for added benefits. With experience and confidence that a relaxed and open state of hypnosis can be reached, tools are soon developed that an individual can use for a lifetime to access the power of his or her own subconscious mind.

There are many levels of hypnosis and various subjective states can be experienced at any particular depth. During lighter levels of hypnosis feelings of relaxation and passivity are commonly experienced. Additionally, there may be slightly altered perceptions or physical changes such as eye fluttering or a tingling sensation in the extremities or a light or heavy sensation in some part of the body. Persons who don't get much of a response at first will continue to learn and develop significant skills within a few weeks of practice.

In the beginning it is common to underestimate the length of time in hypnosis. When asked after an initial hypnosis, many will guess the time as shorter than it actually was. A person who has had a few more hypnotic experiences will usually have a better estimate of time.

The flip side to the occurrence of an initial subjective distortion of time is that the subconscious mind has a kind of built-in clock. When you enter self-hypnosis or when you go to bed at night, your subconscious mind can be trained to bring you back or wake you up at a particular time. One student related giving herself a suggestion when going to sleep at night to wake up at a particularly early hour. She was awakened at exactly the right time by her husband's voice saying, "It's five o'clock." She turned over to thank him but he was sound asleep. The call had come from her own creative subconscious.

In medium depths of hypnosis, the altered state becomes more enhanced. There may be more pronounced physical sensations of heaviness or lightness, or a floating or sinking feeling in part or all of the body. A loss of conscious awareness may occur, or a major change of pain threshold, such as with the experience of "glove anesthesia" in the area of the hands. Various illusions may be perceived through any of the senses. Ability to visualize or imagine suggestions tends to increase with depth.

Somnambulistic levels of hypnosis create more extreme physical and mental responses, such as loss of awareness of most or all of the body. Physiologic responses may include the same kind of rapid eye movements that are associated with dream stages of sleep. Exceptional suggestibility often includes a profound literalness in response to suggestions. Some will have the ability to produce hallucinations, even with the eyes open or post-hypnotically. Complete conscious amnesia may occur.

Hypnosis is a far different state than sleep, but it has been called a sleep of the nervous system. Respiration and circulation slow down, but not as much as during normal sleep states. The brain waves also slow down, though not as slow as the brain waves of delta that are reached during the deepest levels of sleep. The levels of brain waves begin with beta, the fastest, then slow to alpha, theta and delta. Under most conditions of normal waking consciousness, brain waves are primarily beta. In light to medium states of hypnosis, a significant decrease to predominately alpha level brain waves will occur. In deeper levels of hypnosis a person's brain waves may actually go down into theta.

Remember, however, that hypnotic skills develop with practice, so the rules of the above paragraph can be broken under truly extraordinary conditions. An Indian Swami who had been meditating several hours a day for many years was documented on film as having gone into delta brain waves while sitting, his eyes half open. (As a general rule, unless you're focusing on a major trauma issue, the deeper you go into hypnosis the more pleasant the state is, until at deeper levels it can be quite euphoric. This Swami was certainly in a state of bliss.)

There is a rare state of hypnosis far deeper than somnambulism called the plenary trance, that could be likened to almost being a state of suspended animation. The British physician, James Esdaile, produced this state in some surgical patients in India in the 1840's, using a few hours of mesmeric passes as the induction. The patient was kept in the plenary trance sometimes for 24 hours, since this was before chemo-anesthesia had been accepted and hypnosis was the only anesthetic agent. But more importantly, he soon discovered his mortality rate after surgery dropped from 50% to 5%. This was before Lister's campaign against infection, when surgeons washed their hands after surgery, not before. During hypnotic anesthesia the subconscious mind aids the body in developing greater resistance to infection.

In the 1890's a Swedish physician named Wetterstrand reported keeping some patients in the plenary trance for over a week for healing purposes. Leslie LeCron produced this state in more recent times, recording a pulse of 50 beats per minute and a barely discernible breathing rate of only three breaths per minute.

This chapter is a brief introduction to the value of hypnosis and hypnotherapy for the purposes of this book, and cannot be a comprehensive description of the many phenomena and uses of hypnosis. This overview and the following three examples are a sampling, to explain some of the special qualities of hypnosis, which prepares us to better understand the tremendous potential of Hypnotic Dreamwork.

Karen's Story

When I first met Karen she was experiencing a recurrence of symptoms of multiple sclerosis. She had been diagnosed ten years earlier, in 1977. At the time of diagnosis she was blind in one eye and had partial sight in the other. She was informed that within six months she would be a vegetable. Her doctors advised her to go home and get her affairs in order. Karen, who had been raised as a devout Catholic, was in the middle of difficult divorce proceedings. She was particularly worried about her three young children, and prayed that she be allowed to live long enough to see them through school. Amazingly, instead of deteriorating, her symptoms gradually disappeared. Her doctors had no explanation for this turn of events.

Ten years later Karen's husband, a student in one of my hypnotherapy classes, asked if he could bring Karen in as the subject in a class demonstration. Her symptoms of MS were recurring and had advanced, in some ways, even further than before. Her vision and coordination were seriously deteriorating, she was losing dexterity in her hands, and she was about to give up. During our interview she told me that the youngest of her children would be graduating from school in a few months. When I asked if she had been having any other major changes or stress in her life, she said that she and her husband, Kenn, had had to close their business. All three of her children were still at home, she was working more than full time as a bookkeeper, and though she would like some time to herself, she saw no hope of that in the future.

After doing a hypnotic induction we set up ideomotor signals, which is a way of bypassing the conscious mind to communicate directly with the subconscious. Different fingers on one hand can be chosen to rise if the answer to a question is "yes" or "no." Alternative fingers can be used for a subconscious signal that it doesn't know or refuses to answer. Through the use of this type of questioning we were able to determine that Karen's subconscious mind interpreted the cessation of her symptoms ten years earlier as a pact with God that she now had to honor. At the same time there was a part of Karen that had lost faith in God because of her resentment at having developed the sudden blindness. We were also able to ascertain that the onset of her earlier blindness, as well as her current symptoms, had in part to do with the stress in her life. Further questioning revealed that Karen felt a measure of guilt about becoming healthy again.

The session became very long and complex, with conflicting ideomotor signals and subconscious confusion. As the process continued I used Gestalt dialogue between Karen and God to try to break through her guilt and subconscious resistance to getting well again, as well as her resentment of God. There was even some question of whether she still believed in God. Well into the session, I reminded her that if there was no God, then there was no one to keep a pact with. If there was a God, I asked her, wouldn't God be compassionate enough to see that Karen had suffered more than enough already?

After giving Karen some explanation about the sometimes deductive way the subconscious mind works, and that it isn't always rational, I had her do some hypno-analysis to figure out if there was some kind of misconception she had developed as a result of those traumatic experiences. She was eventually able to realize that she had developed the misconception that in wanting to see her kids grow up and getting her eyesight back, she needed to be punished. She continued to assert, however, that "My dues are up. I have to pay." Over and over again we hit dead ends as I kept trying to find ways to help Karen through subconscious blocks. At one point I asked her subconscious mind if she had asked, "Please let me live to see my kids grow up and get through school," or "Please let me die or get worse when my kids grow up." When Karen was able to acknowledge the former, I encouraged her subconscious mind to accept that she was therefore not required to now deteriorate. But she continued to resist, saying she still had to pay. Eventually I was able to help her accept that she could have a pact to live and be reasonably healthy, without repercussions. While she was still subconsciously open and suggestible I ended the session with many positive affirmations of the success she had already had in overcoming the condition previously, the new lasting success she would now begin to have, and the ways in which she could find creative ways to take better care of herself.

Karen began to experience major improvement within the first week, and in the two subsequent sessions I continued to encourage and support Karen on the ways she was now taking better care of herself and the progress she was making. Within six weeks she was free of symptoms, having improved much more rapidly this time. A subsequent Cat Scan years later showed no evidence of M.S. Our sessions were ten years ago and she continues to be healthy today.

This story is a dramatic example of the potential of a variety of creative techniques with hypnosis to affect the subconscious mind. Gestalt dialogue, such as that used with Karen, is employed in almost all of the transcripts of this book, and brief ideomotor methods appear in some cases.

Kenn's Story

Kenn, Karen's husband from the previous story, used his experiences in the hypnotherapy classes and his self-hypnosis to make tremendous changes in many areas of his life during the year he was getting his training.

He came back to see me in 1991 because of a serious injury that caused an anterior curve in the cervical arch of the neck, and had been treated with surgery a year earlier. Instead of getting better, the condition immediately deteriorated further after the surgery. He was so weak that he could not carry a quart of milk one block. He was currently working with a talented hypnotherapist in his town, Charlie Simon, a graduate that I had recommended. One of the effective strategies was to visualize removing the cervical vertebrae area and replace it with stacked tinker toys on wheels that would cause the neck to bend properly. They had made significant progress, but Kenn needed further improvement. His surgeon had seen him recently and recommended immediate surgery, as weakness in the injured areas had caused his head to bend in a way that was pinching nerves affecting his hands and going down into his legs. The surgeon wanted to open up his back and put a brace from the seventh cervical vertebrae to the first, leaving him in a rigid permanent position facing slightly upwards. "I won't be able to nod yes, so I'll just have to say no," Kenn joked wryly.

Kenn's belief was that he had been damaged by the first surgery. But he also wondered whether his sense of deep shame was hindering his body's ability to heal more fully. In his words, "Before I started (hypnotherapy) in 1986 I was a compulsive gambler, excessive drinker, and a three pack a day smoker. I came up with every compulsive, addictive behavior, even eating disorders, and because of all this I feel a lot of shame. I've started recovery and I feel like what might be a stumbling block are my feelings of shame and guilt that go way back." He was waiting to get a second opinion before making a decision about getting more surgery, which terrified him. The original doctor's concern was that without treatment he could become a quadriplegic.

Before doing a hypnotic induction I checked with Kenn about whether or not he could move his fingers to do ideomotor signals, and he showed me the two fingers on his left hand that he could move slightly. Before the hypnotherapy work with Charlie he had been unable to move those fingers at all. He had also been able to get off drugs he had been taking for pain and was no longer chronically constipated, so he had already made dramatic progress in the six weeks since he had started sessions.

After an induction I used the affect bridge (which is also used for Tom's regression in Chapter 19), a technique that taps a person into a particular emotion and then moves rapidly to an earlier memory which is associated with a similar feeling. Kenn recalled being in his bedroom at three years of age and feeling very ashamed. He was being scolded by his mother for wetting the bed. She told him he was a very naughty boy. It was something that had happened many times. He continued to sporadically wet the bed until he was thirteen. It was very embarrassing and he was consequently very shy and self-conscious.

After going to other scenes where young Kenn had been scolded and felt ashamed, I brought adult Kenn back to the earlier scene with his mother and had them engage in Gestalt dialogue. I then asked young Kenny how he felt listening to adult Kenn and had them dialogue. Adult Kenn assured young Kenny he had never done anything wrong, that wetting the bed was a common experience for many young boys and out of their control - there was sometimes even a genetic factor. Young Kenny responded that he would try not to feel the shame. We kept working until young Kenny had more clarity that he was not at fault and adult Kenn was able to realize that he was a good person and could let go of those feelings and the affects they had had on him. Toward the end of the process he said he felt that his mother had done a good job overall and he loved her deeply. She had made a mistake because she was naive. She just didn't know it was something he couldn't help. During hypno-analysis Kenn described not having been able to forgive himself and he now did so wholeheartedly. I gave Kenn positive reinforcements and suggestions for further healing in his neck and back and then brought him out of the hypnosis.

Following the session Kenn continued hypnotherapy and refocused on physical therapy and feeling better about himself. Meanwhile he got a second opinion that confirmed the first. He recognized gradual improvement, and the following month he went to his original surgeon who, with considerable surprise, now said, "Because of your vast improvement I can't justify surgery at this time." Kenn continued to improve dramatically.

Early childhood is a time when we are particularly open and vulnerable to suggestion. Early experiences may teach us that we're not good enough, that the world is a hostile place, that we can't trust people, or that we're likely to get hurt in some way. Very often when we want to make fundamental changes as adults and feel stuck, the problem is that we have been hypnotized by limiting experiences early in life. Such early subconscious conditioning can sometimes last a lifetime.

As the story with Kenn illustrates, when doing hypnotherapy we are sometimes in part doing de-hypnosis. We are helping that

person to let go of negative suggestions or misconceptions that were taken in, often at a young age, and continued to affect his ~~ ~~
experiences. We help that person to wake ~~ ~~
trance he or she has been in. Kenn's exa~~ ~~
because of the physical healing that accompanied the emotional healing, but combining Gestalt and hypnotherapy can routinely cause profound lasting shifts in subconscious attitudes and feelings. Getting in touch with the deeper, greater part of the mind can help in so many ways to unleash the vast potential and abilities that are there.

Frank's Story

When Frank came back from Vietnam he attempted to go to college but dropped out. Initially he made attempts to find work but didn't stick with it. He remained unemployed and lived with his parents. He was addicted to drugs, alcohol and cigarettes. He was overweight, depressed, and had no self-confidence. He hadn't had any relationships and hadn't even been on a date since soon after his return. He briefly tried various therapists but hadn't responded well with anyone. His parents had desperately tried to help him and when they heard of my work, encouraged him to make one more try.

It had been ten years since his return from Vietnam when I met Frank. We started by looking for ways for him to be successful and then taking one step at a time. J.D. Hadfield said, "Suggestion does not consist in making an individual believe what is not true. Suggestion consists in making something come true by making a person believe in its possibility." The first thing I helped him work on was getting into shape while losing weight. With that success, he had the confidence to quit smoking. Then we worked on his issues with drugs and alcohol.

After making dramatic progress in these areas, we worked on building up Frank's confidence to get ready to look for work. His dream was to do delivery work. He felt he would really enjoy being out and driving a truck. He got a delivery job through an employment agency and was very satisfied. He worked hard and diligently, but three months later he was told that although he was doing a fine job, he was being laid off. Frank was angry and felt there was a deal going on between his employer and the agency. He had been retained for as long as he was still paying a large portion of his wages to the agency which had gotten him the position. A setback like this could certainly be an excuse to slip back into drinking and depression, but Frank turned his anger into action. He intensified his exercise program and got right out and started looking for work again. He was hired with forty other people by Federal Express for temporary work during the Christmas season. At the end of the season two people were kept on. Frank was one of them. He's been working for Federal Express for 14 years now.

Over time we periodically worked on various things, including relationship issues. An early example of his progress in this area is when the issue had developed from not having dates, to feelings of guilt because he did not want to continue to see a woman who was interested in him. He eventually developed a long term relationship. We have had a total of about 30 sessions over the years. Currently, like everyone, Frank has his ups and downs. But he is functioning far better than he was when I first met him.

Many causes that bring people to seek hypnotherapy do not involve the kinds of life-changing issues of Karen, Kenn and Frank. But even hypnosis for common issues can lead to major benefits, such as sessions for smoking cessation, which may help significantly lengthen a person's life span. I view the hypnotic state with reverence and consider the role of a hypnotherapist as an honor. I am aware of no greater satisfaction than the service of helping to satisfy a client in making major, lasting changes.

* Complete transcripts of sessions described in Karen's Story and Kenn's Story are included in Randal Churchill's forthcoming book *Regression Hypnotherapy,* to be published by Transforming Press. (This is not the same Karen whose dream is featured in *Become The Dream.)*

CHAPTER 2

Hypnotic Dreamwork:

Subconscious Access Galore

Working with the subconscious mind gives us the potential for deep transformation. One of the vitally important functions of the subconscious mind is dreaming. Dreams are direct existential messages from the subconscious. To enter the dream and work with it directly is an opportunity for profound subconscious shifts.

Although it has not been generally understood, the methods of Gestalt dreamwork, as described later in this chapter, tend to initiate (or deepen) a hypnotic state. This is a major reason why Gestalt methods are so effective. In the early '70's I began consistently adding additional hypnotic techniques to Gestalt dreamwork, and found them to be a perfect match. By further utilizing this spontaneous entrance to the subconscious, we can add even greater value to the techniques of Gestalt.

Dreamwork from the Gestalt Perspective

The vast majority of methods to discover the meaning of dreams are interpretive. The role of the therapist is to analyze the dream or, in some cases, to help the patient or client analyze it. The overwhelming number of books at libraries and bookstores about dreamwork attempt to help the reader understand how to interpret dreams.

Gestalt methods, on the other hand, do not analyze or interpret. Rather than understanding intellectually, the purpose is to experience the dream and feel significant aspects of it at a core level. Dr.

Fritz Perls, primary founder of Gestalt therapy, said "Lose your mind and come to your senses." Rather than analyze, become the dream and all of its different parts. The deeper meaning of the dream is found with Gestalt methods through your heart, your gut, your senses and feelings.

Most people have had the experience of waking up from a particularly intense or frightening dream with a pounding heart or gasping for breath. In spite of being asleep, the body experiences the processes of the dream. Dream images can produce the same physiological affects as the actual event would in reality. As Perls pointed out, when a dream is taking place it is absolutely real to the dreamer. In its own way, it is reality while it is happening.

Your dreams are metaphors for your existence. They are even more than that. Your dreams are direct messages that express your subconscious experience of yourself and the world. The Gestalt perspective of dreams is that every part of your dream is a part of yourself. This not only refers to the different persons in the dream, but all places, animals, objects, body parts, moods, weather and so forth. These parts have been fragmented or projected onto the world. By becoming the part you are taking back the power of the part. Perls, who focussed primarily on dreamwork in the last years before his death in 1970, said, "You are greater than your wildest dreams."

Gestalt helps us own all the different parts of ourselves. Anything you dream about has certain qualities and potentials you are not fully accepting. Persons may not be in touch with their eyes, their ears, their centers, their sexuality, their spontaneity, and so forth. Anything that you become aware of in the dream, even atmospheric conditions or time, is a different part of you that you have projected to one degree or another onto the world. Even a character in the dream which is apparently immoral or repugnant has something of value which the dreamer can incorporate. By becoming the parts and dialoguing between different parts, we take on a certain power that each character has and become so much more than we are when we project those parts externally onto persons or things. Some Native Americans have traditionally identified with different animals or birds and felt the power inherent in that symbol. There are certain advantages or strengths in any character, whether it be survival, cleverness, creativity, playfulness, ability to hide, etc.

Gestalt is an existential therapy predicated on awareness. Using our heads takes us away from the here and now, which we experience externally through our senses and internally through body awareness and emotions. Understandings can and do occur during Gestalt, but are a result of the direct experience of becoming dream characters, interacting with other dream characters, and experiencing our spontaneous physical and emotional processes.

Many who are considered dream experts have stated that there is still so much that we don't understand about the meanings of dreams. But in fact your own creative subconscious mind, which formulated your dreams, knows exactly what they are about, and Gestalt dreamwork is a powerful tool in getting to the answers.

Dreams hold the answers without trying to intellectually figure them out. A formal interpretation could be wrong, or not as important as other aspects of what the dream is about. Unlike different methods of dream interpretation that say a house always means this or falling always means that, in Gestalt dreamwork, dreamers are led to experience what it means for them. The most important meaning is the truth of one's experience. As the therapist, if you feel your client might be missing something obvious you can use encouragement to stay with the feeling and notice if there is also something else. But again, that is turning it over to and trusting the dreamer's subjective experience, rather than giving (or requesting) analysis.

Many persons have gotten value from various methods of dream interpretation, and my statements regarding interpretation are in the context of Gestalt dreamwork strategies. These methods provide us with non-analytic tools which steer completely away from interpretation and are consistently effective in giving us deep understandings of our dreams and solutions to the issues the dreams address. When used properly, Gestalt dreamwork methods produce meaningful revelations time and time again. And they keep the client tending toward hypnotic states, as opposed to analysis, which tends to bring the client out of hypnosis. Avoiding interpretation keeps us focused on direct access to the wisdom of the greatest ally and potential therapist of all, our own subconscious minds, and also allows the potential for deep healing by way of the increased suggestibility inherent to hypnotic states.

Basic Gestalt Dreamwork Methods and their Hypnotic Effects

The first step for the therapist is to have the client describe the dream in present tense while vividly imagining it. Occasionally I may ask the dreamer to describe the dream again more expressively. I sometimes encourage persons to close their eyes and make gestures and movements to experience the dream more intensely. Very significantly, this revivification of the dream bring's the person's full attention right into the subconscious, the part of the mind that created the dream. As discussed in Chapter One, the key to profound, deep therapy is to work with and effect the subconscious mind. By definition, any method that gives us direct access to our inner minds while awake is hypnotic. In other words, this first step in Gestalt dreamwork is a hypnotic induction. (Through many traditional hypnotic inductions, a person initially opens to the subconscious mind by becoming very relaxed and passive. Gestalt dreamwork is one of the many alternative forms of hypnotic inductions.)

Next, the therapist has the dreamer describe himself or herself as being one of the characters of the dream, emphasizing to stay in touch with his or her feelings. If the description is brief, some elaboration may be encouraged. The therapist will usually then have the dreamer become at least one more additional character. This increased identification with specific parts of the dream frequently further deepens the hypnosis.

A very common Gestalt dreamwork procedure is to have different characters dialogue. This is communicated directly in the first and second person, rather than talking to the therapist about the other character. When you dialogue between the different parts, switching and becoming first one part and then the other, this gives the opportunity to work through struggles between conflicting parts (and/or increase communication and appreciation between complementary, harmonious parts), integrating characteristics of each part into a more balanced whole. Questions between the characters are to be avoided or turned into statements. A question is considered a form of manipulation, a way of not taking responsibility. It also is usually a request for an intellectual explanation, which tends to diminish the hypnotic state. The Gestalt dialogue is traditionally done while sitting in a chair, facing an empty chair. It usually works well to have the dreamer get up and switch chairs when moving from one character to another.

Another Gestalt practice is to periodically have the dreamer describe what is happening internally. This is especially good when a person has begun to tap into an emotion, whether or not there appears to be resistance to that emotion. Going inward will tend to take people deeper into hypnosis and deeper into the experience. As the person describes his or her inner feelings you might turn to an inner dialogue to further develop that experience. For example, if a person has begun to make physical movements, you can encourage him or her to exaggerate those movements or become the body part that is doing that, in the same way the person would become a direct character in the dream.

Keep working with dialogue between characters until you complete the communication or get a natural coming together of some of the characters. It is important that the therapist not take sides. What usually happens as you stay with a person in dreamwork is a gradual appreciation and integration of the different sides. The appreciation is automatic with wish fulfillment dreams, but in frustration dreams you initially emphasize the clashing parts and work with those, letting them have total space to be themselves. You encourage each part to express and be itself, whether the part is upset at the other, or afraid, or whatever the feeling is. If the dreamer becomes ready to complete this process, a mutual respect and acceptance often develops between characters at the conclusion of the dialogue.

Most dreams for most of us are frustration dreams or have significant elements of frustration. Both frustration and wish fulfillment dreams are valuable and have their advantages. Working with a wish fulfillment dream, for instance, can be very healing when the subconscious mind finds a discovery or solution, or immerses itself in the joy of its power and sense of accomplishment, or success, freedom, peace or whatever the relevant feelings are. You can also work with such a brief dream segment that it may not be clear at first if there will be something frustrating or challenging to work with. You simply find out by having the person do the dreamwork process.

Combining Further Hypnotic Processes
with Gestalt Dreamwork

If a client wants to work with dreams and hasn't been able to remember a recent dream, the therapist can move right into doing a hypnotic induction to create a hypnodream. (See Chapter 17 for an introduction to hypnodreams.)

Most people are able to do Gestalt dreamwork in the traditional posture, making movements and switching chairs as they switch characters, and so forth. Some persons find this distracting and may become more responsive after receiving a hypnotic induction. Also, the dream may be experienced more deeply and emotionally by some after an initial hypnotic induction, which is one possibility for by-passing resistance or to help someone who is using Gestalt dream-work methods but having difficulty identifying with the parts of the dream. The subconscious connections of this deeper state can bring the dream more to the surface.

If I do dreamwork after a hypnotic relaxation induction I don't have the person get up and switch chairs because that would be dif-ficult and distracting. Instead of switching chairs, I can tap a person on the shoulder or hand to encourage a switch to a different part.

With the integration of hypnosis, we can take traditional Gestalt work further. For example, Hypnotic Dreamwork can include fur-ther integration with direct and/or indirect suggestions. Traditional Gestalt therapy focuses just on the person's process, but there is so much you can suggest for further integration of the process while the subconscious mind is open to suggestion. Actually, the subtle sup-port throughout of the person's process, including encouragement of full expression of each character, is a form of indirect suggestion.

Typically, I keep direct hypnotic suggestions to a minimum dur-ing the process of the Gestalt dreamwork, and once we are at or near the conclusion, I often give various kinds of positive sugges-tions for reinforcement and further integration. However, depend-ing on circumstances, the hypnotic support can take place at differ-ent times during the process, not just at the conclusion. Suggestions at the conclusion can include, for example, encouragement that in-tegration continues to take place in the days and the weeks ahead, and in further dreams. The transcripts of this book include a wealth of examples of the integration of hypnotic suggestions into dream-work.

Sometimes before doing direct hypnotic suggestions, I will begin that process with a few brief hypnotic deepening techniques. The deepening can intensify the suggestibility, and it is also a signal for the client to become more passive and receptive. Additionally, hypnotic deepening can be used to increase the effectiveness of the process at any stage of the dreamwork.

During Hypnotic Dreamwork a dream can be transformed directly into regression when appropriate. Regression work is often valuable when a person is working on a particular issue or recurring pattern, because on a subconscious level, the person hasn't let go of something that is still affecting the way he or she sees and experiences the world. Perls said that a person's experiences are retrieved "not in his memory but in his behavior. He repeats it, without, of course, knowing that he is repeating it."

Traditional Gestalt dreamwork stays with just the dream and the dreamer's here and now experience. But with the understanding we have of hypnosis and regression, we can also return to an earlier similar experience. For example, using the affect bridge, a person can tap into a strong emotion that the dreamwork has brought up, and regress to specific significant experiences that happened out of the dream state at an earlier time. (Examples of how dreamwork can sometimes evolve into a regression can be found in chapters 11, 14 and 19.)

When dreamwork turns into a regression, various regression modalities can be integrated into the work. For example, while dream analysis is not associated with Gestalt dreamwork, encouraging the client to do his or her own brief hypno-analysis at the conclusion of a regression can be important and appropriate. When I lead such an analysis it is usually regarding the understanding and release of misconceptions that the client had continued to be stuck with in the here-and-now experience of himself and the world. I am usually able to help keep this self-analysis very brief so that it normally does not interfere with the hypnotic state.

Any additional form of hypnotherapy can be integrated when appropriate. For example, there are various ways ideomotor questions are used in the transcripts of this book to request information or get feedback from the subconscious. Other hypnotic tools selectively used herein include grounding and centering techniques, indirect suggestion, hypnotic metaphor, time distortion, bibliotherapy and inner child processes.

Providing a Supportive Presence

As has been stated, even without a formal induction, Gestalt dreamwork tends to initiate hypnosis. It's important to understand that people in hypnosis are in an extremely receptive and suggestible state. I consider it a sacred place that needs to be honored and respected. I do not consider it appropriate to ever criticize someone in that state. Examples of Perls' work show that he was a very critical practitioner at times, and some of the other early Gestalt therapists followed his example. But criticism can be reframed, as many therapists have discovered over the years. The therapeutic process can get stifled in a non-supportive setting. To give a client an environment of love and acceptance is to allow that much more potential for Gestalt to develop into its full capacity to do great work.

Dialogues in the dreamwork transcripts of this book demonstrate that there are many ways to communicate in a non-judgmental manner. The therapist provides greater opportunities by being supportive. Within the Gestalt process itself, for example, persons can be encouraged to continue a dialogue that has become frustrating so that they may become more aware of what they are doing that is causing that frustration. If a client is confused he or she can be helped to come to a better understanding more effectively through patience than through criticism.

Common Steps in Hypnotic Dreamwork

1. The dreamer describes the dream in present tense while vividly imagining it. Sometimes it may help to describe the dream again more expressively, including making gestures and movements to experience the dream more intensely.

2. The dreamer describes himself or herself as being one of the characters of the dream, endeavoring to stay in touch with his or her feelings. Then the dreamer becomes at least one more dream character.

3. Have some of the characters dialogue directly to each other.

4. Periodically have the dreamer describe what is happening internally. Sometimes an internal dialogue may develop from this that is a similar process to the dialogue of dream characters.

5. Keep working with steps two through four with selected characters until there is understanding and acceptance, or a completion of the communication that each side needs to make.

6. Any hypnotic process, such as ideomotor questions or regression methods, can be integrated when appropriate.

7. Brief further hypnotic deepening techniques may sometimes be used to increase identification of the dream or therapy process, or to initiate a detailed hypnotic suggestion period.

8. Hypnotic suggestions are given for further integration and acceptance.

9. Give suggestions for returning to normal awareness, followed by a posthypnotic interview.

CHAPTER 3

Dream Recall, Lucid Dreams and Hypnosis

Dreams can be fleeting and disappear from conscious memory quickly. Many persons rarely or never recall their dreams, but everyone dreams every night. Dreaming is a natural and necessary function, and EEG machines can document the periods of time each night that an individual's dreams occur. Sleep deprivation studies, in which a person is allowed to sleep but kept from dreaming, have shown how important dreams are to mental health and well-being.

Sleep states go through cycles. In the beginning of each cycle the sleep drops until it becomes deep, then lightens toward the latter part of the cycle. Dreaming takes place in the lighter stages of each cycle when brain waves are less slow, generally during stages of rapid eye movement (REM) sleep. The first dream period typically begins about an hour and a half after falling asleep.

Preparation for Improved Dream Recall

There are various methods that can help increase dream retention. Dream recall can usually become a habit with practice, even for someone who previously hasn't recalled any dreams for years.

Through hypnosis, we can use some of the most effective methods for recalling dreams. The hypnotherapist can give hypnotic suggestions for improving dream recall in conjunction with other methods, such as those described below. Self-hypnosis can also be used to give autosuggestions for dream recall, and this can be especially beneficial to do at bedtime. Keep expectations reasonable. It is unrealistic for a person who hasn't recalled dreams for years to expect to remember dreams, and remember them vividly, the first morning after this is hypnotically suggested. (Although this can happen.) Plan on gradually developing habits of dream recall with a dream journal, expecting as the days and weeks go by that you will be remembering your dreams with increasing frequency, detail, and clarity.

If you are not a novice just beginning to recall your dreams, you can give yourself a suggestion for a particular kind of dream, such as a dream about finding a solution to a certain issue in your life. Remember, however, that your subconscious mind on it's own will automatically choose to dream about important issues in your life.

Many persons have reported spontaneously having increased dream recall, without even trying to achieve that, within a few weeks of beginning a daily practice of self-hypnosis. The increased connection between the conscious and subconscious minds that occurs during hypnosis tends to open these same communication lines for better dream recall upon awakening.

Another method is to read something spiritually positive and inspiring before going to sleep. This can help raise your awareness beyond the concerns of daily life and tap you into the wisdom of your subconscious, which is the part of you that will ultimately find the best solutions to those concerns through your dreams. Praying can also be a beneficial spiritual habit at bedtime. Praying or spiritual reading habits would be of obvious benefit in other ways, especially at bedtime, partly because the value of these activities may be increased through heightened suggestibility if the hypnogogic state begins to take effect.

Awakening and Remembering

To help with dream recall, have your dream journal, which can be a pen and paper or tape recorder, handy next to your bed. Upon awakening, turn off your alarm if necessary, close your eyes, and return to or stay in the same physical position. If you awaken naturally, not because of an alarm clock or other external stimulus, you have probably been in light sleep and therefore dreaming. Even if you awakened by alarm clock, if this was after a fairly normal length of sleep, the odds are at this late stage that you have probably been dreaming. When it is possible, waking naturally without the aid of an alarm clock is recommended to assist with dream recall.

If no images of your recent dream come to mind, continue to lie still and stay relaxed. Slow your breathing down or keep it slow, and clear your mind. Allow any dream images to come to your conscious mind. You may find it helpful to move your closed eyes back and forth repeatedly, left to right and back, which is similar to the rapid eye movements which occur in dream sleep. As any images begin to come up, allow them to be. Feel that you are attracting the images to you, rather than chasing after them. Gently move from image to image. Continue as long as you wish, or as long as you are remembering more and reconstructing the dream. With practice, you will sometimes recall long and very detailed dreams. However, it is important to realize that any memory whatsoever, no matter how brief, can be successfully used for Hypnotic Dreamwork. If you are beginning to develop dream recall, be satisfied with any glimpse into a dream. If you recall a feeling but no dream memory, stay with the feeling. The feeling may lead to a dream segment. Let any images come that will.

If you do not recall anything, continue in your relaxed state and think a few key words one at a time, with several seconds or more to focus on each, such as: person, place, travel, building, house, outside, animal, object, emotion. If at any point such a category begins to trigger a dream memory, stay with it to develop the memory further. If the thought of "person" gives you a sense that you were doing something with someone, or going somewhere with a group, or having a dialogue with a few people, stay with that sense. A subset of category words can sometimes help at this point, such as man, woman, child, friend, family, co-worker, stranger, famous person, old, young.

As you are continuing to recall the dream or dream segment and preparing to begin to reach for your journal, it may help to mutter a few descriptive words about the dream to keep the dream in your mind during this shift. Then go ahead and write or speak into the recorder.

The vast majority of people who use these techniques will begin to remember their dreams. Some who still don't remember within several weeks may be resisting looking at some aspect of their existence.

Whatever the reason for continued lack of dream recall, you can respond by doing a hypnodream or some uncovering hypnotherapy work.

Awakening and Staying in the Dream

Lucid dreaming takes place when you become aware that you are dreaming and stay in the dream. The difference between a lucid dream and dream recall is that recall occurs after the dream as you are coming to consciousness from a dream state, or in a flash of memory later. You can go over details that are remembered and you may be in touch with certain emotions from the dream, but the dream itself happens outside of your conscious awareness. The drama unfolds with you as a character interacting with other characters and/or the environment.

In a lucid dream you come to awareness and stay in the dream, thereby having the possibility of some influence in the action or plot and outcome. The lucid dream is a state that is as real as life, except that you have fewer limitations. Because you are aware that you are dreaming, you can do things you are ordinarily unable to do or afraid of. You can create a fantasy, be anything you want to be, or leap off of tall buildings and fly. Lucid dreamers, however, report varying degrees of absolute control. A lucid dream can be a kind of a dance that occurs between your dreaming subconscious and the part of you which is aware. As one lucid dreamer reported, "It's a balancing act. You can say you want this or that, but you may be surprised by what you get."

An important element of lucid dreaming is that it gives the dreamer an opportunity to practice meeting difficult situations with awareness and creativity rather than habitual reaction. A habit is something that has become stored in the subconscious realm of our minds that we continue to do - sometimes consciously, and often unconsciously. If you have been driving a car for many years, for example, you don't consciously think about every time you change gears or press on the gas pedal or brake. You respond automatically from your subconscious mind. With continuing practice in lucid dreaming, a habit of awareness develops which can spill over into waking life as well.

The key to lucidity in dreaming is the awareness that you are dreaming and not awake. In the normal dream state strange things might be happening, but in spite of that it seems to be reality at the time. You think you are awake. Even if you have a fleeting suspicion that you might be dreaming, you don't check. Just as you can program yourself to recall dreams, once you have mastered the art of dream recall you can progress even further by programming yourself to check in while dreaming and become lucid.

Techniques for Checking In

A good method for checking in while dreaming is to make it a habit to look for signs. Look around and notice if things are in focus or clear. Look at something, look away, and then look back again to see if it is the same or has changed. When looking at something with words while dreaming (whether that be a book, magazine, office building or package of food), the words will be unclear, disorganized or moving . Look down at your clothing or look at your hand and ask yourself, "Am I dreaming?" If you are awake, you will of course know it. And if you are dreaming, you will also know it.

One way to begin to establish the habit of checking in while dreaming is to periodically ask yourself at random in your waking state during the day, "Am I dreaming?" or use one of the checking techniques listed above. It might seem silly at first because you are well aware that you are awake, but what you are doing is establishing a habit that can carry over into your sleep state.

An added advantage is that "checking in" helps us to stay more lucid and conscious during the day - so we can become more aware in our waking lives, and not go through the motions of life with little thought or consciousness. In effect, this technique helps us to "wake up" to life.

Stephen LaBerge, founder of the Lucidity Institute, says frequent lucid dreamers "wake up" more often in the waking state and realize, "Oh! *This* is what's happening to me." He practices the simple technique of trying to remember to touch the door frame whenever passing through a doorway, while asking himself, "Am I dreaming?" It helps him to stay awake in life and also to become lucid whenever he walks through a door in a dream.

More Methods for Developing Lucid Dreams

In addition to the periodic check in during the day, we can use the altered states that occur just before falling asleep at night and when waking up in the morning to seed the thought of checking in to see if we are dreaming. After inducing self-hypnosis or when in the hypnogogic state just before falling to sleep at night, give yourself the autosuggestion that it is your intention to recognize and check in when you are dreaming. Begin to create a dream and visualize yourself being lucid in the dream, asking yourself if you are dreaming and answering yes. Tell yourself that as you become lucid, you will remain in the dream. Pick a theme or action and say "I'm now going to..." For example, a lucid dream of a departed loved one can be as inspiring as a real visit and help persons who are struggling to cope with their grief and sense of loss. Or a lucid dream can be used as a form of rehearsal to increase performance and skill in such things as public speaking or sports. Give yourself the suggestion to become lucid again during that last dream stage of sleep in the morning just before waking up, and drift off as you begin creating your dreams.

After waking up from a lucid dream, use your dream journal in the same way that was discussed for dream recall. Keep your dream journal or tape recorder by your bedside. Say a few words about your dream out loud or to yourself to help you with the recollection as you reach for your journal or tape recorder, and begin to write or speak into the recorder.

Hypnotic Dreamwork with Lucid Dreams

In lucid dreaming your subconscious mind connects with your conscious mind and you become simultaneously aware. In hypnosis that connection is also made. In many ways the two states can be similar. Hypnodreams, which will be described in Chapter 17, can be virtually identical to lucid dreams, especially in the deeper levels of hypnosis. Acquiring the skill of lucid dreaming is another way to strengthen the connection between the subconscious mind and conscious awareness. In the beginning you might realize, "I'm dreaming" and simply follow along passively as the dream unfolds. This in itself is beneficial because dreams reflect your subconscious experience of yourself and the world. In fact, a wish fulfillment dream can be like positive auto-suggestions, and going along with the dream can intensify these healing qualities. With continuing experience you can take more control, helping meet challenges, determining where you want something to go and even choosing the subject matter. At the furthest end of the spectrum you might even be able to recall your waking life and direct your dream to pursue some interest or to creatively tackle some current issue. Remember, however, that your subconscious mind on its own will automatically choose to dream about important issues in your life.

Returning to lucid dreams later for Hypnotic Dreamwork, with a therapist or alone, will have the same common steps (described in chapter 2) as working with a regular dream or an elicited hypnodream.

* The dream is recalled in the present tense
* The dreamer becomes different characters and describes himself or herself
* Selected characters dialogue directly with each other
* The dreamer periodically may describe what is happening internally
* Hypnotic deepening and suggestions can be given
* Any further hypnotherapy processes can be integrated when appropriate

In addition, there are times when Gestalt dreamwork techniques can be brought directly into a dream when the dreamer becomes lucid. In a lucid dream the conscious mind has tapped into the subconscious and the expanded potential for meaningful personal transformation exists. Becoming lucid in a recurring dream, for instance, can be an opportunity to work on a major ongoing issue. A nonrecurring dream can also have great significance, but a recurring frustration dream is emphasizing that an important issue continues to be unfinished and is begging to be worked out.

From the Gestalt perspective, every character in the dream is a part of the dreamer. If a recurring dream happens to be a nightmare, for example, no matter how frightening a character or situation might be, by becoming lucid the dreamer has the awareness that he or she can't be harmed. Rather than run, the lucid dreamer can turn and face the monster and communicate with it. The dreamer can face his or her fear and dialogue with it, which is therapeutic in itself, and begin the process of understanding, growth and integration. Further dreamwork can also be done later.

The conscious mind is the tip of the iceberg. The other "ninety percent" is accessible through the subconscious mind, the seat of the emotions, imagination, memory, habits, intuition, and the pathway to the superconscious. Dreams are an important link between the conscious and subconscious mind and lucid dreaming, like hypnosis, forges a strong connection. With the powerful combination of hypnosis and Gestalt dreamwork, we can truly "become the dream" and experience the joy of waking up to much more of our full potential.

CHAPTER 4

Kay's Dream:

The Kidnapped Boy and the Goldfish Messenger

RANDAL: Tell your dream with your eyes open or closed, whichever is easier for you. Describe your dream as though it's happening right now, using the present tense.

KAY: Okay. I'm a young woman. There is a bus load of relatives waiting for me and my mother has come to me. She is rather agitated because I'm not ready to get on the bus yet and periodically she comes to me in the dream and says, "You know we've been waiting for you for hours and we can't leave until you're on the bus." I understand that she is embarrassed and upset because I'm not on the bus and she's losing face with the family. (Kay begins to cry and then laughs) God, do I have a load on this! So I understand that but things keep coming up that I have to do before I get on the bus. One of those is I have to shower and dress for whatever occasion that is. Another is that I come across a favorite cousin that I was partially raised with and I wind up assisting her in renovating a condominium.

RANDAL: Just a little side track. (laughter)

KAY: Right! And then another thing happens, which is my favorite part of the dream. I'm called in to help solve a mystery. The staff from a restaurant found me and had me come to the restaurant where there is a woman who is a detective. She's gone there for dinner and when the soup course comes, instead of soup, she has a bowl of water with a white goldfish in it. The goldfish is the clue but she doesn't know what it means so they call me. I know already when I get the phone call that the fish has been sent through the sewer system by a five or six-year old boy. (Kay is overcome by emotion and cries quietly for a few moments)

RANDAL: Stay with your feelings, that's fine. (Kay gasps) Breathe down into your stomach. An important part of Gestalt is going inside yourself.

KAY: Yes. So he's being held hostage and the only way he can communicate with the outside world to let them know is to... (Kay pauses unable to talk momentarily) I can't believe I've got all this stuff around this. So he takes his pet goldfish and sends it down the sink. And it comes up in the restaurant where this detective is and one of the people in the kitchen is aware enough to realize that that fish has to go to that detective because she will get the message. Then they also know when she doesn't get the message that they need to call me in to tell them what that means. (Kay cries and sighs deeply)

RANDAL: Keep breathing.

KAY: After I had this dream I felt very elated all day long. I'm kind of surprised that there is all of this going on around it now. That was about it. The boy was being held by two men and a woman but I didn't see that much of them. I knew he was being held there and that he had sent the goldfish.

RANDAL: Close your eyes and become that boy and feel what that feels like to be held hostage. (Kay is crying)

KAY: He was actually fine with it.

RANDAL: Become the boy.

KAY: I'm okay with it. I see... (deep sigh and tears) that I'm dealing with irrational people. (laughing and crying) They won't let me do anything as obvious as use the telephone so I have to think of a way to get a message out. I need someone to come and assist me because they're bigger than I am and I can't quite pull it off to just escape on my own. So I think of sending the goldfish out.

RANDAL: How does it feel to send the goldfish out?

KAY: (Kay pauses and tears run down her face) Well, I don't really want to lose the fish but it's the only thing I can think of to do and if it works the goldfish will be unharmed and I may even get it back. I just have to take that chance.

RANDAL: And how does it feel to take that chance? How do you feel about your goldfish?

KAY: (crying and speaking with some difficulty) I love it. It's very pure and beautiful and calm.

RANDAL: Become the goldfish. The boy has already described you. How do you describe yourself?

KAY: I'm a messenger. I'm silvery and white. I move very surrealistically in the water. I have a long tail fin. I'm a very pretty fish and I'm timeless.

RANDAL: How does it feel to be on this mission to try and save the boy? Going through the sewers as I recall?

KAY: (laughing) Well, it's all right because I've been through a lot before. It's just like one more mission. There's plenty of water going through the system so it's not really that bad. It was quite brief and it turned out very well.

RANDAL: So that feels okay. Any other feelings about doing this mission? Here the boy is kidnapped and you're trying to deliver a message. How does it feel to be a part of that?

KAY: That feels good. Having a purpose.

RANDAL: Good. Now I'd like you to become one of the kidnappers. Is there a main kidnapper or are all three of you together? Become the one that is either a leader or the one you recall most vividly now.

KAY: (pause) It was not a good idea to do this. (laughs) These other two, even for me their energy feels...my energy is not all that together, but these other two people are all over the place. Whatever the original idea was, it's like there is no plan. It's a mistake. Neither of the other two have really evolved as the leader in this situation which means I'm going to have to be the leader and that's not what I had in mind. I was just going along and I thought somebody had a plan but it doesn't look that way. And now we've got this kid here and I don't want to do anything to the child. I mean, what are we doing here? What is this?

RANDAL: (Randal pulls an empty chair around to face Kay) Okay, the child is in front of you. What do you want to say to the child that you kidnapped?

KAY: We didn't really know you were going to be here. (Kay speaks haltingly with a lot of emotion) You weren't part of the plan and to tell you the truth we don't know what to do with you. (pauses to cry)

RANDAL: Breathe down into your stomach.

KAY: The best thing for you to do is to just stay cool because I don't want to hurt you. And I won't. But I don't know about those other two people. They're not too stable so I don't know how this is going to turn out. Just stay calm.

RANDAL: Uh huh. What do you feel inside your body? Go inside your body.

KAY: Some tension.

RANDAL: Where do you feel that tension?

KAY: I feel tension in my stomach.

RANDAL: "I'm tensing my stomach."

KAY: I'm tensing my stomach.

RANDAL: (to class) Notice how she is now taking responsibility. Rather than feeling some tension she is tensing her stomach. What else do you notice? What else are you doing inside your body?

KAY: (laughing, then crying) Looking to see how I feel. When everything around me doesn't make sense that's where I look to get my bearings, so I'm doing that.

RANDAL: Well, just keep doing that. Feel your body.

KAY: I'm trying to figure out how to get the other two people out of there and just leave the whole situation. Leave the boy and walk out.

RANDAL: Let's bring these other people here now. They're right in front of you. What do you want to say to them?

KAY: We need to leave. We don't belong here. You may have had some idea about what was going to happen here or what you were going to do but this is not the time and place. We have to leave without disturbing anything. We've already disturbed the boy but he's okay. Now we just have to leave. You may not want to but that's what has to happen.

RANDAL: Good. Now I'd like you to switch and be one of the other two kidnappers. What do you want to say in response?

KAY: Well, that doesn't make much sense. We were going to do something here. There was some reason why we came but I can't remember exactly what it was now. I suppose we could just leave.

RANDAL: Okay, let's switch sides now. What do you want to say in response to that?

KAY: That's good.

RANDAL: Is it clear now that you are just going to leave? Is there any question or anything you need to say about how this is going to be done or does that feel finished?

KAY: We'll just tell the boy that we're going to leave and that's it. We're not going to do anything else. We apologize for upsetting him. We're going to leave now.

RANDAL: Let's bring him here now. He's sitting right in front of you. The others have agreed to leave and now you're here with the boy. What do you want to say to him?

KAY: We're leaving now and we're not going to bother you any more.

RANDAL: Is there anything else you want to say to him right now?

KAY: I don't understand why we were here but we're leaving.

RANDAL: All right. Switch sides and become the boy. (Kay switches chairs)

KAY: Okay. I wondered what you were doing here. (laughing) It kind of looked like you didn't know what you were doing. I guess since you're leaving and nothing really bad happened, in a way it was kind of exciting. I was scared before but I actually kind of liked it. So you're going to leave now. That's great.

RANDAL: Good. Does that feel finished or is there anything that you want from that person?

KAY: I think you and your friends ought to find something else to do. (Randal and Kay laugh)

RANDAL: Good idea. Let's switch and see what this person says. (Kay switches chairs) Is this person a woman or a man?

KAY: This is a man.

RANDAL: So how do you feel in response to what the boy just said?

KAY: I think it's a good idea. I think he's right.

RANDAL: "I think you're right."

KAY: I think you're right. You're a pretty smart kid.

RANDAL: Okay, let's switch back over here. (Kay switches chairs) Be the boy again and this time I want you to bring your gold-fish here. Your white goldfish. What would you like to say to your goldfish?

KAY: (laughing) You did a great job. And I'm really glad to have you back.

RANDAL: Wonderful.

KAY: (sigh) I was worried about you but I knew you could do it.

RANDAL: Switch. (Kay switches chairs) What does the goldfish say?

KAY: It's my job.

RANDAL: And how do you feel, goldfish? Do you feel like you accomplished something and do you feel satisfied?

KAY: Yes. I did my job.

RANDAL: Good. How do you feel in your body right now?

KAY: I feel fine. I'm relaxed. I feel pretty calm.

RANDAL: Take a deep breath and fill up your lungs. On the exhale send a wave of relaxation down your body as I push down on your shoulders. (Randal moves behind Kay and puts his hands on her shoulders) As I rub your shoulders feel yourself going deeper. As I very gently rock your head feel yourself going deeper. Continue being the goldfish. You are the goldfish. I'm going to count from three down to one and at the count of one your eyelids lock tightly closed. Try to open them on the count of one but you'll find the harder you try the tighter they lock together. (Kay sighs and cries softly) It's good to cry. Three, two, stuck tightly, one, go ahead and try. They're stuck together. (Kay tries to open her eyes) Okay, stop trying and feel yourself go deeper. (Kay cries harder now) It's so good to cry.

Feel the joy of being a hero. You really helped to save that boy that you love so much. (Kay continues to cry and Randal rubs her shoulders as he talks) Feel the joy of your own heroism, your own bravery. You said it's just a job but you were going through those sewers, you know? (Kay laughs) Your life was in danger and you made it. Be aware right now that you have that in you, that you can do whatever you want to do. (Kay alternately laughs and cries)

Just think how great you're going to feel accomplishing anything you want to accomplish. As a healer, as an intuitive, as a hypnotherapist, you just do it. You move forward from one achievement to the next. In your life, also, when you have something to accomplish, when you have a challenge, when you want to have fun, whatever it is, you do it. That beautiful white goldfish. You go through sewer water if you have to, and you come out clean and pretty. What a powerful attitude.

Now be that boy. Wow! Same thing for you. Do you realize you're a cool kid? You got kidnapped and you actually had a pretty good time with it. I think you're tapping into a lot of awareness that these people were pretty stupid and thoughtless but they didn't mean to be bad.

KAY: Uh huh. They were telling me it just got out of hand.

RANDAL: And you helped them just by being yourself. But besides recognizing these people for who they were, more importantly, you're a hero. I mean what did you have to communicate with? Absolutely nothing, but you had your goldfish! Hey, you are one creative boy. What are you going to be like when you grow up? Even more incredible? Is that what's happening in your life? You're becoming more and more incredible with every passing month, with every passing year as you are continuing to mature.

KAY: In a way, I guess that's true.

RANDAL: Well, you're only five or six years old and just think. This is just an early stage for you. You've got a long way to go. It may be hard for you to even imagine all the things you are going to continue to accomplish as you mature and develop and expand. And what a wonderful attitude – "Actually it was kind of fun for me." (Kay laughs) How many kids your age would do what you have done? Just feel good about yourself and know that you are years ahead of your time. You have great things to accomplish. Great adventures ahead. You can feel your adventuresome spirit and your cool and your creativity in working this thing out with your goldfish. You kept calm and brave in this process. The vast majority of processes in life aren't going to be this tough and you're going to do just great.

I want you to be Kay now and hold that boy (Randal places a pillow in Kay's arms) and tell him whatever you would like to say to him. (pause) You don't have to say anything. You can just hold him, that's fine, too. (after another long pause Kay cries in sobs) That's good, so good to cry, as you know. Such a release. It feels so good.

KAY: You did a really good job and there's a lot that you won't understand as you grow up but that's okay. You don't have to understand all of it. You have a really clear view and you see what's required in a situation. And you're sure of yourself. You know yourself. Even if you don't understand, that's okay because you have other things that will help you. Stay with those and that will carry you through.

RANDAL: Right. If you don't understand what's going on around you, you have all those other special parts of yourself. You have your confidence and all those aspects that will carry you through.

KAY: And you are very brave.

RANDAL: Be this boy now and talk to Kay. Feel the love she's been giving you and the good energy and the wisdom. What would you like to say to Kay?

KAY: I knew you would understand.

RANDAL: You're quite a team there. And your goldfish, too. All right, do you want to relax now? (Randal takes the pillow away) That's right, breathing down into your stomach. Stay centered. Just take it in. Know that you can do self–hypnosis any time you want and get in touch with those parts of yourself - the boy, the goldfish, all of that beautiful aliveness and heroism and cleverness and trust. How about that trust? Just trusting that everything would work out. When you have a challenge you just take it as a job and you do it very well. You use all of your creativity, your intuition, your life's experience, your guts, your strength, your intelligence, your heart. Feel your body. Feel the strength, the clarity, the peacefulness. Feel your health and vitality.

When I count to five to bring you out of hypnosis you feel all the more of that aliveness. You feel yourself being very present and having a nice balance today in your contact and withdrawal. You can reach out and pay attention to what's going on in the class and if you need a few moments sometimes you can go inward and notice how good you feel. You're going to have some beautiful dreams tonight. You may remember some of them in the morning. You're going to continue to have dreams that further integrate this process for you. Wonderful, tremendous parts of yourself. Remember to take time tonight and tomorrow night after both classes to have some peaceful meditative space for yourself. You just did a beautiful job and it's time to sit back and bask in that feeling of success. You deserve it.

Okay, getting ready now. Number one, slowly, calmly, and gently, becoming more and more alert, awake and aware. Number two, continuing to come back. Take your time, perhaps enjoying the sound of the rain in the background. Number three, continuing to come back. Nice, slow, deep breathing but more and more invigorated. Number four, getting ready to open your eyes. On the next number you're fully alert, rested and refreshed. Coming back, number five. All the way back.

KAY: (laughing and stretching) Thank you very much!

RANDAL: You're welcome and thank you very much. Just sit here for a minute and get used to having your eyes open. Great job. Just like that boy and the goldfish. Before you sit down I'd like you to take a look at the beautiful people in this room. (to the class) While she's looking around let's give her a hand. (applause) I'll be very happy to answer any questions but Kay has had a profound experience and I don't want to get out of our hearts and into our heads just yet. Let's take a break and you can ask questions afterwards. (looking out at the class) Oh, I'm talking without my glasses. I can see! I can see! (from the audience: laughter, "Hallelujah!")

RANDAL: (after a break) During the dreamwork, there were other places we could have gone and other characters that I could have had her become, like the sewer system. (laughter)

KAY: Thank you for not choosing that!

RANDAL: You're welcome. You can experience any aspect of a dream. Being the message, for example. The characters we worked with were obvious choices, like the fascinating goldfish and the boy. We also worked with the kidnappers. People can face their dark side but in this case these kidnappers weren't as horrible as most. Her characters did not have to really struggle much with each other. They were very cooperative. For a frustration dream, there was an extraordinary lack of resistance during this session.

Gestalt dreamwork is considered a full package but hypnotic procedures can add greatly to the process. At the end of Kay's Gestalt process, I added hypnotic deepening and post-hypnotic suggestions for further integration. I gave Kay various suggestions, knowing she would accept whatever fits for her. (to Kay) I wonder if you'll be surprised at how much does fit for you? (laughter) All right, so I throw in a few suggestions. Is that an interpretation? No.

Just making random comments. (more laughter) But that was after she did this whole process herself.

Kay has done a lot of work on herself and is an experienced therapist. She was well aware that crying is good, but I still reminded her as a reinforcement for her subconscious. If there are any residual emotions from childhood it's always good to encourage the expression of them, even when you know the person intellectually understands that.

It was interesting when I was addressing Kay as the boy during post–hypnotic suggestions that he spontaneously talked in response to me. Normally during suggestions people tend to be passive, but occasionally a child will verbalize aloud in response. When I said, "Be that boy," she really became that boy to the point of acting as such a feisty kid might act in hypnosis.

Kay did a beautiful job. She stayed with her feelings and rarely blocked them. The exception I noticed is that she occasionally stopped breathing, which is not unusual. Many of us do that sometimes when we start to feel pain. If you're not breathing you're not as aware physically and emotionally, so as therapists be prepared to remind people to continue breathing deeply. That's a good idea during any form of therapy.

Q: When you were working with Kay I noticed you kept bringing those chairs closer together. I wondered if there was any particular reason for that?

RANDAL: I started out with the chairs farther apart because I didn't know what the kidnapper was going to be like. If he was really like "Ahhh" (Randal grimaces and looks threatening) then I wanted her to have a little space from that. (laughter) Then the kidnapper said, "Oh God, I guess I really blew it, didn't I?" That's not so bad, so I brought them closer together. If you feel that there could be some extremely negative energy then that extra distance can be nice.

Q: (to Kay) Do you feel a need to go back on that bus and address any of the relatives or do you feel resolved with it now?

KAY: In the dream I never got on the bus. I had other work to do before I could get on.

RANDAL: This felt quite profound for Kay and it was a fairly detailed dream. She was feeling much more energy as she expressed the part of the dream that had to do with the goldfish messenger and the kidnapping. That seemed to be an especially urgent issue for her. The bus may be even less relevant now because she has dealt successfully with something that was more important. If she's really curious several days from now and wants to know about the bus, that would be an intuitive sign that there is something more that can be explored. We may have gone beyond the bus and since I don't know, I don't want to try to dredge something up that may no longer even be an issue.

Q: (to Kay) Did you feel like there was a connection to the inner child and the message?

KAY: I feel like I'm still integrating and I think that will keep happening, but I did have a very distinct feeling of being that child in a way. And I had a distinct feeling at the end of the process that I had grown up while we worked. I think a part of me was still stuck back there, rejecting those crazy adults and feeling like I didn't want to be a crazy adult so I opted to be a kid. Part of the process for me was to grow up and let those crazy adults go away.

RANDAL: Also the child part of you can enjoy all the more being a child, too, in the process of growing up. Over time you'll gain insights from your own background and experience in therapy without trying to analyze, "Oh yes, this is what's happening between my adult and child," from the Transactional Analysis viewpoint, for example. (to questioner) Your question was a request for Kay to intellectually try to interpret the meaning of part of her dream. I encourage us to be true to the Gestalt process and avoid analysis. (to Kay) Right now, for you to enjoy the experience of "something is happening" without trying to figure it out, exactly as you've been doing, feels just right.

KAY: Thank you so much. I feel really good. I feel like I changed and I'm looking forward to being in my life in a different way. (applause)

Interview One Week Later

RANDAL: How have you been doing?

KAY: Well, it's been an interesting week. A couple of times I thought about sitting down and working further with the dream, but like you said before, it wasn't there in that shape anymore. I had already taken it in and there was nothing else to do with it. But some good things happened. I've made overtures to my son to do some hypnotherapy with him, maybe just a relaxation, and he's said, "Yeah, I want to do that," but he hasn't had time. And this week he finally did. I worked with him and I also did some work with my husband. Interestingly, the work I did with my husband was about a brave child. It was a real mirror. I feel like the work you and I did together got me to a place where it allowed those two things to happen.

Another thing I noticed is that when I do collage work I always put a fish in. Whatever else is going on in the collage, there is always a fish in there somewhere and that's been true for a number of years. I think the dreamwork is connected. Also, there are some things in my life that are integrated now in ways they weren't before. For example, I notice I feel less need to justify and explain myself to people.

RANDAL: That illustrates an important point. It isn't necessary for a dramatic event to happen. You're someone who was already quite confident, but you now feel deeply secure about yourself. You have all of these attributes that you can express whenever you need to. A lot of that is going to be subtle because you don't need to go from A to Z. For you it's a matter of being that much more confident and powerful and secure. Not needing to explain yourself is a perfect example of that.

KAY: Yes. Before I felt like I always had to justify myself and I would give all this explanation before getting to my actual purpose. I just didn't need to do that this week. I was much more direct but without being threatening or aggressive.

RANDAL: That's all the more powerful.

KAY: And I noticed something else. Previously when I've been working on my art, there has been a little voice that says, "I can't believe you're spending your time doing this. You must be crazy. It's just like child's play. Blah, blah, blah..." and "Are you sure you should put that color there?" A continuous, invalidating, negating babble. And when I worked on a piece this week my mind was quiet. I'm sure some of you have done art work or some project where you get in the flow. It's not even a matter of "Oh, yes, this is the right color." You're just in the flow and questions don't even come up. I had an extended period of two or three hours with that and it was fabulous.

RANDAL: That's great. Are there any questions for Kay?

Q: At the beginning of your dream your mom was waiting for you with a bus load of relatives. Is your mother still alive and have you talked to her since the dreamwork? Or do you feel a shift with her from your own perspective?

KAY: My mother is alive and I haven't talked with her this week. Usually we would talk but we didn't because her phone wasn't working. Then her phone got fixed and our phone went out of order. (laughter) I can tell you that the older I get and the more I learn, the better my relationship is with my mother. I used to be very angry about a lot of things and I'm working that out.

RANDAL: We didn't deal directly with your mother in the dream but perhaps there is some synchronicity that your phones went out. Sometimes it will be appropriate for you to talk together and other times not.

KAY: Yes, I agree with that. My mother has twelve brothers and sisters so I have a huge family and more cousins than I can count. It became clear to me at an early age that if I took on as much involvement with the family as my mother had in mind for me, that could be my whole life. Somebody is always getting married, having a birthday, dying. It's like "Get me out of here!" because I could be swallowed up by family acknowledgment and involvement. That's been an ongoing issue.

RANDAL: One thing you've obviously had to learn is how to be selective. Although people might expect and want things of you, well, we're not in this world to live up to other people's expectations.

KAY: Right! It's not always easy to do. I know that she wants me to participate at certain times but I'm not always willing or available. I do participate a lot and I enjoy it when I do, and that's a new development in, I would say, the last ten years.

RANDAL: And of course that part of the dream wasn't about your mother, it was just represented by your mother. It was a part of you. I suspect this part has already begun to become more fully integrated.

CHAPTER 5

Rachel's Recurring Dream:

Back in the House of Israel

RACHEL: I've had a recurring dream for the last seven years. It's almost always the same and there is nowhere to dialogue because it's a very short segment. I tried becoming the part and becoming myself in the situation so I could tap into the feeling and every time I think I have dealt with it, after a few months it comes again. What can you do when there is no real dialogue?

RANDAL: Do you want to work on that now?

RACHEL: I'm scared but I want to.

RANDAL: It's up to you. I could give you an answer or we could do some work on it if you feel comfortable doing that in the group.

RACHEL: I feel like it's time. It's been seven years.

RANDAL: Great. (Rachel comes up and sits opposite Randal)

RACHEL: I want to tell you that it's a very humiliating dream for me.

RANDAL: I salute your courage in coming up here. In the process of working through the dream you can get into those feelings. Whatever the feeling is, you transcend the power it has over you by feeling it, facing it, and opening yourself up to becoming it.

RACHEL: And I'm doing it publicly.

RANDAL: Yes. In just getting up here and having the courage to work with this in front of all of these people now, the healing process has begun. You started to say that this is a recurring dream you've been having for seven years and you're having a problem with it because of the lack of dialogue. Even though you're familiar with doing some dream work, you've gotten stuck with it. Is the dream exactly the same each time or is it somewhat different?

RACHEL: Parts of it are the same and parts are different.

RANDAL: Okay. Please describe the dream.

RACHEL: I always find myself in Israel, where I came from. I'm in my parent's house. My grandmother is there. Every time the house is different. Sometimes my brothers are there and sometimes they are not there. The rest is pretty much the same.

RANDAL: Now tell a dream you've had in the last few months.

RACHEL: I had two this week.

RANDAL: That's close enough! Say it in the present tense as it's happening now. You don't need to say anything further about what's recurring or what's not. Right now this becomes your reality of your dream, of your experience, exactly as it occurred this week.

RACHEL: I'll close my eyes because it's easier for me. Suddenly I'm in my parent's house in Israel and I don't know what I'm doing there because I'm supposed to be here. It's like I'm cut off from the reality of the United States. All of my friends, everything is there in Washington.

RANDAL: Say rather, "I don't know what I'm doing here, I'm supposed to be over there in the United States." So go ahead, you're in Israel now, in your parent's house.

RACHEL: I don't know what I'm doing here. I have no money. I don't like to live here. I'm dependent on them again. I don't have my own space. I don't know what to do for work. I'm helpless. I have no friends. I'm lonely and I don't have anyone. Okay, what should I do for money? Maybe I'll go back to archeology. No, I can't go back to archeology. I don't want to do it anymore. I haven't done it for many years so I'm not competent anymore. No one would want me. I can't really find anything I can do for money. I'll do hypnotherapy. No, I can't do hypnotherapy because I'm not a psychologist and you can't do hypnotherapy in Israel. Why am I here? I don't know why I am here. That's it. All of this humiliation, that's part of my thoughts in the dream. I feel very humiliated and lonely because when I left Israel I had my career, I had my Ph.D. in archeology, I had my own house, I had lots of friends and now I have nothing. (Rachel opens her eyes)

RANDAL: Back when you were in Israel the first time, you had all these things. How long have you been in America?

RACHEL: Eight years.

RANDAL: So now you're back in Israel and you have nothing.

RACHEL: I'm like homeless, like a bum. I have nothing. And I have not anything to make money in the world. I am completely helpless.

RANDAL: Being in this dream now, is anybody there with you at your parent's house?

RACHEL: Sometimes my parents and my grandmother are there. Usually they are silent. I know that they're there. Sometimes I'm with my brothers. They share a room in the house and I think, "How come they're here? They're already married." I'm aware in the dream.

RANDAL: Okay, you're aware in the dream. You're aware right now. What are they doing here? They're already married and they're in the house. What part of the house are you in right now?

RACHEL: I'm just looking at the house. It looks like a simple house. It's like an apartment. It looks like a place we stayed for a short time. It's very simple and functional. I'm walking around to see what's there. I'm in the living room now. There's not much furniture there.

RANDAL: You're not seeing anyone around at this particular moment then?

RACHEL: I can feel my mother and my father over there.

RANDAL: So they're around but you're just wandering around in this functional house.

RACHEL: And I feel terrible. I feel like, how can I be here? I'm not supposed to be here. I feel like I went back in time and I'm trapped here.

RANDAL: So who or what has put you here? Close your eyes and we'll talk to that. (Randal moves an empty chair in front of Rachel) Let's put this in front of you and talk to the person or thing that put you here. What do you want to say?

RACHEL: I don't know why you brought me back here.

RANDAL: "Why do you bring me back here?" You're in Israel now, be right in the middle of that. You can feel and sense the house around you. Your father and mother are over there. Your brothers are staying here, whether they're here at the moment or not. And here you are with no money, no property, no work. (Rachel's expression looks pained and she is shaking her head as Randal talks) Talk to whoever or whatever did this to you.

RACHEL: Why did you bring me here? I don't belong here. I don't want to be here. It doesn't make sense. I feel like you brought me to a nightmare. Who are you?

RANDAL: Now I want you to get up and switch places and be whatever it is that brought you here. (Rachel switches chairs)

RACHEL: (pause) It's very hard.

RANDAL: Stay over here. This is where your power is right now. Go inside your body. Keep breathing down into your stomach.

RACHEL: I feel like I'm terrified to get into my body.

RANDAL: This is what brought you over here. You are that person or thing or whatever it is. You're terrified to get into your body. What do you feel in your body right now?

RACHEL: I feel a lot of energy right here. (Rachel moves her hand down her body)

RANDAL: Okay. A lot of energy all the way up and down your torso.

RACHEL: Here is like a big opening, a big rush of energy (motioning from the top to the bottom of her torso), and here (motioning around her head) it's like I have no head, like it's just space. Like I'm spinning.

RANDAL: So be that big rush of energy. Is it better for you to stand up or sit down here? (Rachel stands up) You are one big rush of energy. (Rachel is breathing heavily) That's right, breathe down into your belly. Breathe all the way down into your toes. Stay with it. (tears are running down Rachel's face and Randal removes her glasses) You're doing great. Feel that rush of energy coursing through your whole body. Are you in touch with that energy?

RACHEL: It's only to here (Rachel motions to under her chin). It hasn't gotten here yet (motioning to her head).

RANDAL: It's from the bottom of your chin to where?

RACHEL: I can feel it in my toes.

RANDAL: All the way down to your toes. Feel that energy there. Keep breathing down into your stomach. Breathe down into your toes. Feel that energy coursing up and down your body as if you are that energy yourself. (Rachel's head is shaking)

RACHEL: Can you tell my mind to be quiet, please?

RANDAL: You tell your mind to be quiet. There is a gap between the head and the body. You are the energy. Put your head on the chair there and tell it to be quiet.

RACHEL: Please be quiet. Please don't take me out of this process because I want to get it.

RANDAL: All right. Now I'm going to have you switch and be Rachel's head over here. (Rachel sits in the chair) You are the head over here, speaking to this energy that's coursing through the body. Go ahead. Shake your head. Be Rachel's head. What do you want to say to this energy here?

RACHEL: I don't like this energy.

RANDAL: Say, "I don't like you."

RACHEL: I don't like you. I like to figure things out and I can't figure you out. I like to be in control. I like to understand everything. You're pushing me away and I don't like it.

RANDAL: Now get up and switch sides. (Rachel gets up and faces the chair) Keep standing. Be this rush of energy now. You heard what Rachel's head just said to you. What do you say in response to that? She doesn't like to be pushed away. She doesn't understand you.

RACHEL: I think you just bullshit a lot. You like to say all kinds of things and figure things out and it doesn't take me anywhere. What takes me somewhere is feeling my body, being in my body. My body knows better than you.

RANDAL: Excellent. Feel the power that you feel being in your body. (Rachel smiles) All right. What's that smile? Does it feel good?

RACHEL: My mind is now this small. (Rachel makes a circle with her thumb and index finger)

RANDAL: Let's put your mind on the chair and see what it has to say. (Rachel sits in the chair) Now be that mind that is smaller.

RACHEL: I'm small but I'm still smart. I'm strong and I'm still here.

RANDAL: What do you want to say to that energy? How do you feel toward that energy right now?

RACHEL: I have to admit, you don't feel so bad anymore.

RANDAL: It helped, what it had to say?

RACHEL: It feels okay. I feel like I trust this energy.

RANDAL: Say, "I trust you."

RACHEL: I trust you and I don't need to protect you.

RANDAL: Get up and switch and be that energy. (Rachel stands up and faces the chair) Talk to Rachel's head.

RACHEL: It's here. (Rachel taps her head)

RANDAL: Good, you've got your head back in place now. The part of you that is that energy, what do you want to say to the head? (to the class) Notice the integration. This is what it's all about.

RACHEL: Thank you for listening and cooperating and maybe we can do something together.

RANDAL: Excellent. So we've come all the way to an appreciation and a respect. Anything else you want to tell the head?

RACHEL: You're very smart and you have helped me out many times.

RANDAL: Yes, you need that head. Now head, can you say something further that you appreciate about that energy over here?

RACHEL: I have appreciation for it because it's also smart. It has its own intelligence and I like smart.

RANDAL: Okay, now you've got the two of you together. The whole is much greater than the sum of the parts. You've put yourself in Israel without any money, without a job and all that. You've got all of your power. You're feeling yourself really integrated.

RACHEL: Right.

RANDAL: So Rachel was asking you what you brought her here for. Do you have an answer for her? Let's find out what the opportunity is here. What are you accomplishing by going to Israel now?

RACHEL: To teach her to create something from nothing.

RANDAL: Very good. You're telling me this woman is that powerful, to create something from nothing? (Rachel starts to cry) I'll bet you she is. Go inside yourself, Rachel. Go inside that part of you that can create something from nothing. (Rachel sobs) Feel how good it feels to cry. What greater power in the world can there be than creating something from nothing? You're doing it right now. Breathe down, all the way down to your toes. There's never been anyone in the world that is just like you. You're very special. And you are right now creating something from nothing. Every moment you are becoming that much more of a new person and using that much more of your full capability. You've got the power within you to create marvelous things. How many people have created something from nothing? You're one of those that can do it and are doing it. Talk about growth. What greater opportunity is there than that? Go inside your body now. What do you feel?

RACHEL: I feel a rush of energy throughout my body. It feels like I'm more inside my body. I feel more contact with the earth.

RANDAL: That's great. You can take even more responsibility for that by saying, "I'm contacting the earth." That is you initiating it now.

RACHEL: I'm contacting the earth.

RANDAL: "I'm sending rushes of energy through my body."

RACHEL: I'm sending rushes of energy through my body. I'm making contact with lots of parts of my body. I feel that this is my house.

RANDAL: Say that again.

RACHEL: I feel that this is my house.

RANDAL: You don't have money and other things, but now you have a lot, including this home. Talk about what you have and who you are.

RACHEL: I have all this intelligence which is light and love and beauty, and it's creative.

RANDAL: Light, love and beautiful, creative intelligence. Sounds like the greatest riches in the world to me. You can do anything with that - on any level. If you want to make money, you can find ways to make money. You find ways to get security, to get love, to develop your relationship with yourself. You can have all of this that is you. All of your soul, all of your life's experience.

RACHEL: I'm already doing it.

RANDAL: And you're already doing it. Rather than be afraid of it you can take joy in it and trust the miraculous. This is wonderful, this emerging work that we just evolve with. And that's life. That's what you're doing. You're doing a beautiful job of it. (Rachel opens her eyes) Wow, your eyes look beautiful. (to the group) Look at Rachel. (to Rachel) Take a look at the people out there.

RACHEL: It's hard to see without the glasses but I can feel.

RANDAL: Look with your third eye. You can also put your glasses on.

RACHEL: No, I don't want the glasses.

RANDAL: All right. I'm with you. I don't have my glasses on either. (looking toward the audience and squinting) I sense someone over there. (laughter - then Randal looks back at Rachel) Look at those eyes, that beautiful face. Look at that receptivity and openness. You

can all see that. (to Rachel) Without your glasses, just make eye contact with some of the people, whoever you would like to. (Rachel
makes eye contact with several people) Do you still feel good without your glasses?

RACHEL: Yes. (she continues to make eye contact with various
class members)

RANDAL: Great. You can see enough. You can see plenty. You
can see with more than your eyes, too. You can feel with your heart.
A lot of different parts of you are taking in that energy. Feel those
beautiful people out there. Hey, I'm having a good time. All right.
Let's go over here. (Randal and Rachel walk over to the other side
and look at the people) Is there anything you would like to say to
Rachel?

SEVERAL GROUP MEMBERS: Welcome home!

RACHEL: Thank you.

RANDAL: You can say it with your heart and your gaze as well.

RACHEL: This is great. (Randal and Rachel hug and the class
applauds)

RANDAL: A lot can be done in a brief session. It brings people
into themselves and their different parts. This was a fine example of
the integration of those parts. I also would like to acknowledge the
group. I've seen people do profound work, experiencing transfor-
mations and even miracles in private sessions. But group energy
often adds something to this process. Not only the specific thing
that we did at the end with Rachel, but the presence, attention, and
support of the group. I want to thank all of you for that. Are there
any questions?

Q: At what point do you know that the session is ended? Rachel's
face just lit up, but how do you know you've taken care of this recurring dream?

RANDAL: I don't think there is a magical point at which dreamwork is ended. There is often more that can be accomplished in the
way of integration, but in this case it was obvious that there was a
major completion. She got it. She was getting value at many stages,
but when she reached the point of saying "This is my house," that
was very thorough integration. "Now my head is on my body."

I like to get some form of completion when I do a session, even
in cases when there is much more work that needs to be done. You

can give encouragement and reframe the session in a way that will acknowledge the person for what they've accomplished and seen. A hypnotic suggestion might be, "You are continuing to experience more deeply and understand all the tools you have to continue to integrate this process into your life. You're making many breakthroughs today and tomorrow and all through the week, so that when we have our next session you'll be able to communicate many realizations and experiences and new ways of acting, thinking and feeling." You can even suggest further healing dreams of whatever kind to make greater and deeper and more powerful integration of these experiences.

Rachel's dreamwork came to a very clear and heartfelt stage that feels complete and finished, but it's not always so obvious. She had already come a long way when she started to tap into that force of energy and I could have finished with that, saying, "Great, you're starting to feel that now, and in your own life you can work with this." If you get to a point like that as you're doing dreamwork, that's a very significant step.

Commentary

This brief session takes a step beyond the previous dreamwork with Kay, by working with a split within Rachel. Gestalt process often leads beyond dialogue between characters to dialogue between parts of a character in the dream. The character could be the individual who had the dream or any aspect of the dream.

At the end of the dreamwork I gave some post-hypnotic suggestions without adding hypnotic deepening because the hypnosis Rachel had naturally entered while doing the dreamwork had already been dramatically strengthened by the emotional intensity and breakthrough of awareness she was processing at that moment. She had spontaneously entered a level of consciousness that opened her potential for maximum results.

Postscript: Rachel Writes Three Years Later

When I attended your Dream Seminar and worked on my dream, there was a point that fostered an inner shift and also deepened my rapport with you. That was when you asked me, "So who or what has put you here?" That was the mystery and the cause of my feeling helpless. The not knowing how I got there, "seemingly" against my will. Bringing it directly to the "hot seat" was refreshing and took me by surprise that you could pinpoint it so simply. I felt appreciative and I knew that I could trust you.

The real inner split was between my heart that missed my country and my practical mind which warned me of my inability to make a living in my country of origin, with the new skills that I acquired in the United States. Within a month after our session I had another variation of the same dream. The major difference was that this time I was more in touch with my power, and felt capable of making a living, in my country of origin. Since then, I haven't had any similar recurring dream.

CHAPTER 6

Susan's Dream:

Rosemary's Baby

SUSAN: I'm in a castle that reminds me of the castle in the Wizard of Oz, only it's nicer. I'm in a beautiful room. There are stone walls but there are also golden tapestries and draperies and things like that. And there's a big, soft bed. It's very nice. The next thing I remember is a feeling that there was something wrong and there was a man...

RANDAL: "And now I'm starting to have a feeling that there is something wrong..."

SUSAN: Something is wrong and there's a tall man with brownish curly hair, dressed almost regally. He's like a king or something, wearing golden and purple robes. But when I look at him I get almost a holographic image. I'm seeing him and seeing the two of us together and he changes and he becomes... (pause) I can see the face of a wolf. I know that he is not good. There is a very definite feeling that this is wrong and it comes to me that he is the devil and he is hiding in this image of the kindly king in regal robes. I don't know what he wants but I'm not really afraid. And we're still walking down the corridor and talking and I'm pretending not to notice that I see him as a wolf.

Then it comes to me that I'm going to be part of a ceremony, the birthing of the anti–Christ. And I'm still not really worried. I know that my lover is out on his bike and he's going to be home soon and he'll help me get out of this situation. I'm not concerned. Now the wolf face has changed and I'm not seeing him as a dark wolf. I can see quite clearly that he is a white wolf and he is walking upright as tall and as large as a man.

I make my excuses to go to my room to get ready for dinner and when I get there Bob is there, but he's asleep on the bed and that's very unlike him. I know that he's always awake and alert after a ride and very active. It troubles me that he's sleepy. I feel again that there's something wrong here but I wake him up and tell him all about what's going on. I'm telling him to help me. "I want you to come and we've got to get rid of this guy. We've got to save mankind," or whatever. I don't know that that's what it is, but we have to do this together. He's agreeing and I take him with me but he's so lethargic. And we get back to this wolf/devil, whatever he is, and I realize that the reason he's so lethargic is that the devil has already gotten to him. He is under the devil's spell and he can't help me. He basically is turning me over to the devil, and I'm still not afraid because I know in my heart that I can save both of us. I will be able to talk my way out of this. I'm beginning to speak to the wolf/devil, talking him into letting us go. As I begin to come up with the reasons why we should be let go and why this is not going to happen, I wake up.

RANDAL: As you're talking him into letting you go, do you feel that you're really getting somewhere?

SUSAN: Uh huh. I feel it in my heart. I know everything is going to be okay. I know that I can get us both out of this jam.

RANDAL: I get goose bumps from this dream. This is powerful. I'd like you to start by describing yourself as if you really are the castle. Describe your qualities.

SUSAN: Okay. I'm very large and I'm very strong and I'm very ancient. I've withstood everything and I will continue to withstand. These humans may come and go but I'll still be here. You can add tapestries to me to change my appearance but I'll always be here.

RANDAL: How does it feel to be this castle?

SUSAN: It's nice.

RANDAL: All right. Now be the wolf. Describe yourself.

SUSAN: I'm still very powerful and I'm going to win. I'm tricky and I'm sneaky. I'm going to have my way at all costs and I don't care who gets hurt because that's the way it is.

RANDAL: How does that feel, being this part that says "I'm going to win."

SUSAN: I like winning, like anyone. But the idea of winning at all costs troubles me greatly. The idea of hurting someone to win is a burden.

RANDAL: You say it troubles you greatly. Do you feel that as the wolf or are you talking as Susan now?

SUSAN: Susan.

RANDAL: Okay, be the wolf and describe how it feels to have the kind of power that you wield and to be the kind of person or thing that you are, this wolf/devil pretending to be a king. How does that feel?

SUSAN: It's actually a physical sensation of strength and power. But it doesn't sit well in this body.

RANDAL: Uh huh. I want you to have the courage for the moment to be that. And I'm wondering, since he is standing and walking in the dream, if perhaps you could be standing up? (Susan stands up) Remember you're just playing a part here. Have the courage to feel the power of this creature and all of the different qualities, negative and positive. Power has its positive qualities, it's a matter of how it's used. Feel what it feels like to be this creature. Describe what you look like and what you do, really experiencing that.

SUSAN: Okay. I do love my strength and the power that I wield. And I'm beautiful and I know that. The facades that I put on are merely for show but I'm beautiful. I'm a huge white wolf. My goals are my own and they may not be appreciated by others but they are mine and I will hold on to them. I believe in what I'm doing.

RANDAL: Very good. (Susan sits down) It's important for you to be that, understanding when you experience the different parts that you don't take it literally in every single aspect. You were just describing things that are power points for you and you can use them as you work this out. And you can find ways to use them in your life, that are positive rather than negative.

There are many fascinating possibilities here, including playing different parts of the castle and Bob and the robes and so forth, but I'd like to go right to the end of the dream. Come over here, please. (Randal directs Susan to sit in a chair opposite where she was standing) I'd like you to be Susan and talk to the wolf creature just as you were doing when you woke up. I'd like you to start having that dialogue with him now.

SUSAN: I know who you are and I can see you for who you are and you cannot control me. It doesn't really matter what you do to me physically, you will never be able to take control of me. And you will never control my child nor have that child because it will always be mine. It will always be a part of me. And the goodness that I have within me can overpower you.

RANDAL: Very good. Now switch and be him.

SUSAN: I don't like him.

RANDAL: I know you don't like him. That makes it all the more important. The way to transform this part is to become this part. Let yourself get into it. In the beginning you're going to be every single aspect of this part and we'll see where it goes.

SUSAN: (pause) I can't even come up with good arguments. I think that's the hardest part.

RANDAL: Stand up. You did a good job standing up. (Susan stands up) Now you're in the shape of this white wolf in his beautiful robes and you're about to do this ceremony. You're in your power right now. This is what you are determined to do and yet you have someone who has caught you and knows exactly what you're about, whether you've been fooling other people or not. You want to do the ceremony with Susan and she's saying no way. Now what do you say?

SUSAN: I say that I'm a god and I have more power than a mere mortal and I will do as I please. No one can stop me.

RANDAL: Very good. Switch. (Susan sits down) All right, Susan, this guy says he's a god and he's got much more power than you, a mere mortal. What do you say to that?

SUSAN: I don't believe in the power of evil. I believe that evil is within us and therefore anything that you can throw at me is already within me. I can win because I just have to change it around. I just have to turn it into a positive and you can never win.

RANDAL: Great. Now switch. Be this guy. I think it's good for now that you continue to stand up. (Susan stands)

SUSAN: The evil that is within all of us is stronger than the good and I can still win because mortals are weak. They give in to the evil because it's easier or because it feels good.

RANDAL: You're doing a great job. Now switch and be Susan.

SUSAN: Well, it's true that evil is often tempting but it doesn't have to be given in to and I choose not to give in to it. I'll follow my own destiny and will not allow others to take control.

RANDAL: Good. Switch.

SUSAN: Whenever you are weak I will be there waiting.

RANDAL: Okay, switch.

SUSAN: I understand that and I will be ready.

RANDAL: All right. Let's see if there is anything further he has to say.

SUSAN: As will I.

RANDAL: Switch and be Susan. Is there anything further you have to say? (Susan shakes her head) How do you feel now? This guy is so confident.

SUSAN: So am I.

RANDAL: I feel that. That's great. Now as I understand it, in this dream you're about to give birth, is that right?

SUSAN: No.

RANDAL: Isn't this a ceremony about the birth of the anti–Christ? What were you going to have to do within the ceremony?

SUSAN: I would eventually be the surrogate mother.

RANDAL: Okay. Was the ceremony going to be to get you pregnant, for the anti–Christ? (Susan nods) I get it, like "Rosemary's Baby". Sit down and close your eyes. I want you to feel the confidence that you have. Here's the devil, someone more than a mere mortal and he can't touch you. Feel your strength. Where does that come from? (Susan gestures to her heart) Good, from your heart. Feel your heart expanding and becoming very powerful. Feel that radiant energy. I'm going to count from three down to one and at the count of one your eyelids will lock tightly closed. At the count of one try to open your eyes but the harder you try the tighter they lock and the deeper into hypnosis you go. Three, two, stuck tightly, one. Go ahead and try but they're stuck together. (Susan's eyebrows move but her eyes remain closed) That's good. Relax, stop trying, and go deeper. Now I'm going to pick up your left hand. Just let it hang loosely in mine. When I drop your hand send a wave of relaxation down your body. Now I'll pick up your right hand. As it drops feel yourself go even deeper. That's fine. Take a nice, deep breath and fill up your lungs. On the exhale send a wave of relaxation down your body and feel yourself go much deeper. That's good. Now another deep breath. On the exhale send another wave of relaxation down your body. That's good. One more nice, deep breath and this time go five times as deep. Way down, way down. As I massage your shoulders feel yourself going deeper. Feel your grounding cord going from your perineum right down to the center of the earth. Feeling pure light shining down on you and feeling the most light of all coming from within your heart and radiating outward.

There have been countless people throughout history that have resisted evil and you are one of those people. You use this to your advantage in the way so many others have. You use this as an opportunity to stand up and be strong and clear and to be all the more virtuous, all the more dedicated, all the more honest, all the more powerful. You have stood up to this very powerful creature, robed and beautiful and thought to be a king, that has been fooling a lot of people. But you have seen through his disguise and that makes you more powerful than him. In standing up to him you gained those qualities that are good – including qualities of power and beauty and clarity of purpose. You take on only that which is good and you let go of the rest. The more confident he becomes, the more confident you become.

Just like millions of other people who have done this very successfully, you continue to hold your power and strength. Each situation in which you find yourself, you continue to make a good and clear choice. When you keep speaking the truth, your word begins to become law in the universe. I honor you. In the face of this creature that has been so terrifying to so many people, you are confident. You're not going to buy into him. You know that you have your soul and that you are victorious.

Now I'd like you to look at what you can do in this situation in which Bob has been under the spell of this creature and you are confident that you can save him. Bring Bob here now and tap into what you are doing for him. Perhaps it's going to be very easy. When I tap your shoulder you can describe what you are doing to help get Bob out of the situation. Three, two, and one. You can speak.

SUSAN: I'm just holding him and loving him.

RANDAL: All right. I'm bringing Bob here now. (Randal places a pillow in Susan's arms) You can hold him and love him. Is there anything you'd like to say to him or would you like to be non–verbal now?

SUSAN: I want to tell him that he has the strength, too.

RANDAL: Say, "You have the strength, too."

SUSAN: You can make it. (Susan caresses the pillow)

RANDAL: Switch and be Bob. (Randal touches Susan on the hand - Susan will stay in the chair rather than switch chairs during the remainder of the process) What does Bob say in response to that?

SUSAN: He's afraid. (tears start to run down Susan's cheeks)

RANDAL: So be Bob. Say, "I'm afraid."

SUSAN: I'm afraid.

RANDAL: Be Susan. (Randal touches Susan on the shoulder) Bob is still afraid. What do you want to say to him?

SUSAN: I'll help.

RANDAL: Make it present tense rather than what you're going to do. Tell him what you're doing now to help.

SUSAN: I don't know what to do.

RANDAL: Yes you do. Stay with it. Bob's afraid. He needs your help. Is it helping him that you're holding him?

SUSAN: Uh huh.

RANDAL: Good. So you're helping him. You do know what to do. (Susan nods) Does that feel sufficient for the moment? The best thing you can do for now is just hold him? (Susan nods) Good. Hold him. Love conquers all. You're healing him right now by holding him. It's just what he needs. Sometimes in life, Susan, you don't need to know what to do next. You can just do what your heart tells you to do right now and it all sorts itself out. When the next situation comes, what needs to be done emerges. And maybe the next thing to do is to continue holding him for awhile longer. You're doing great. Loving and supporting him is also healing for you. It's good to give your love. Tap into the tremendous power in your heart that is radiating out and know that that is having a profound effect. Sometimes it takes time but the ice is melting. (Susan nods her head) You can feel that now. You know that. You know just what I'm saying. He's healing. He's clearing. Those former effects are wearing off. Now switch and be Bob. (Randal touches Susan on the hand) Is there anything you'd like to say to Susan right now?

SUSAN: Just be there.

RANDAL: So, Bob, does this feel good, having Susan hold you? Are you starting to feel less afraid and more secure now? (Susan nods) Feel what it feels like to be Bob, to feel the beautiful love and comfort and strength Susan has to give you. Know that she's one hundred percent there for you. Know that you are getting more power and more courage and more strength and more freedom and more clarity and more self–determination with every moment. Now be Susan (Randal touches her shoulder) and feel that radiant energy coming from your heart. (Susan's head nods slightly) Know that the more you give the more you receive and that there's an infinite supply. It's coming from your heart and from your soul. (Susan takes a deep breath)

That's right. With every inhale you're breathing in the life force. With every exhale you're exhaling any tensions. You're radiating that energy out and healing him. And sometimes nothing needs to be said. Just feel. Just be. And sometimes, just like Bob, you can be afraid, and that's okay. Just stay with your heart. It all sorts itself out. The heart is victorious. You deserve love. You deserve to give love. You deserve to be a loving, healing force in the world. A good, loving therapist. A good, loving friend. A good, loving person. Especially a good, loving friend to yourself. You give this loving energy to others that you choose to, and to yourself. Now be Susan. Be in your body. What do you feel right now?

SUSAN: Okay.

RANDAL: You feel fine? (Susan nods) Stay with that. Isn't it wonderful that sometimes the best thing to do is just to be? To be with your center, to be with your heart, to be with your love. And it works. Stay present. You are getting more powerful by the moment. You have all the time in the world. Breathe down into your stomach and into your heart. Now switch and be Bob. (Randal touches Susan's hand) Let's see how Bob is doing now. Get in touch with your body and your feelings and tell me what's happening with you.

SUSAN: I'm okay too.

RANDAL: Feeling better and better? (Susan nods) Great. It's working. You deserve it, Bob. You're healing. Look at how far you've come. You were under the spell of that powerful creature who says he's immortal, who says he's better than people. Now look at you. You've opened up to Susan's love, the love of your dear friend. She has healed you by you opening up and allowing that healing between you and her to take place. Do you realize how far you've come? Enjoy it, Bob. Take it in. Feel the love that you feel for Susan, who has saved your life because she loves you very deeply. She went up against the devil, took you away from that creature and saved you. And part of it was that you saved yourself, too, because deep down you had the power to be receptive to her love.

Talking to both of you, Bob and Susan. Your subconscious mind continues to learn a great deal. It continues to learn how much you gain in your life as you remain open to the love that is there. Seek and you shall find. Reach out and you have resources around you. You have your friends, you have your family, you have each other. You find ways to make your love work, to transcend to new and greater experience. You experience new and greater affection and joy and power. Heal deep down. The nurturance, the giving and receiving, how good that is for both of you. The more you give, Susan, the more you receive. You deserve all the good that life has to offer. How are you doing, Susan? Feeling fine?

SUSAN: Uh huh.

RANDAL: Good. How are you doing, Bob? (Randal touches Susan's hand) Feeling fine? (Susan nods) Now you're even more powerful because there are two of you. You're together. You're walking away from that attempt at a ceremony. I'd like you to feel that power. Take a look at that creature over there. Is there anything that you'd like to say to him at this time? (Susan shakes her head slightly) Nothing? That's fine. He obviously sees the power that you have together so you can get a sense of what's going on. Is he walking away? What is happening here as you get a completion?

SUSAN: We're walking away.

RANDAL: Okay, feel yourselves walking away together. You can go anywhere you want. You're going to a good and nurturing place for you and Bob to continue to enjoy each other and yourselves and your love and your strength. Get in touch with where you are going and when I touch you on the shoulder you can describe that.

SUSAN: It's a big, beautiful room.

RANDAL: Is this a big, beautiful room in the castle?

SUSAN: No.

RANDAL: This is elsewhere.

SUSAN: Uh huh.

RANDAL: Is this like a sanctuary for you?

SUSAN: Uh huh.

RANDAL: Good. You're going into a big, beautiful room. It's a sanctuary room in your own place far away from there. How does that feel?

SUSAN: Good.

RANDAL: Know that you and Bob can go there together any time you want. You can also go there by yourself or with any other friend. Your subconscious mind continues to learn a great deal and continues to find ways to tap into sources of power and wisdom within you that know what to do and how to do it.

Now I would like you to show me your "yes" finger please. (Susan lifts her right thumb) Okay. Please signal your "no" finger for me. (Susan lifts her right index finger) Okay, as we are concluding this process now, Susan, I'm going to give you two possibilities and either possibility is perfectly fine. I'm going to tap into the wisdom of your subconscious mind because your subconscious mind knows the answer to this. I don't. We can just complete this now and have you be secure in this very beautiful place. Or the alternative would be to look at that creature from a distance and get a sense at this time if there are any further positive aspects of that creature that you would like to take on to help the love and the good things that you have. Would you rather stay here in this beautiful place, just you and Bob, and continue to let that creature be far away? (Susan lifts her right thumb) Yes. That's fine.

Look over there and see that you are separating yourself from the creature and gathering the success of the good. Over millions of years of history human beings have come so incredibly far. Once again, good triumphs over evil as you continue to find ways to successfully thrive on the love within you, giving and receiving that love.

Is there anything you would like to say or to ask, Susan, before I bring you up out of hypnosis? (Susan lifts her right index finger) You signaled no. Thank you. I know how good it is now to just feel that loving energy between you, to feel how far that love can go. It can be life saving. That deep inner knowing of the power of love is always there in your subconscious. You can come back to this beautiful sanctuary by yourself or with Bob or with anyone else, including tapping into the wisdom of God, the wisdom of the spiritual energy and love around you, any time you want.

I'm going to count from one to five. With each number that I count you become more and more alert, awake and aware. At the count of five you open your eyes, feeling fully alert, rested, refreshed and invigorated. Number one, slowly, calmly, easily and gently, begin returning to your full conscious awareness once again. On number two, more and more alert, awake and aware with each number. (Susan begins to rub her eyes and Randal removes the pillow she has been holding) On number three, more and more alert, awake and aware. Number four, getting ready to open your eyes. On the next number opening your eyes, feeling fully alert, fully rested, fully refreshed. Number five, wide awake. Welcome back. (pause) How are you doing?

SUSAN: Great. Thank you.

RANDAL: You look great.

SUSAN: You gave me the power of the wolf so I didn't need to talk to him again.

RANDAL: Good, so you had already completed the integration. It didn't surprise me when I asked you if you wanted to go over that and you signaled no. It felt like you had all of that power and you didn't need to receive any more. This integration can take place in a lot of different ways and sometimes without having to own it more directly. You found your own way to get that power. Love triumphs again! The good guys win! (applause from the class)

Q: I'd like to explore more about working with the negative character. In this specific case you let her gain the power of whatever positive qualities this character could give her and the rest just went away. If you have any other negative characters, should you do healing with them?

RANDAL: There are various ways that you can work with negative characters and in this case, my God, this was the devil! I don't know how much the devil is going to compromise. Susan found a way to get the power and let go of that which didn't fit. She succeeded in integrating the parts of him that were of positive use for her.

Usually, even in working with a character that is a murderer or a monster, direct growth within the character can be gained during the dialogue. In many cases the character eventually begins to compromise. That begins a healing process as the reality sets in , with a new respect for the other character and a recognition of a mistake or a need to change. In whatever way it happens, there is a coming together or a growing or learning by the character. In this extreme case the response came in an interesting way, but most commonly the characters come together more directly within the dialogue. (to Susan) I was trying to couch my suggestions and communication in a way that it would fit if you were a devout Christian who, as some Christians do, believed in the devil in the traditional sense, or that it would fit with whatever your belief system was.

SUSAN: And it did do that.

RANDAL: Good. Thank you, Susan.

Commentary

Ideomotor activity refers to the involuntary capability of muscles to respond instantaneously to thoughts and feelings. Ideomotor signals are an excellent method for eliciting information directly from the subconscious. The ideomotor form of finger signals was used briefly in this session and will appear again in many of the dream-work transcripts of this book. This quick method of "checking in" is the most common purpose for ideomotor responses during these Hypnotic Dreamwork sessions, as opposed to more complex explor-atory ideomotor questioning such as was described in Karen's Story in Chapter One.

In whatever form used (finger signals, pendulum, automatic writing, etc.), ideomotor skills need practice to be developed. Susan and other participants within these transcripts respond very readily to ideomotor questioning because of their experience, being either previously trained hypnotherapists or well into a thorough hypno-therapy training by the time of their dreamwork. Responses to brief, unprefaced questions such as those found in these transcripts, if given without significant prior practice, would often be answers from the conscious rather than the subconscious mind. There are several books included in the bibliography that thoroughly explain various uses of this important hypnotic tool.

Post-Session Dreamwork One Week Later

RANDAL: (to Susan) I am holding this beautiful letter you sent me about all the realizations you got about the dream. Is there any-thing you'd like to share with us now about your insights?

SUSAN: I had three dreams on two different nights and the third one really startled me awake. It seemed like it should have been fearful but it wasn't. Everything worked out fine. I asked myself, "So was that it? I'm not supposed to be afraid of something that startles me because it's not really fearful and everything's going to be okay? If I've got it, would you just let the dreams go?" Then the next night my dream was about a house that I've been creating progressively in my dreams over the years. When I first went into the house there were some rooms that were not right so I've been changing those rooms in different dreams. The house comes back and each time it's modified a little bit to be more like what I want.

RANDAL: That's great. You keep remembering this particular dream and it keeps evolving, showing your shifting experience.

SUSAN: Well, that's what I finally discovered with this sequence. The house is me. The front house is the conscious me and this has been working pretty well but there was this other place behind, kind of in a cellar and dark. It was furnished and decorated but it wasn't really a very nice place. It was livable. Apparently that is my subconscious and over the years it has grown. It's above ground now and it's become a guest house. And after this request to my subconscious to let the dreams go, this part of the house has furniture now.

RANDAL: Can you describe the latest version of this house?

SUSAN: The house now is perfect so I've moved off into the guest house. And the guest house is fully enclosed. It looks nice now. It was still bare inside up until this and now it has furniture. As I go through I think, "Wow, I've got all these new, neat things. Hey! I've got a computer. I didn't know I had a computer. Look at all the furniture! And another TV. I could put that in my real bedroom in my real home. I've always wanted a TV in my bedroom." So all of these things were my psychic presents. I have all these new toys.

RANDAL: That's a lot of furnishings to get in one day. You've been a busy young lady! Since you're having such wonderful, vivid dreams and they keep evolving so rapidly, I would like you to take a minute to describe yourself as the house that now feels finished and that you no longer need to reside in. Become that house and describe yourself.

SUSAN: It's a really nice, big house. Very roomy. It has everything that you need and everything is in the correct place. When I was this house before there was a big, long corridor and the rooms went off of it. They weren't in any coherent fashion. They weren't functional or convenient. You could get to them but it was a long way and it was a nuisance. There was this big, huge room and it could have been such a beautiful, functional room but it was torn up. It had stairs going up here and down there and things built in to where they were so solid that they weren't movable. There was no flexibility to the room. "Here I am and you can't change me." So I tore out all of that and opened the whole thing up.

RANDAL: "I tore all of that out and I've opened all of myself up."

SUSAN: And I've made myself more flexible. I have movable parts now. They're not stuck in one place. I can move the table over to this side and enjoy breakfast by the window, or I can move it over to this side and have it by the fireplace, or I could make a little conversation center down here by the fireplace. Or I could bring it back farther to make more space to allow for more company. I can make it more intimate or as open as I want.

RANDAL: "I can be as intimate or as open as I want." This is some great progress.

SUSAN: One, two, three dreams in a short time like this. It's funny, but I'm assuming that something is going to happen. That I'm going to be startled. I just have to remember that it's nothing that can really hurt me and not to be afraid.

RANDAL: Sometimes positive things can startle you, too. For example, it might be about how pleasantly surprising or how easy something is or how smooth or expansive you feel or how ready you feel to move forward.

SUSAN: The house is actually an evolution that has been going on for several years.

RANDAL: Well, it's been evolving very quickly lately. Now describe yourself as the guest house. Describe what you're like.

SUSAN: I'm finally furnished.

RANDAL: How does it feel to be furnished?

SUSAN: Kind of nice. Very homey.

RANDAL: "I feel very homey. I feel very..." what? What's the feeling of being furnished besides being homey?

SUSAN: I'm livable and I'm comfortable. All of my furniture is soft and cuddly and my colors are earthy. Lot of greens. There is nothing dead or dying in there. It's very alive.

RANDAL: "There is nothing dead or dying in here. I'm very alive."

SUSAN: And it's very nice.

RANDAL: "I'm very nice." (applause) Say it, come on.

SUSAN: I'm very nice.

RANDAL: So, you enjoy being both places. You enjoy being the other house and you enjoy being the guest house.

SUSAN: We are very much attached now.

RANDAL: (Randal holds up Susan's letter) Can I quote from part of your letter?

SUSAN: (Susan nods and points to a place in the letter) By the way, I did this and it did work.

RANDAL: Good. (Randal reads from the letter) "I think the best thing you did was intuitive. During the hypnotic suggestion you said that today was all there was and to not worry about what comes next. That was exactly what I needed to do. Today I love, tomorrow will take care of itself." That's great.

SUSAN: And I went home and I loved all week end. I didn't criticize and I didn't argue and I didn't allow anyone to pull me off center. I just loved and I did fine.

RANDAL: I'd like to summarize a couple of things you say in this letter. You were identifying with the castle as being your spirit, the wolf as being your power, and the evil being your fear of your power. The changes from king to dark wolf to white wolf you were experiencing as facades that you wear for fear of your power. You can accept it and not be afraid of all of your power because the good within you is stronger than the evil. Beautiful.

SUSAN: That's part of what I love so much about this kind of therapy. I always worry about projecting what I want or perceive someone needs. This method allows you to simply accept the person as they see themselves and to help them to work on what they want to work on in their way. Not my way. Not, "this is the way I think Randal should go and therefore I'm going to just tug gently." No matter how gently, it's still a tug and it doesn't allow that person to grow and develop their own furnishings. This process helped me to work on myself.

RANDAL: Great. Thank you, Susan.

Postscript: Susan Writes Three Years Later

Since the dreamwork I have had a couple of other dreams that had the same tone, i.e., I needed to love and accept myself more and that things would always work out for me if I did. It isn't always easy for me but I continue to strive in this area.

I had a feeling that I knew what "startling" thing was waiting out there for me. I have known most of my life that I have some psychic abilities but I have always kept them locked away. When I was young it was because I didn't want to be different. As I got older, I feared the responsibility of knowing something and not being able to change the outcome. Anyway, I recognized this as a part of me and knew I had to be able to accept all of myself if I was ever to be truly happy. Once I opened up to my abilities I started to receive more information, and sure enough, found it wasn't so scary after all. Thanks for all your help and support.

CHAPTER 7

Patrick's Dream:
Pulling the 747 Jet

RANDAL: Is this a fairly recent dream?

PAT: Actually it's from the past but it's so vivid that it comes right back when I talk about dreams. I've had many scary dreams and this one is not frightening, but it's fascinating to me. I seem to have never forgotten it. It's as vivid today as if it happened yesterday.

RANDAL: A dream can be a series of metaphors or it can be an overall metaphor for something that is very key about our lives. This dream sounds like a very powerful metaphor. I'd like you to describe the dream in the present tense. You can do it however it is most comfortable, with your eyes open or closed. Try to be there as vividly as you were when you were having the dream.

PAT: I'm nine or ten years old and I'm at the top of a hill. It's a nice, suburban winding street, but it isn't a suburb setting. The street is normal width with two lanes, one direction each way. There aren't any houses that I can see and all along the street there are trees. I don't know what you call them but they grow about twenty or thirty feet tall and are sometimes used for wind blocks. They're placed down the street at regular intervals and they're all about the same height. It looks like an evergreen. I'm at the top of the hill and I'm pulling behind myself a 747 jet. (laughter)

RANDAL: You're at the top of the hill and you're pulling this plane? You're walking?

PAT: Yes, I'm pulling it and it's not overpowering me. I don't have to hold it back. Actually, it just came to me that I'm on a decline. I never thought of that before.

RANDAL: That helps, doesn't it? (more laughter from the group) You're actually going slightly downhill, then?

PAT: The rope is over my right shoulder and it's taut, so there is resistance. But the most fascinating thing to me in the dream, and I just giggle at it all the time, is that it's a full size 747 with a bubble on the top and everything. The wing tips are barely two inches away from the trees. I don't refute the physical aspects that this is only a two lane street and I know that everything is in proportion, but it still fits. It's full size and I'm pulling it down the street and it seems to be going down straight without wiggling or wobbling or anything. It's not touching the trees, it's just going perfectly down the street.

RANDAL: Is that it? Is that the end of your dream?

PAT: The only other thing is that I don't see or hear anyone, but there is a feeling of a booming voice saying that I can't do what I'm doing. (class laughs)

RANDAL: Does this voice that you're hearing seem to be coming from out there or from within your head or what?

PAT: It seems to be coming from outside of me but there is no actual person.

RANDAL: So there is a feeling of a voice saying, "You can't be doing that. This is impossible!" How does that feel for you?

PAT: It feels very natural and easy. I'm not struggling. Everything is so real. This is as real for me now as it was years ago when I had the dream. I'm not in wonderment. I hear the voice and I'm not fighting it or saying "You're wrong." I'm hearing the voice and I keep going on with whatever I'm doing. If I want to use the word "task", I go on with my task. I just keep at it and the one thing that has come up new right now is that this is a street with a decline, but the rope is taut.

RANDAL: So there is a slight down hill slant and you're really pulling on the rope but the slope is helping.

PAT: Yes, there is resistance and I've got to pull.

RANDAL: So it feels good to be doing this task?

PAT: Oh, it feels great.

RANDAL: Good. I'd like you to close your eyes, Pat, and go inward. Get the feeling of taking one step after another, pulling that giant 747 behind you. Being nine or ten years old and feeling the power of doing that task. Not only pulling that gigantic plane but pulling it so perfectly that it moves without touching the trees. Go into your body and feel what that feels like.

PAT: I feel very powerful and very much in control, in that the plane is reacting to my pulling it. It's not guiding itself. I am doing everything to the plane and there is a feeling that it is letting me do this. It's not fighting me.

RANDAL: Excellent. Now I'd like you to be the plane. Say, "I am a 747" and describe yourself.

PAT: I am a 747 and I am huge. I have a very smooth skin and it's glistening in the sun. I'm silver. I have many, many windows. I particularly feel proud of the bubble. (Pat laughs and the group laughs with him)

RANDAL: "Of my bubble."

PAT: I feel very proud of my bubble. My wings are heavy and they're projected back. They're down sloping but I feel very stable and I'm really glad that this small boy is showing me where to go. I feel like I can just let go even though I'm huge and it looks like I could roll and get out of control. I feel confident that this little boy is going to guide me where I need to go. I feel some sadness about it. (tears begin to run from Pat's eyes and Randal hands him a tissue)

RANDAL: What is it you feel sadness about?

PAT: It seems like I've given him a very big task.

RANDAL: Okay, let's talk to the boy now. You feel some sadness for him. The boy is out here in front of you. Tell him now, "I really feel sad for you that you have such a big task." Go ahead and say it.

PAT: I know I have a lot of force and power and I know you're worrying about it, but as you can see you're in full control. You can see that the line you have attached to me is taut. I'm not getting out of control and I'm not going to run you over. I respect you very much for taking on this task. I'm cooperating even though I'm so much bigger than you. I trust you to guide me down the street.

RANDAL: Now switch and be the boy. Move into this other chair and talk to the plane now.

PAT: Boy, you are big. I feel so honored to do this. I look back and I realize that there is a slope to the road and you could run me over. I feel very awed that you respect me and you're allowing me to do this. (Randal hands Pat another tissue to wipe his eyes) I see the plane smiling at me. I'm aware, I'm a little boy, just how beautiful it is.

RANDAL: Tell that to the plane. Tell the plane the positive feelings you feel about it.

PAT: (wiping his eyes) You're so big but your lines look so neat and together. You look really old. I'm awed at how big and massive and together you seem to be. Everything is defined. There are no squiggly lines. Everything is so clear and precise. And your cooperation is incredible. I'm just wondering what you're doing this for. Why are you allowing me to pull you?

RANDAL: Switch and become the plane. Just sit there and take that compliment. Feel that sense of awe that you are appreciating this boy and now he is appreciating you so much. Just be there and get a sense of feeling the warmth of this boy respecting you so much. How does that feel?

PAT: It feels great.

RANDAL: Now he was asking you a question. What is your response?

PAT: You're small, but I trust your foot steps. You don't stumble. You take one step after another. You feel secure and trusting and you know where you're going. I've seen the curves on the road and I know there is a slight decline and we could really get out of control. I'm massive, I weigh tons, but I'm going to allow you to have control through this line that you have and I won't put any more strain on it than you can handle. You're very competent in what you do. I'm trusting you. I like you very much.

RANDAL: Switch and be the boy. Now it's time for you to just take that in. Here is this great big, powerful plane that trusts you very much and respects you for what you are doing and how you are doing it and how much you are helping out. How does that feel?

PAT: Wow. It feels very natural and it feels so good to cooperate. It feels incredible, this cooperation and trust.

RANDAL: How does it feel to tell the plane your feelings?

PAT: It's beautiful. I'd like to feel it's shape. (Pat's hands stroke an imaginary cone shaped nose) I can feel how big and smooth you are. You work so well within yourself. All your systems are integrated and all your electronics. You know where to go and how to land. Sometimes you don't even need a pilot. There is an auto pilot that can take off and land by itself. Incredible. I never realized before that there wasn't a pilot in there.

RANDAL: Switch and become the plane now. Take in the appreciation of the boy that you respect so much, who has been helping you and is in such awe of you. Accept it. Accept everything that you are, this magnificent creation that is so smooth and self–contained and in so much control.

PAT: Wow, thank you for your compliments. I fly well, I land good, and I take off great. And it's true that I can do this on my own but sometimes I think I need a guide... (Pat wipes his eyes) and I'm glad you're here today. I'm glad you're here because I was feeling a little concerned about the slope. I realized that someone had asked me today to take off without a pilot and I really needed a guide. With all my sophisticated equipment and electronics and guidance systems and radar, I needed a guide today. And you came and helped me, and I thank you very much for being here. Even though you're very small, I needed a small guide. I couldn't have taken off without your help.

RANDAL: Now switch and be the boy. Take that in! You are getting so much appreciation for such a big task and you're really honored to take it on. You deserve it.

PAT: I never realized it before, but all through my remembrance of the dreams, there were no doors...and a door just opened. (Pat pauses to wipe his eyes and continues talking while sobbing quietly) I've been invited inside... (Pat's voice tapers off)

RANDAL: That's wonderful. Look at that beautiful plane opening itself wide open to you. Steps are down, the door is open. You can continue to take your time and admire it or you can walk on into the plane.

PAT: I'd like to go in.

RANDAL: All right.

PAT: (laughing) I haven't flown this plane for years.

RANDAL: This dream is very relevant. It's no accident that the dream came so clearly to you today. The time has come. You have been pulling this plane for years and you deserve to go in. (Pat sobs and wipes his eyes)

PAT: I'm halfway between sorrow and joy. Somewhere in the middle there. I want to stand at the bottom of the stairs and just savor this.

RANDAL: This is your moment. You can savor it as long as you want. The time has come. You have pulled this plane far enough. It was the plane's turn to let go all that time and now it's your turn to let go. Relax. The plane is about to take you in. You've done a real good job. That plane is so proud of you. The whole town is proud of you. You maneuvered that big, important plane and you did it so well. You were so proud to do it, to have that responsibility. You've taken that on and you've done great. You took it right through that town all these years and you've kept it right on track. You've done your job. Take a long time to enjoy yourself. It's going to be the plane's turn now. The plane has a lot of adventures coming forth.

PAT: I feel like I'm about two feet off the ground.

RANDAL: Good. You're going to be further off the ground in a little while. Feel yourself on top of the world. Are you still standing at the bottom of the steps looking up at the beautiful plane?

PAT: I want to put my hand out and touch the railing.

RANDAL: Go ahead. What does that feel like?

PAT: It feels like the greatest wealth in the world to me. It seems like the game shows that I always laugh at, "Come on down, Pat! Come on down!"

RANDAL: You hit the grand prize! Great. Feel it.

PAT: Oh yeah, it feels good. I want to walk up the steps.

RANDAL: Your time has come, Patrick. Walk up the steps. What does it feel like?

PAT: It feels like the steps weren't built to code. They're a little bit steep but that's okay. I like the steepness. They seem to be just the right pitch.

RANDAL: Going up at a steep angle that's just right for you. How does it feel stepping up these steps now?

PAT: Well, I'm a little bit shaky. My legs are shaking. It's been such a long time.

RANDAL: Stand up now and make the motions of walking up these steps here. (Pat gets up and goes through the motions of climbing steps) That's right.

PAT: Yep, they're a little bit off code but they sure feel good.

RANDAL: All right.

PAT: I can see the door now. It's flung wide open and inviting me into the inside.

RANDAL: That's great. Are you already in front of the door?

PAT: I'm on the top step and I'm looking in. The whole inside of the plane, as far as I can see, is carpeted in a purple velvet.

RANDAL: Beautiful.

PAT: What's inside is a huge library of all the books I ever wanted. I don't even need to go into the library, it just feels good. Both sides of the plane hold all the books and to the left is the door to the cockpit where we sit down and fly. That's where I want to go. I want to go and sit down and see it.

RANDAL: And you know the plane is very happy to have you do that.

PAT: Before when I was the plane I said I know about the slope we'd been on, but now the plane feels on solid ground. It feels to be on the runway.

RANDAL: Good. So let's get over to the cockpit there. Come on over and have a seat. (Pat, who has been standing, goes over to the chair and sits down) You're sitting down now at the seat in the cockpit. How does it feel?

PAT: It feels like one of those big captain's chairs that wrap around your body and you sink into it. It contours. It feels so very comfortable.

RANDAL: Feel those beautiful contours and the way you sink into it. Just settle yourself in and look at the magnificent control panel and everything you see around you. How does that feel?

PAT: It feels great. It's got all these controls on the panel. It feels like it was contoured for my hands, like when you squeeze clay in your hands and get a mold. When I put my hands on it, it was just made for me. It just fits my thumb and the way my hands lock here on the controls.

RANDAL: Take it in. This is your life.

PAT: I'm realizing that two years ago I gave up my books. I know now that my books are behind me. I gave them away for the purpose of wanting to know what I know and not what other people know. I feel this is a great place to be. The whole library is behind me but the first place I wanted to go is the cockpit to put my hands on the controls.

RANDAL: You can go back to that library any time you want. The plane is on the runway and you've got your hands on the controls. Does this feel like a completion or do you want to go further?

PAT: It's complete.

RANDAL: Okay, just hang out there at the controls.

PAT: It's fascinating – all the lights and the switches. All the dials. I seem to know how to use them all. (Pat sighs)

RANDAL: You do know how to use them all.

PAT: Somehow. There is this big instruction manual sitting right beside me. I know it's there but I don't need it. It feels so good to sit here on level ground. The plane is permitting me here. I can sit here for as long as I want.

RANDAL: That's wonderful.

PAT: Whew! Thank you.

RANDAL: Thank you. (Pat stands up and they hug) Let's give Patrick a hand. You just took us for quite a ride.

PAT: That was a helluva ride. I never imagined this would happen.

RANDAL: (to the class) This was a wonderful example of a wish fulfillment dream that spontaneously developed further during the dreamwork. Pat got to deeply experience the different parts and their mutual appreciation. Then lo and behold, a new development took place. The door that had never been there before dramatically opened. Suddenly Pat was on the runway – he had pulled the plane all the way.

(to Pat) As you had done prior to that, you totally appreciated every step - staring at the plane and spending time with it. Walking slowly up those steps and stopping at the top. Going inside and looking around and discovering your library. Walking to the cockpit and sitting down and really experiencing yourself as the pilot of your life. You have gone to several new levels. New shifts and opportunities in your life will be easy and natural. I want to acknowledge you for letting go and being so spontaneous and present. I love your enthusiasm. You came right up here and wanted to work with this dream and it paid off.

Commentary

A basic tenet in Gestalt work is that you don't help your clients. You allow them to find their own resources. For example, you don't give ideas about what one character might say to another during a dialogue. That is their work. But while Patrick was continuing to find his own way, his wish-fulfillment dream began developing in an exceptionally emotional and meaningful manner. Therefore the hypnosis he had entered by initiating the dreamwork had spontaneously deepened. Because of these factors, I began to increasingly interweave positive hypnotic suggestions, encouraging him to become even more aware and to take this profound experience even further. By continuing to develop his dream it had evolved into a hypnodream. (See Chapter 17 on hypnodreams.)

The integration of hypnotherapy with Gestalt dreamwork adds the power of interjecting positive suggestions at various points when appropriate or at the end to strengthen and expand on the work. This session contrasts with the previous three of Kay, Rachel and Susan, in which the direct hypnotic suggestions were given at the conclusion, distinct and clearly separated from the rest of the dreamwork.

CHAPTER 8

The Return of Sharon's Recurring Childhood Nightmare:

The Broken Blinds and the Staring Stranger

SHARON: I had this dream last night.

RANDAL: Don't you have anything more recent than that? (laughter) Okay, well that's what we'll have to go with.

SHARON: This is very interesting to me because there is an aspect of it that is part of a recurring nightmare I used to have as a child.

RANDAL: So there is still something that your subconscious mind is wanting to work through from that. That is obviously very significant.

SHARON: (laughing) That's why I jumped up here. It's time to deal with this. In the dream I'm in the house on Fremont Street where I grew up. I'm in my bedroom for most of the dream. My mother and father are there. I'm in my twenties. In this bedroom there is a window on the south side and a window on the west side. The window blinds aren't shutting properly. They just won't close, so I can't keep people from seeing in. The window is the part of the dream that is part of the childhood experience. I can't get them closed because the blinds are broken. I look out and I'm really angry that they haven't been fixed. I look out one window and I don't see anyone but I try to close it and it won't close. Then I look out the other one and there is a girl standing there.

Another part of the dream is that my parents live in the house also, and off and on during the dream there are different men that I sleep with. I may or may not have a sexual relationship with them but they're walking around nude all the time. My parents are aware that the men are in the house and they're different people. If I do have sex with them I have absolutely no emotion about it, I just go through the process. And I have the sense more that these people are my brothers. They're in and out and I just don't think anything about it. One of the people is a fellow I went to high school with, which I didn't have any particular relationship with. I just knew him. He ran with a group of guys and I ran with a group of girls and we saw each other sometimes. Then there are other things that pop up about this recently in the recurring dream.

RANDAL: You're about to describe aspects about this dream that are recurring for you?

SHARON: Yes. They've been recurring in dreams in recent months. So in living with my parents, I'm also going to school. And I'm going to school for a Ph.D. in a subject that I have absolutely no interest in whatsoever. I'm just wasting their money. I go to classes and I don't take the exams or try to get any kind of scholarship. There are two classes that I'd really have to concentrate on if I wanted to get the degree. The rest of the classes I think, "Oh God, these are so easy, why even bother." But one of the classes I think I would have a lot of difficulty with is calculus. And the other one is something similar to that but I don't remember what it is. That's all I remember about it.

RANDAL: Besides the parts that have been recurring in recent months, there was some aspect of the dream that occurred when you were just a girl?

SHARON: Uh huh.

RANDAL: Which part was that?

SHARON: When I was a girl I would have a recurring nightmare. In the dream I would be in my room and I would sit up in the bed and look out the window. There would be this man standing there. I could see the man's face and he'd have a hat with a brim on it and he would be looking at me and gradually break into a smile. The smile would get bigger and bigger. The more frightened I became the more he would smile. I would actually be screaming with my eyes open but I wouldn't be awake. My sister was in the bed with me and mother would come running into the room. That's the part of the dream that's recurring - the window and somebody out there looking in.

RANDAL: Was the girl that was out there in this recent dream staring at you?

SHARON: Yes.

RANDAL: Was she smiling at all? Did you notice that?

SHARON: No.

RANDAL: But she was staring. When you say girl, are you talking about a child or a teenager?

SHARON: A child. She wasn't as young as the child I was.

RANDAL: And the recurring aspects in recent months, do they have to do with your being at your parent's house and going through this Ph.D. program that you're not really interested in?

SHARON: Yes.

RANDAL: I'd like you to be the girl that's looking in the window and describe yourself.

SHARON: I have brown, kind of curly hair. It's cut short. I've got brown eyes. I mostly just see my face. (pause) I'm trying to get in touch with how old I am. Maybe I'm eight or eleven. Something like that. Rather than describe how I look I think it would be easier to describe how I feel.

RANDAL: Describe how you feel.

SHARON: I feel hurt.

RANDAL: You feel emotionally hurt?

SHARON: Uh huh. I have a sense that I'm not wanted there. I'm shut out and I'm not wanted in the house with the people.

RANDAL: Are you referring to Sharon's house or do you mean a house you live in which is a different house from the one you're looking at?

SHARON: I don't have a home.

RANDAL: How does that feel?

SHARON: Lonely. Abandoned. It's funny, I have a sense that inside the house it's warm and wonderful. Being as I'm that person and I'm also the people in the house I know that's not true.

RANDAL: But being just this one character right now, it sounds like this is what you're longing for. The home looks inviting and that's why you're looking at it.

SHARON: Yeah, because there's a yellow glow from the light inside and light to me means warmth. It means being safe, belonging.

RANDAL: I'd like you to switch now and be the character that is Sharon. You are in the house and you are dealing with the blinds that are broken and won't close. You're looking out the window and seeing someone looking in. How does that feel for you?

SHARON: I'm very angry that the blinds haven't been fixed by now. When I look out the first window and there is nothing out there but just the grass and the house next door, then I'm very pleased. That was the window I used to see the man in. Then when I look through the other window I expect to see someone there but I don't expect it to be the little girl. Regardless of age or gender or anything else, I don't want anybody looking in my windows. I don't want anybody invading my privacy unless they're invited. They're not to force themselves.

RANDAL: Talk to this girl who is looking in your window and tell her how you feel about that. The girl is sitting in this chair here. (Randal indicates the empty chair facing Sharon)

SHARON: I'm sorry but I don't like you looking in my window. You don't belong here. There's got to be some other place where you belong because you don't belong here.

RANDAL: I'd like you to get up and switch chairs. Now you're the girl. Respond to what Sharon just said.

SHARON: Where am I supposed to go? What am I supposed to do? I want to find where I'm wanted. If I knew of another place I would go because I know you don't want me. I really don't want to come in if you don't want me.

RANDAL. Switch again and respond.

SHARON: I'm not responsible for you. I don't know where you belong. This is your problem and you figure it out for yourself but get away from my window.

RANDAL: Now be the girl.

SHARON: Can't you see that I'm not grown up yet and I don't know where I'm supposed to go? I've only been with you and I don't know where else to be.

RANDAL: Tell Sharon what you want from her. Tell this woman whose window you're looking into what you would like.

SHARON: I agree that I don't belong there and I don't want to be there anymore but I don't know how to detach to go wherever it is.

RANDAL: Switch and be Sharon.

SHARON: Then you've got a problem because I'm not going to let you in.

RANDAL: Tell her what you want from her even if it's repeating something you said before.

SHARON: I'm tired of you looking at me. I'm tired of you expecting things from me. You're an aspect of my past that just doesn't belong here anymore. You don't belong with me anymore.

RANDAL: So say, "Go away!"

SHARON: Go away.

RANDAL: Switch.

SHARON: I understand you don't want my loneliness. You don't want my sense of abandonment that I have held for you. You don't want this uncertainty, this indecisiveness, this fear of letting go. You don't want any of that stuff that I have here for you. I get it and I don't blame you a bit. I just don't know where to go. I want to go somewhere where somebody wants all these things. There's got to be a place for me in the world, too.

RANDAL: Do you have a name?

SHARON: Molly.

RANDAL: So what do you do now, Molly?

SHARON: Well, I've got to say that I feel good that you don't want me around any more. I feel good that Sharon doesn't want all this stuff that I carry anymore. I think just by having said that, you told me to go away, that I no longer fit, and I really hear that. It's interesting that it makes me happy since I have all this other stuff that I carry but that's been my purpose all along. As soon as you were ready to release and let go that's all you needed to do and I can be gone. I can go and I'm just going to go into the ethers, more or less, and when I'm called on, when somebody else needs or wants these things that I carry, they can call me forth and I can be there for them. I feel good about that. That's my part in the world.

RANDAL: Very good. What is it that you have to offer if someone calls you?

SHARON: I think you would call me aspects of the dark side and I think to experience these things is healthy and beneficial. It's part of the human condition, part of being alive. I just give people experiences of those conditions.

RANDAL: So you are some aspect of the dark side?

SHARON: Yes.

RANDAL: How does that feel?

SHARON: I like it. I'm serving a purpose in the world. I really feel good about it.

RANDAL: "I feel good about myself."

SHARON: Definitely. On earth you people talk about yin and yang, the light and the dark. You think there should never be any darkness but there's a time for me and a space for me. Whatever somebody came here to experience, I can join and help them with their experiences. There is nothing evil or bad about me really.

RANDAL: You said a few minutes ago, "It's time to go into the ethers."

SHARON: Uh huh.

RANDAL: Go ahead and do that. Disappear into the ethers. (after a lengthy pause Sharon makes various movements and whooshing sounds, then becomes passive again) That's good. Just be there in the ethers and know that you serve a purpose. You're absolutely a part of us. And know that while many times you will not be appreciated, what matters is that you can appreciate yourself. You are important. It is good to be the dark side manifesting yourself where appropriate. There are certain ways of expressing the dark side that are very constructive. You can give yourself a chance to manifest in ways that are useful. Breathing down as you are, deep into your belly and into your chest, how do you feel right now?

SHARON: I feel clean. I'm not the dark side. The dark side has gone.

RANDAL: So who or what are you right now?

SHARON: An empty space.

RANDAL: How do you feel to be this empty space?

SHARON: Perfect.

RANDAL: Great. Go inside your body and notice if you have an awareness of anything or does it just feel like clean, empty space?

SHARON: I feel a slight tingling but other than that I'm just space.

RANDAL: How does it feel to be clean, empty space?

SHARON: I don't think it's something you humans can understand.

RANDAL: I'm going to give you a chance to just be that right now. You don't have to say anything or do anything. I agree, I think it's something that most human beings don't understand. Just be that clean, empty space. (pause) Please get in touch with your finger signals. What you're going to experience right now is time distortion. You're going to have this huge amount of time to be this clean, empty space. Time is going to accelerate so that every second is going to be the equivalent of a minute. One minute gives you a full hour or more to totally enjoy the feeling of being clean, empty space. And when you feel finished with that, when you are totally satisfied and you're ready to move on, you can signal with your "yes" finger. When I snap my fingers begin. Three, two, one (Randal snaps his fingers), begin. (two minutes pass and Sharon raises her "yes" finger)

Good. Feel your strength, Sharon. Time is returning to normal now. Feel this tremendous sense of peace and quiet and clarity. This is a part of you that you come back to and use. You can gain from this strength, this well, this space, this quiet. This is going to the very center of your being to help you be grounded and centered. When you're with someone, whether it be socially or as a therapist, you are totally present, but with your own center, your own detachment. You can be compassionate and detached simultaneously. You also give yourself time each day to experience this feeling or similar feelings of being perfectly peaceful, calm, quiet, clear.

You are part of Sharon and you can handle anything. Feel the center of power and wisdom within you. See Sharon in this dream, in that room, and the girl you were concerned about has gone away, disappeared back to the ether. You are there with Sharon. Is there anything you would like to say to Sharon, to that part of yourself that is there?

SHARON: Welcome. I've been waiting for you. It's time for us to be together, to unite. We have work to do in the world now, that's why it's time to come together.

RANDAL: This time when I touch your right shoulder you're going to switch and be Sharon. What is your response?

SHARON: I know. I don't think I need to say anything else.

RANDAL. You don't need to. That's fine. Just be there with her. Welcome home.

SHARON: (pause) I feel very complete.

RANDAL: Just come back at your own rate. Take your time and come back when you're ready with all of this that is you. Come back here with us in this room. (after a pause, Sharon opens her eyes and laughs)

SHARON: Was I an interesting specimen?

RANDAL: I wouldn't call you a specimen. You are most interesting. (class applauds) You look beautiful.

SHARON: Thank you.

RANDAL: Is there anything you want to share with the group about your experience? You don't have to share anything right now. You may feel non-verbal and that's fine too.

SHARON: There are things I'd like to share with the group. For one thing, I had no idea who that little girl out there was or what she represented to me until I started to get into the description. And I had no idea that she had a name, which she did. It was just a beautiful experience. It was perfect. Things to let go of and things to look forward to.

RANDAL: That's great. Let's stop for now. I feel it would be good to give yourself some time. You've just had a profound experience.

RANDAL: (after a break) There were various images in Sharon's dream we could have explored. I was particularly interested in focusing on a recurring part. I was fully expecting to have her become the broken blinds as an integral part of that, but there was so much that developed immediately about the girl outside the window. Working with the girl felt complete even though we didn't directly gestalt other aspects of the dream. Sharon was so clear with what she became that I even hesitated to bring her back to be Sharon, but I felt it would be good to continue that integration. Perhaps she might go back to explore other aspects of the dream at a later time, but for now where she went was so profound. It was time for her to own that and be that. It felt like the perfect place to stop.

SHARON: It felt really good that you were able to extract everything without leading me. You said "What do you want to tell the girl?" and I said, "I want her to go away. I don't want her here." I was saying those words and you said, "Tell her to go away." You gave me a direct order to be very succinct and just do it. I was trying to scoot her away without being bad.

RANDAL: You were trying to be nice about it.

SHARON: Yes, and you said forget that and just do it. Another point is that Molly got very clear about her value before you ever said anything. She just started smiling and realizing she had a real value which is extremely important.

RANDAL: Yes. It's great when you begin to acknowledge your-self before I do any acknowledgments or add hypnotic suggestions. I can then reaffirm what you feel, anchor it more deeply, and help expand it.

Commentary

Time distortion, an interesting hypnotic phenomenon with many uses, is worked with in this chapter and with Delores' Hypnodream in Chapter 18. According to Cheek and LeCron, all major hypnotic phenomenon were discovered by the middle of the Nineteenth Cen-tury with the exception of time distortion. The ability of a good sub-ject to speed up or slow down time tremendously in hypnosis was discovered by Dr. Lynn Cooper in the early 1950's. He documented, for example, that experimental subjects could solve a problem in ten seconds that would normally take ten minutes. Accounts of a drowning person recapitulating whole segments of his or her life within a few seconds are examples of spontaneous time distortion.

Interview One Week Later

RANDAL: Any thoughts or feelings since you did your session, Sharon?

SHARON: Yes. A couple of days later I had another dream that turned out to be very related to that one and I worked with Marcy (one of Sharon's classmates) on it. In this dream I was in a very white room and I remembered the work you and I did when I talked about the space that was clean and empty. In working with Marcy, I de-scribed it as pure and expansive. There was a switch in the white space and she wanted me to be the switch and I said "No, I don't need to be the switch because I know what it means." When I came back out she asked me about the switch, and it was that those two dreams are like the integration of yin and yang. The switch goes back into clean, empty space or I can switch and go into the place of purity and expansion. They're sort of the same.

RANDAL: They're a similar kind of space but different complements to each other?

SHARON: Yes.

RANDAL: That's great. My intuition is that your dream made a dramatic emotional impact.

SHARON: Definitely. It was about freedom, too. Freeing myself from the old stuff when Molly left. Also it was very spiritual.

RANDAL: Yes, and as I mentioned before, the parts that where recurring had clearly major significance, especially from the childhood nightmare. There had been partial resolution since it was no longer a nightmare, but the blinds were broken and there was the staring stranger. Way back it had been a man that kept giving a bigger and bigger smile, but it changed to the girl who was associated with the dark side. In fact those two images weren't all that different from each other because that man that was so disturbing for you was an aspect of the dark side. So these were unfinished issues that went all the way back to childhood. Your resolution feels very important.

SHARON: As a girl this dark side seemed very intimidating and frightening. When I saw the girl at the window she probably represented the same qualities as the man, but the image was no longer overpowering to me. As an adult I've developed to the point where those things are not so frightening, and with your help, could easily handle that. Thank you very much. (applause)

Postscript: Sharon Writes Nine Months Later

I continue to be amazed at the results which can be achieved when working with a skilled hypnotherapist. Thank you so much for assisting me to understand, appreciate and release Molly. Since that session, I've had no further dreams with aspects of either people looking into windows at me or of any frustration or efforts to go to school or take classes. Powerful stuff!

Chapter 9

Cheryl's Dream:

The Magic Bus Appears in Mexico

CHERYL: I don't usually wake up with a dream that is this vivid in detail and the details didn't seem all that important, but it somehow felt significant. After waking from the dream I felt a lot of emotion all day .

RANDAL: Even though it hadn't seemed that important you still felt an ongoing emotional response. This is a very significant dream.

CHERYL: In the beginning of the dream I'm deciding to get on a bus to take a ride around the city and I have a little dog with me. The dog is wearing a jacket or sweater. It's really a cute little dog and it's very smart. It's also very well behaved. I'm very fond of it in my dream. I don't have a dog in real time.

RANDAL: Yes you do. This dream is now your real time. Stay in the dream.

CHERYL: Okay. I'm on the bus with this little dog. After awhile I notice that the bus isn't moving and I realize it hasn't been moving for some time. We're just sitting here. We had gotten on the bus for a very early morning ride around the city and I realize that I need to be home by nine o'clock for an appointment. I also notice now that the bus is much roomier inside. It's more like a train and people seem to be lounging around. So I go up to ask the bus driver what time the bus is going to be back to the street I need to get off on and he says, "Well, what street is that?" I'm trying very hard to remember where I live and I come up with the cross streets and tell him. He says, "The bus will be back there around nine o'clock."

I go back and sit down and look at my watch. It's about a quarter to nine and I think, "Well this bus doesn't look like it is going to move. It's not going anywhere." Then I realize, "Oh my gosh. Does he mean nine o'clock tonight? I'm going to miss the whole day." I go up again and say, "Excuse me, but did you mean nine o'clock this evening?" and he says, "Well, sure." I think, "Oh, no. This can't be because I have to be home by nine o'clock this morning." I ask if there are any other buses or any other way I can get home and he starts to tell me but it sounds really complicated. Then he says, "Why don't you just go out? There are some lovely market places around here. There are a lot of really nice things to do during the day." So I looked out or stepped out...

RANDAL: "I step out." Keep it present tense.

CHERYL: I step out and realize that we must have really traveled some distance because this looks like Mexico. The market place is a food market and it's very dusty and dry. The food looks really interesting and I'm feeling kind of hungry anyway. In the meantime I'm out of the bus and I've taken off my jacket and I notice that the clothes I'm wearing match the little jacket my dog is wearing. We're a nice team. Now I'm outside of the bus and some children are holding the leash of my little dog and I'm marveling at how well mannered he is. He's so bright and he knows just what to do. These children are holding the dog for me while I make a decision about whether I'm going to go and enjoy the market place or whether I've got to figure out this complicated way to get back. And then I wake up.

RANDAL: When you wake up what are you feeling like? Do you realize that now you're in Mexico and you're not going to get back for your nine o'clock appointment? Or are you still trying to get back?

CHERYL: I'm undecided. I woke up not making a decision. I don't know if I'm going to try to figure out how to get back. It's very complicated.

RANDAL: All right. I would like you to be the bus. Describe yourself as the bus – what you look like and where you're going.

CHERYL: Well, I'm a bus. Starting out I'm an ordinary bus, traveling on a regular route that's just making stops around the city like it always does.

RANDAL: "Like I always do..."

CHERYL: Like I always do. But as I go on my space really expands and I'm much roomier and lighter inside. Everything is brighter.

RANDAL: "I'm brighter..."

CHERYL: I'm brighter. I'm much more opened up than when I started out and I don't have to go anywhere. I'm not going to stay on the same schedule. I'm not even going to go anywhere right now.

RANDAL: Well how does that feel? Do you like being this bus? Do you like how you've evolved?

CHERYL: I like this new bus better.

RANDAL: "I like myself better as the new bus..."

CHERYL: I like my roomier, more open, lighter self better and I like that I'm not on such a schedule.

RANDAL: I'd like you to stand up, if it works to stand up. Be in whatever position you want to be in, but I'd like you to feel yourself being this bus. (both Randal and Cheryl stand up)

CHERYL: Well, how I would really be the bus is not standing up at all. I would be the bus like this. (Cheryl lies on the floor with her arms spread open)

RANDAL: Okay. Feel yourself. Are you this bus as you have evolved now?

CHERYL: I'm the big, roomy bus.

RANDAL: The other bus that was keeping a schedule was you before but this is you now. Feel that expansive, roomy quality and describe yourself again as the new bus.

CHERYL: I don't have that sense of being confined any more. I'm much more expansive. Time doesn't have the same value or constraints, so I'm much freer as this bus. But at the same time that I'm moving less there seems to be more movement going on inside.

RANDAL: How wonderful. Does that feel good to you?

CHERYL: It feels much more natural – less artificial. It feels more in tune. There are less boundaries from outside about how I am.

RANDAL: Good. (Randal helps Cheryl up from the floor.) Now let's go right to the end of the dream. Have a seat. (Cheryl sits facing an empty chair) Now you're Cheryl. You had actually gotten off the bus. You've been walking around a marketplace in Mexico and you're debating whether to go back. Is there anything you have to say to the bus?

CHERYL: There is something...what I'm feeling is a lot of emotion for no apparent reason. I'm feeling it very strongly looking at the bus because...boy, there's just a lot of intense emotion going on right here (patting her chest).

RANDAL: Close your eyes. Describe what's going on right now in your body.

CHERYL: A lot of stress.

RANDAL: Where?

CHERYL: Right here (pressing her solar plexus).

RANDAL: In your solar plexus area. When you say a lot of stress, is there a movement? Is something stuck?

CHERYL: It feels like a lot of quivering. A lot of motion.

RANDAL: Okay, I'd like you to stand up. (Randal helps Cheryl up) Have your whole body do what's going on in your solar plexus area. Become that whole energy, that movement, in whatever way your body can act that out.

CHERYL: It's just quivering. (Cheryl holds her arms out and shakes all over)

RANDAL: So quiver now...yes.

CHERYL: I'm quivering like this inside.

RANDAL: Now exaggerate that. Really get into that motion. (Cheryl shakes more rapidly) Breathe down into your stomach as you do it. (pause) Now relax. Go into your body. (Cheryl stops quivering and her hands make fists) What do you feel in your body? It might help to have a seat here.

CHERYL: (Cheryl sits down, hands still clenched) I'm feeling tense.

RANDAL: When I said to relax I noticed your hands. Go ahead and tense your hands. Where else do you feel tense? All over or just in some areas?

CHERYL: Well, now I feel tense all over. I was quivering but now I feel tense and it's related to that choice. I think... (Cheryl puts her hand to her forehead) Oh, I said choice didn't I? I was thinking of the decision, about coming back or not.

RANDAL: Uh huh. Let's go to that decision about coming back or not. Is that what you're feeling tense about? (Cheryl squirms on her chair) Keep feeling the feelings in your body. That's good.

CHERYL: Okay. What I am feeling is that...this is a significant time of year. Actually it's a significant date in my life. Tomorrow is exactly five years from the time I had advanced cancer and the doctors were telling me I was going to die within a few months. And this whole decision and choice feels like it's related to my having to come back or not. Before this dream it felt like a very resolved decision.

RANDAL: So what are you leaning toward here? The part of you that's sitting in this chair, does it want to come back or not? You're going to dialogue with yourself now. I'd like you to say to the other part of yourself, "No, I don't want to come back," or "I want to come back."

CHERYL: No, I don't want to come back. I don't want to go back to that very restricted schedule. I don't want to find the bus that takes me back. It's too complicated. It takes me back into just what I'm trying to get away from. I want to stay with this more expanded bus that is taking its time and is here in Mexico. I want to go visit the market place and I don't want to go back.

RANDAL: Switch parts and see if there is a part of you that wants to go back.

CHERYL: (pause) Who am I now?

RANDAL: Do you feel there is some part of you that would like to go back instead of enjoying this bus and this place?

CHERYL: Oh, there's a very responsible side that says "You've got an appointment at nine o'clock and you need to be there. You need to be reliable. You always are reliable." I need to show up.

RANDAL: All right, let's switch. Respond to the Cheryl who wants to keep the appointment.

CHERYL: So what is going to happen? What possibly is going to happen that is going to be so terrible if you miss the appointment?

RANDAL: Okay, switch.

CHERYL: There are people that are relying on you to be there. In fact they need you so you have to be there. And if you're not there all these people are going to be let down.

RANDAL: Switch.

CHERYL: I think they won't be let down. I think that by not being there they will find the strength in themselves to work out what they need to.

RANDAL: Switch.

CHERYL: I don't know who I am.

RANDAL: That's because you're integrating it. You are the one who was saying that you need to go to these people for their appointments. And then the other part just reasoned that she thinks it will work out for these people if you don't show up.

CHERYL: I think I'm ready to stay with you. I think I don't need to be there for them.

RANDAL: How does that feel?

CHERYL: I guess it's not such a big a deal. I don't think it was ever as critical as I thought it was.

RANDAL: You can let go of that, right? Come over here to this chair and put the bus over there. Is there anything you'd like to say to the bus that brought you here? The new expanded version.

CHERYL: You've got to stay off the old route. This new route is certainly much more comfortable. Stay here in the market places of Mexico.

RANDAL: Switch and respond as the bus.

CHERYL: As a new expanded bus I'm enjoying the diverse people and animals I'm attracting. I'm traveling with much more exciting company than I was.

RANDAL: Good. Would you like to switch and thank the bus for having brought you here?

CHERYL: Yes. Thank you for bringing me on this journey and for taking me off that other route. This is certainly a much more exciting journey that you're taking me on.

RANDAL: And do you want to switch and see if there is any appreciation the bus would like to show you?

CHERYL: Well, you're welcome to come aboard anytime.

RANDAL: (standing and beginning to move behind Cheryl) Take a deep breath as I begin to rub your shoulders. (Cheryl closes her eyes) As you exhale sink deeper down. (Randal pushes down as Cheryl exhales) We'll do that a couple more times. (as Cheryl takes a second deep breath, Randal continues) Many wonderful changes are taking place as you shift to this new perspective of expansiveness and flexibility. You're taking time to smell the flowers, to enjoy being here now. You're enjoying going by your own time, enjoying the new experiences you're having in life, of going into a new stage of life. There is a whole new world to explore. You are the new, expanded bus. Feel those feelings as you identify with the bus, of lying there and being so light, so expanded, so open. When you go to bed tonight and in the next few nights, you can continue to identify with other images in the dream. You can be the dog that is so bright and so aware. You can become time and experience your new sense of time. You continue to get more realizations and insights from your dreams. You've already done therapy and this will further integrate the experience.

As you're ready you can come back now, slowly and gently. (pause) This is a great stopping point. After all, you have a good parking place and it'll be close to lunch time soon in more ways than one. (Cheryl opens her eyes)

CHERYL: Thank you. (Cheryl and Randal hug)

RANDAL: (to class) When something within the dream evolves, my intuition is usually to go toward the latter form. When I said to become the bus, Cheryl started from the beginning and then evolved into the new expanded version. I felt it was more appropriate to work on where she had come to, rather than on the earlier version. I thought at first of having her become the very smart, well-behaved dog with the matching jacket, but she can do that on her own if she wants.

CHERYL: I want to see what it's like to be that dog. It was a very special little dog.

RANDAL: Yes, I encourage you to do that tonight. Gestalt dreamwork is easily done on ourselves. There definitely are other things you can explore about your dream. What we worked on was a major issue and there may be others. The issue of you and the bus and the shift that you are experiencing in your life was quite profound. Does it feel that way to you?

CHERYL: Yes. What surprises me is the emotion that came up. On the morning of the dream I did some hiking up in the hills and I felt very emotional. Tears were running down my face. It was hard to get in touch with what it was until we just did this work. I realize now that I was somehow connecting this time of year with the anniversary that is coming up tomorrow.

RANDAL: I don't know if you've heard of the anniversary syndrome, but when someone has a traumatic experience the feelings can come up several years later at the same time of the year. The death of a parent, for example. Even though the doctors had said you were going to die soon, you resolved it. You had a lot to deal with at the time of that tremendous shock, even though you eventually worked it out.

CHERYL: Everything you just said is true. Words really have an impact on people. Even though I didn't accept the death sentence that was given to me, I still feel that part of me has doubt and says, "Maybe my doctors were right."

RANDAL: You mean you were thinking that at that time, five years ago?

CHERYL: There is still a part of me now that has a little bit of doubt that maybe they were right and I'm dying after all. That feels a part of what this dream was about — making a choice between going and staying. As I'm thinking about it now, five years is the magical number that is sometimes given as a measure of whether you're going to make it or not. I think that's where this is all coming up from. I know I've made it a point these past few years not to make any long term plans in my life.

RANDAL: This was such an incredibly powerful experience at the time. You described in a previous class how your doctor told you in detail about the radical surgery he wanted to immediately do and other repair work that was going to be done after that and the possible side effects that could lead to other problems. When you refused to do it, one doctor was so shocked that he insisted you have a psychiatric test. And in the months following that you began your long journey toward health and here you are in the pink of health. That had to have an impact even if you didn't buy it, so that some part of you was still superstitious and somewhat afraid of that.

CHERYL: That's exactly what I'm feeling. There was a point when I experienced a sense of emotional and spiritual healing, but I didn't know whether that was going to manifest as a physical healing. That little bit of superstition you just mentioned shows how powerful words are when they come from an authority figure. In many cases people manifest exactly what is predicted. I remember thinking, "Well, wait a minute. It's possible that I might die of cancer, but it's not inevitable." Even though I hadn't been trained in hypnosis at the time, I recognized the power of a negative suggestion.

RANDAL: In fact you said you knew how depressed you were feeling and if you had gone through that radical procedure you believe you would have died on the operating table.

CHERYL: Yes. I knew within myself that there was no way I wanted to live in the condition I was going to be left in. I felt quite strongly that I wouldn't survive surgery.

RANDAL: (to class) I think this is all very relevant. We have not digressed because this is the big issue that was brought up by the dreamwork. (to Cheryl) You received a lot of negative opinions and you thought you had worked it through, but there was still this residual effect after five years. Already I know you are feeling a lot of relief from what you just did, but also you will continue to feel further relief and the joy of that. Beautiful story. Thank you very much.

Postscript: Cheryl Writes Three Years Later

It's amazing how pivotal that dreamwork was as a turning point in my acceptance of coming back and embracing life. In the two years since then I've accomplished so many things and laid the groundwork for a beautiful and fulfilling future. Every once in awhile I catch myself getting caught up in the hectic schedule of that original bus and know I need to stop and get back into a healthy balance.

I did go on to work with the cute little dog in the dream that always knew what to do, and experienced it as a delightful combination of my inner child and my higher self. I continue to tap into that - a playful kind of innocence that is open and trusting on the one hand and wise and knowing on the other.

Chapter 10

Questions and Answers

The following are actual questions and answers taken from the transcripts of this book.

Q: Why is dreamwork so important?

A: Dreams are existential messages from our subconscious minds that are more than symbolic of our lives, they *are* our lives. They are the essence of how our subconscious minds see ourselves and the world. If a major shift or breakthrough has not occurred since, any fairly recent dream is significant. When you work through issues in the dream, you are inevitably working through issues in your life.

Q: Could you give a definition of the word Gestalt?

A: Gestalt is a German word that has to do with wholeness. The whole is greater than the sum of the parts. Think of a car. If parts are scattered here and there it's much less powerful than when all the parts are together in just the right way. The same is true for a human life. Gestalt has to do with becoming whole and complete, able to use our full capabilities.

Q: Is the moment a person awakens particularly significant?

A: When the dreamer wakes up spontaneously during an unresolved dream, as opposed to waking up by an alarm clock or something external, it's called the impasse. Waking is a last resort. You have not found any other solution. In a frustration dream your last resort is to escape from it so thoroughly that you wake up out of the dream. It isn't really escaping, but at the moment you can get yourself temporarily out of the quandary that you're in. "What in the world do I do now? Where do I go?" You can wake up from the dream.

Q: Are recurring dreams particularly important?

A: A dream doesn't have to be recurring to be a very important message, but recurring dreams are always particularly significant. The subconscious mind is emphasizing, "This is a big issue here and it continues to be unfinished. Let's work through it!"

Q: If Gestalt doesn't include analysis, how do you deal in hypnosis with a repetitive dream? What do you search for?

A: By having your client become the characters in the dream, he or she gets realizations without intellectually trying to figure it out. Whether it's a repetitive dream or not, the realizations come, usually immediately. Even when persons don't figure out directly what a particular dream has to do with their lives, they are working things out to integrate the different parts toward greater harmony.

If my client's session evolves from dreamwork into regression therapy, the regression work could eventually include a very short period of hypno-analysis (primarily self-analysis by the client, with myself there as a support person), which I don't do during the process of the dreamwork itself.

Q: Do the parts always come together in Gestalt dialogue?

A: In my work they almost always come together in one way or another. Let's take a very unusual and extreme example. I did dreamwork with a man who described being with a girl that he was trying to save. He and the girl were being chased by a tall, obese, ugly murderer. They ran through parks and buildings and ended up in a hotel.

The man who was being chased grabbed a broken bottle and was somehow able to pin down the man who was twice his size. He held the bottle to his neck and said, "Leave us alone! I don't want to hurt you but just leave us alone!" And the other man said, "No, I'm not going to leave you alone. I'm going to kill you," and then he woke up. I had him dialogue with the murderer and after much switching, the pinned–down man still would not compromise in any way , even repeatedly telling him, "You're going to have to kill me or I'll kill you." Suddenly my client screamed and smashed the broken bottle against the man's neck and killed him. I had him continue the process. "Be the dead man. What do you want to say?" And the dead man said, "Oh thank you! I needed that." And my client suddenly got it. He had started a successful business eight or ten years ago and it had been of great value, including leading to his marriage. Now it was time to move on. The man who had been chasing him was this job, but now he really wanted to change his profession. It was time to let go and that was what this dream was about. So this process, in an ironic way, led to a harmonious conclusion. In some way or another, there is usually an integration.

In some cases a person may remain partially unfinished, but any realization has value. What a person is to discover may not all occur in a single session. If an issue is not totally resolved at the conclusion of a session then the work can continue in life or in the next session. The object during dreamwork is not to get to a point where you get the realization. The object is to become selected parts of the dream at a deep level and experience that for its own intrinsic value, owning each part. Realizations often come when you are not looking for them. You can keep getting realizations when you're not intellectually trying to figure it out but by just experiencing it.

Q: Can this empty chair dialogue in connection with the dreamwork be done with oneself or does it require an operator or a therapist there with you?

A: It would require that you know Gestalt work and that you could have that part of you that is detached tell yourself to switch characters and so on. The more you do it, as therapist or client, the more natural it becomes. I would not recommend that anyone do a regression to a traumatic experience alone. But dreamwork tends to bring you into a lighter state of hypnosis that encourages more control and stays in the present with a dream. The subconscious is obviously ready because it has been attempting to handle the issues by creating the dream. Be prepared for the possibility that strong feelings may come to the surface.

Some people may find, if they haven't done much work on themselves in therapy or on their own, that they have a hard time feeling or expressing a particular kind of feeling, or being around someone who is expressing that feeling. Whether the feeling is anger, grief, fear or whatever, it is a sign that there is unfinished business. In that case it would be valuable to do some hypnotherapy sessions to begin to work through that. Once that process has begun the person may be more comfortable with any images associated with that feeling that come up in the dreamwork. In general, mentally and emotionally healthy individuals have the potential to do a lot of good work with their own dreams.

Q: Can you work on a dream if you only remember a small part of it?

A: Even the tiniest part of a dream, such as a single image, can be worked with. For example, I worked with a man who could only remember a moment from a dream in which he was standing in his home town of Sacramento looking out at the horizon and he was impressed with a certain building. That was all he had. I had him become the building and it turned out that he was a beautiful old court house. It was a wish fulfillment dream. He gave elaborate descriptions of his elegant, well-decorated rooms.

"Go inside to where the court proceedings are going on. How do the people feel about you?"

"They feel very good. I'm here to see that justice gets done."

I wasn't looking for anything that was necessarily negative or positive, but I had him check out the electrical and the plumbing and so forth, and things were working fine. There ended up being no necessity for dialogue between any of the parts of the session that he experienced. He was like a new man afterwards. He was standing tall and positively radiant after the experience of working with that one moment.

Q: I realize that Gestalt dreamwork has to do with integrating different parts. Does that always mean that the person ends up understanding the dream?

A: A major purpose of Hypnotic Dreamwork is helping your client work things out between different characters to help own, balance, strengthen and integrate the parts. Improving the interaction between parts has its own intrinsic value, even when the dreamer does not make a conscious intellectual association with a current relevance as it applies in his or her life.

In addition, experiencing a dream by becoming different parts will periodically bring about a satori, a mini enlightenment experience of "Aha!" when the person gets the connection between this dream and some aspect of his or her experience. As an example, I did dreamwork with a woman who was going through many changes. She had been a homemaker during all of the time she had raised children. Now that they had left home she was going on to graduate school and was also in a hypnotherapy training in which I was the guest instructor. We worked with her dream about a very powerful wild stallion that had been totally free and was now being taken somewhere in a train. It didn't know where it was going but felt okay about it, realizing it had been free all these years and now it was time for something else. The woman went back and forth, becoming the train and becoming the horse, and dialoguing between them. She expressed frustration that she still had no idea whatsoever what this dream was about. I told her that was fine and encouraged her to stay with it. A few minutes later she suddenly realized the obvious and exclaimed, "Oh! I'm that stallion!"

It's important to let the person get it. If people don't consciously experience the meaning of their dreams immediately in this way that's fine too, because they're working out the valuable process of integrating different sides of themselves through Gestalt dialogue.

Q: Is there ever a time when a person just isn't getting something that you can tell them or at least give them a hint?

A: There may be times when a person is almost there that you help them. That is something I would rarely do, but I know it can work. My introduction to Gestalt dreamwork was through a series of dream therapy groups in the late sixties, when I was seventeen. I remember having a dream that took place at a Renaissance Faire. My teacher was Ann Boyne, a truly sensational Gestalt dreamwork therapist who has since retired. At one point she said, "Well, don't you get it about this dream?" I'd been making all kinds of realizations but she continued to be excited about the dream itself, and I looked at the big picture and said, "Well, life is a Renaissance Faire." And she said, "Randal, *you* are a Renaissance Faire!" I just loved her comment. I immediately made the connection with so many colorful, playful, creative, joyous associations that were a part of my experience of such a fair.

Q: How would you handle it if someone came in and said, "I had a dream about you."

A: I would work with that. "Become Randal." If you tell me you have a dream about me, that dream is not really about me. I'm a character in it and this character may have some qualities that the dreamer assiciates with me, but the dream is about you. You're identifying or projecting certain qualities onto me that you have the option of integrating into you. Within that framework I can see working on anything whatsoever a person comes up with in dreamwork.

Q: In a dream are the different personalities always parts of yourself, or can they be your interpretation of how a particular person is and what they represent in life?

A: In some ways it might be an interpretation of that other person but what's relevant in Gestalt work is that whatever else it might be, it's also a part of yourself. It always works to own this part of yourself and become that part in the dream.

Q: From a brief therapy standpoint, is dreamwork the kind of work you might do if you felt somebody needed to do some regression or uncovering to come closer to a goal they want to attain?

A: That can work very well. Dreamwork can be a link whether you're doing counseling or hypnosis or bodywork or any form of therapy. It can be a valuable way to get down to core emotional issues that might be blocking someone from their full potential in some area. In addition it may lead to a regression, but often can lead to resolution without necessarily needing to do further regression work.

Q: If a dreamwork session turns into a regression to a difficult experience, would you take sides in that case?

A: As a rule, it's a mistake in any kind of Gestalt work to take sides, not just when doing dreamwork. When going back in regression to childhood and dealing with an excessively critical parent, for example, it's natural for many to identify with the child and want to confront the parent with a statement such as, "Don't be so harsh to your child!" But people need to discover the power within to find their own resources so that part doesn't remain "a helpless child" when difficulties arise.

Another reason not to take sides in this regression example is that there is a critical parent inside the person. What happened in the past is only relevant regarding how the issue is influencing the person's life now. A highly critical inner parent might be playing out in a relationship or at work, for example, as well as through self-criticism. A person can be stuck with these mental expectancies and habit patterns. If you take sides it can stifle the process of integration and growth that needs to take place between the two extremes.

You can have a very critical parent on one side versus a helpless child on the other that has no idea how to take care of itself. If you're supporting the helpless child without the critical parent, then the person is going to be stuck with a helpless child part and the critical parent part will not just disappear. There is something to be gained from aspects of each side. By integrating and bringing together the power of both extremes, the two sides begin to compromise and mature, and you help to create balance in the whole person.

Q: Can Gestalt dialogue and dreamwork help a person deal with anxiety?

A: Gestalt dreamwork taps people into here and now experiences and gets them out of anxiety. Anxiety is defined as the gap between the present and the future. We never know what's going to happen in the future so it's fantasy. Ironically, doing dreamwork can get people out of fantasy into the reality of the present.

Q: You've said that during hypnosis people only accept the suggestions they want to accept. But you've also said that a lot of the problems people have were caused by the fact that they had been hypnotized into negative beliefs, often at an early age, and that you are in effect de-hypnotizing them. Can you clarify that?

A: I was referring to the traditional therapeutic structure of a situation as opposed to life in general. Anyone seeing a hypnotist knows that he or she could become highly suggestible. That helps the person to be aware. The purpose of the therapeutic context is to help the client make positive changes. That's very different from, for example, the highly emotionalized state of a four-year old child being beaten severely by a drunken parent. That child is especially open to suggestion at such a time and learning all kinds of negative things. That kind of hypnotic state can be very damaging, especially early in life when a child is so suggestible. In a therapeutic context you can offer strong support to help counteract negative expectations and belief systems resulting from past trauma.

Q: Is it that people are being hypnotized from childhood on and then during hypnosis therapy they get de-hypnotized from the negative? Or is it that the more recent suggestion is on top and the old program is lying underneath? If that's the case, then does the top layer wear off or do you have both and sometimes you go one way and sometimes you go another?

A: Hypnosis is not so simple as waving a magic wand. We have entrenched neuropathways in the brain and many associations. When a person has something very strongly embedded in the subconscious you can begin to work with it and sometimes get incredible results even in one session. But most commonly when someone has been this way for most of a lifetime you will do a series of sessions in which you reiterate and deepen the suggestions as well as deal directly with underlying issues and possible regression work. The therapy might also entail the use of ideomotor methods to elicit information from the subconscious, such as through finger signals. There still may be some tendencies to feel the negative associations but you can use many methods, including teaching the person self-hypnosis for positive reinforcement, to continue to weaken the old negatives and give more and more support to positive imagery and expectancy.

Q: I have heard that the ability to be hypnotized decreases with age. Is that true?

A: There is some slight truth in that but individual differences are greater than age differences. A better than average subject who is eighty may respond at least as well as a less than average subject who is ten. Beginning around age five, the ability to be hypnotized in the traditional sense does tend to increase and hits a peak around the age of eight to ten, when children can be passive but still have such vivid imaginations. Their minds haven't become cluttered with all the complications that come up for adults in the course of a day and a lifetime. It's more like a gradual hill than a mountain peak, and then there is a very gradual tapering off as the decades go by. Also, accumulated stresses may cause someone to need a little more time or to not go quite as deeply. But almost all of my octogenarian clients have responded well.

Q: Is the outcome of a session affected by doing the work in a classroom situation?

A: There is often added value in doing therapy within a classroom setting because of the presence of the group, and sometimes, also, the opportunity for feedback from the group. The energy in the room that comes from the people that are there, and the love and bonding that often develops in our classes, are all factors that create greater opportunity for growth and transformation.

Q: Is a person who is hypnotized going to reflect the hypnotherapist's prejudices? For instance, if the hypnotherapist is strongly prejudiced about how something should be resolved, is the person who is hypnotized vulnerable to that?

A: A hypnotherapist who has expressed expectancies about what could happen or could be the cause of some issue can frequently influence the client. Many therapists are far more influential than they realize, and this often happens throughout the health and counseling professions, not just in the field of hypnotherapy.

The individual has to be able to identify with the suggestions to respond. For example, suppose I'm working with an individual regarding an addiction. We've worked through some underlying emotional issues, and this person has apparently reached the stage of readiness to quit the addiction. I may choose to give various suggestions for alternative forms of healthy behavior and attitude that I have carefully selected that appear to be appropriate for the person. The person will go with the ones that are most subconsciously desirable. By giving several alternatives, the subconscious can choose which suggestions to begin to accept and integrate.

I can give an example that happened nearly twenty-five years ago with a client who was one of my first natural somnambulists. She came to me to work on improving her dance skills, and responded very well to the therapy. She also would go so deep that all she would remember was part of the induction. Then at the very end of the counting to awaken, she would become consciously aware again. After our third hypnosis session I asked, "Well, how was that for you? Did you remember anything this time?" "Actually I do remember something. I got very annoyed when you said that I was every bit as good of a dancer as my instructor. I know damn well I'm a better dancer than her!" She informed me that she got very wary at that time and stayed conscious for about thirty seconds before she decided I was on the right track again. That's an example of how any therapist who is doing his or her best may hit something that doesn't fit, and yet the client is in control and will accept that which is felt to be appropriate.

There tends to be an emotionalized desire to respond to the suggestions of the hypnotist. The more in rapport the hypnotist and the client are, the more there is desire to follow an acceptable suggestion.

But if the suggestion is the ideal of the therapist yet it isn't right for the person, the person can find many ways to not follow it. The person may even consciously think, "I haven't thought of it that way but if the therapist thinks this is a good idea, I don't see any reason why not." But then the subconscious mind can easily avoid getting behind it.

Q: There are so many choices you can make about where to go in a dream. How do you avoid leading somebody and yet find out where they are and if they're able to go further?

A: It is appropriate to have your client become any aspect of the dream at all. As long as you are neutral with each character and not trying to find solutions for your clients, you can support them in finding their own solutions without interfering. Your purpose is to help a few parts in the dream come alive, communicate, dialogue when needed, and begin to integrate so that your clients can move toward actualizing their full potentials. The procedures of Hypnotic Dreamwork I've outlined work well to these ends.

If you're not sure of the value of developing a dialogue in one place, there may be something more significant elsewhere. It can be effective to have your client move on to different characters. You can jump around to different scenes without being jarring or disorienting to the person. If you think about Gestalt dialogue, first you're one side and then the other. One side can be crying and the other might be frustrated or angry. Just as persons can usually switch easily between characters, they can immediately shift to a different part of the dream.

Q: What if a session starts to go in a certain direction and the person lets you know they don't want to go there?

A: If a person doesn't want to go somewhere, I won't force it. That's the bottom line, and we can shift to a different direction instantly. However, there are times during a Gestalt dialogue that to be supportive it may be appropriate to encourage a fearful part to face the feeling. "Express yourself. You can do it. Tell your father how you feel about how he's been treating you." As an example of a compromise, I could possibly direct the person out of the experience but focus on a more current version of the same issue. For example, I might say, "I'd like you to focus on someone in your life now that you feel is being unfair to you and stand up to this person." Depending on the circumstances, I could also move on to an entirely different issue, or to some form of healing imagery.

As another example, a person may say, in an angry voice, "No, I don't feel angry at her." If the anger is obvious, there is strong denial. It can sometimes be appropriate to encourage that person to break through, instead of holding all that tension inside. Even though it may initially seem catastrophic to the person to express the feeling, there are times to encourage the realization that expression in the right circumstances is much healthier than being stuck in resistance. The person may have been feeling the anger all along but internalizing it in a damaging way, and the breakthrough can be very valuable.

I'll add that I don't feel a person should have a particular feeling. When it's obvious that there is a lot of tension, I don't always know at first what the person is feeling. The important thing isn't so much that the client necessarily has to feel a particular emotion. What is important is that they stop hurting themselves - their bodies and their minds and their spirits. But I always keep as my intention to work in a way that is true to the unique qualities and needs of the individual, and there are many circumstances in which there are solutions other than expression of a particular feeling, even when the repression of that feeling is one of the issues.

Chapter 11

Christine's Dream:

Crawling Over the Six-Inch Hurdles

Introduction to the Use of Regression
in Dreamwork

The subconscious mind stores memories and the emotional associations of those memories. A hypnotic regression is any experience in hypnosis in which memories from the recent or distant past are revivified. There are many forms of hypnotic regression, and many potential benefits. What is relevant to this book is the kind of regression that may spontaneously spring from a Hypnotic Dreamwork session. While I never initially seek to switch from the dream to a regression, dreamwork can naturally develop into regression. Gestalt works extremely well with hypnotic regression, as it does with dreams.

In addition, it is interesting to realize that since a dream is reality to the subconscious while it is happening, to vividly recall a dream is actually a form of regression.

Three of the sessions within this book spontaneously evolve into regressions: the dreamwork of Christine in this chapter, Liz in Chapter 14 and Tom in Chapter 19. The initial reason for regression development with Christine and Liz will be obvious. Both spontaneously verbalize the connection to past experiences. The purpose of regressing Tom may not be as apparent. When he becomes a dream character in the beginning of his session he spontaneously gets stuck in an emotional reaction. He has a difficult time switching to become the other character, as per instructions. It quickly becomes clear he is having an abreaction, which is a highly emotionalized reliving of a past experience. The affect bridge is used at that point to have him stay with his feelings and return to the initial sensitizing event.

Much of the value of these three regressions will become more apparent as they progress, and all include additional explanation by way of the post-session discussions and questions and answers.

Christine's Dream and Regression

CHRISTINE: I had a dream last week that had to do with getting things accomplished in my life. I have a hard time doing things.

RANDAL: It has at least something to do with that but let's see what evolves. Go ahead and tell the dream in the present tense. Try to imagine and feel it as if it's happening right now.

CHRISTINE: Okay. I was looking down at a scene...

RANDAL: "I'm looking down at a scene..."

CHRISTINE: I'm looking down at a scene and I'm aware that there is a person lying on the ground trying to get over these hurdles that are about six inches high with her body. She's wiggling around like a worm. I know it's me because these hurdles are hurting my body.

RANDAL: Even though you're watching this other person, it's hurting your body?

CHRISTINE: Yes. And there's a woman over her and she's saying, "Come on, you can do it!" I know that that's part of me, too. Then there's a man over here and I can't really see him, he's more in the background. Then I realize I'm more like a rabbit. I see my body being like a rabbit and sometimes being a rabbit. This rabbit is trying to get trained to jump over these hurdles. Then I woke up.

RANDAL: This is sometimes a person that is you, and sometimes it's a rabbit?

CHRISTINE: Uh huh. And also I have a pet rabbit and several years back I had a drum experience where the power animal that came to me was a rabbit. It was a metaphor.

RANDAL: Are you having a harder time as a woman or as a rabbit?

CHRISTINE: A harder time as a woman in the position I was in. I was on the ground like a worm trying to get over these hurdles. A rabbit can just go like this (Christine bounces in her chair), but as a woman it was like being paralyzed or something.

RANDAL: Thank you. I would like you to become that woman and my thought is to have you actually lie on the floor in that position. If you would be more comfortable you can stand up, but I would like you to get into that position either lying or standing, and make those movements as though you're going over these hurdles.

CHRISTINE: Okay. (laughing) I'm going to do the floor thing.

RANDAL: Good for you. I'll get down here on the floor, too. (Christine lays on her stomach, her arms are at her sides, and Randal sits beside her) I want you to feel as if you are attempting now to go over these six-inch hurdles. (Christine is wiggling and with a jerk turns on her side) You're having to squiggle and turn on your side and leap a little, even though you're lying down. Feel how difficult that feels. (Christine is resting on her left arm now and rolls to her other side, wiggling and moving head first, inching along) You're wiggling along, as you said, almost like a worm.

CHRISTINE: (laughing, rolling onto her back) It might be easier this way. (Christine continues to wiggle, slowly inching forward)

RANDAL: You've come a ways. Not exactly like the Olympics currently taking place in Atlanta (laughter from the group), although it may feel just as hard. Close your eyes and go inside your body. What do you feel right now?

CHRISTINE: Exhausted. Tired. It hurts.

RANDAL: Some part of your body hurts?

CHRISTINE: Not right now. (Christine sighs) But if I keep doing it this way it's going to hurt. I'd just like to get over these hurdles without it being so painful. I want to be able to go faster without feeling it so much.

RANDAL: (touching Christine's shoulder) Now I want you to be the hurdle. Describe yourself as the hurdle.

CHRISTINE: (continues lying on her back) You can't get over me.

RANDAL: Say that again.

CHRISTINE: You can't get over me.

RANDAL: (touching her shoulder, as he will continue to do each time she is to switch) Be yourself again. What do you want to say in response to the hurdle?

CHRISTINE: I can hardly get over it. It's just too big.

RANDAL: Say that to the hurdle. "I can hardly get over you. You're too big."

CHRISTINE: I can hardly get over you. You're way too big. I can see your top but I can't begin to climb over you. You're not like a mountain, you're straight up and straight down. You're not like a gradual thing. And you're sharp. You hurt.

RANDAL: Switch and be the hurdle. What do you say?

CHRISTINE: I can't respond.

RANDAL: Describe yourself as the hurdle - what you look like, what your shape is, what your purpose is. Say whatever you want to say about yourself.

CHRISTINE: I'm immense...and tired. I put thoughts in your head. I'm black.

RANDAL: Tell Christine what kind of thoughts you put in her head.

CHRISTINE: I put thoughts about fear. "You can't do it. No matter how hard you try, you can't do it."

RANDAL: Be Christine and respond.

CHRISTINE: Yes, I can do it. You're not telling me the truth. You're not real. You think you can make me be afraid but no matter how long it takes... (Christine cries and catches her breath) I'll get over you.

RANDAL: Good.

CHRISTINE: So you're getting smaller.

RANDAL: Go inside your body. What do you feel right now?

CHRISTINE: I feel like I'm paralyzed on one side. I feel like I can move on my right side but not on my left side. I don't know why that is.

RANDAL: You don't have to know why. Just say "I'm paralyzing my left side." That's a way of taking responsibility.

CHRISTINE: I'm paralyzing my left side.

RANDAL: Feel yourself doing that. Get into that feeling in your left side. (Randal picks up a pillow and holds it in front of Christine) I'd like you to take this pillow, grab it with your right hand since your left hand is paralyzed, and do something to paralyze the pillow. Paralyze it now.

CHRISTINE: I'm paralyzing it.

RANDAL: Say that to the pillow, "I'm paralyzing you."

CHRISTINE: I'm paralyzing you. You can't move.

RANDAL: Breathe down into your stomach and feel yourself paralyzing that pillow. Put all that energy into the pillow to paralyze it. That's good. Breathe. Now relax and set the pillow aside. Go inside your body and what do you feel? Is it the same or is it different?

CHRISTINE: I don't feel as much fear. It's changing a little bit.

RANDAL: What's changing?

CHRISTINE: I was shaking in my body before but I'm not shaking in my body as I was.

RANDAL: Good.

CHRISTINE: I think I could use my left hand if I just wanted to, but it seems like I'm hypnotized.

RANDAL: Uh huh, well, perhaps you are. (laughter from Christine and the group) The harder you laugh, the deeper you go. (more laughter) You're doing great. So even though your left hand is relaxed right now, your whole body is relaxed, you're not feeling that paralyzed feeling. The golden rule in Gestalt is, "Do unto others as you do unto yourself." You just took that paralyzed feeling and put it out into that pillow. You released a lot of that feeling. Take a look at those hurdles. How do you feel about those hurdles now?

CHRISTINE: They seem smaller than they were and I realize that trying to get over those hurdles the way I was, was a strange way to do it. In the dream that's the way it was but it doesn't seem that I have to do it that way.

RANDAL: Let's imagine that you're continuing to have the dream and let's say that this dream is reality. You've been attempting this strange way of trying to get over these hurdles and now that you're recognizing this, what do you want to do?

CHRISTINE: I just want to stand up and step over these hurdles.

RANDAL: Well, do you want to stand up and step over the hurdles?

CHRISTINE: Yes, but I would like to know what the hurdles are.

RANDAL: Make a statement to the hurdles along those lines: "Tell me what you are."

CHRISTINE: Tell me what you are. Why are you here?

RANDAL: Be the hurdles. What do you say in response?

CHRISTINE: I'm your mother.

RANDAL: Now switch and be Christine. (addressing the group) Is there a box of Kleenex around?

CHRISTINE: Are you suggesting to me... (the whole group breaks into laughter)

RANDAL: (joking) I just needed to blow my nose. (more laughter) It's always good to have these here. Be Christine now and talk to your mother. What do you want to say to her?

CHRISTINE: You can't do that to me.

RANDAL: Let's turn that around and make it an even stronger statement, saying "I won't let you do that to me."

CHRISTINE: (forcefully) I won't let you do that to me.

RANDAL: Explain to her what you're not going to let her do.

CHRISTINE: Stop me. I won't let you stop me.

RANDAL: Good. Do you call her mother or mom or what?

CHRISTINE: Mom.

RANDAL: Be mom and respond to Christine.

CHRISTINE: I don't want you to be that way. I really want you to grow. I'm sorry that I stopped you when you were a child.

RANDAL: Say "I'm not stopping you now."

CHRISTINE: I'm not stopping you now.

RANDAL: Good. Now switch and be Christine.

CHRISTINE: I'm going to have fun. I'm going to grow. I'm not going to be so strict on myself.

RANDAL: Switch and be mom.

CHRISTINE: I'm going to get out of your way.

RANDAL: Instead of that being future tense let's turn it into present tense. "I'm out of your way."

CHRISTINE: I'm out of your way.

RANDAL: Now be Christine.

CHRISTINE: I'm going to step over.

RANDAL: Let's turn that into the present tense.

CHRISTINE: I'm stepping over now.

RANDAL: I want you to visualize stepping over.

CHRISTINE: I'm stepping over with my right foot but my left foot is having trouble getting over. It's hesitating and dragging.

RANDAL: Become your left foot and left leg. Describe yourself.

CHRISTINE: I'm dead. I'm paralyzed. You have to help me.

RANDAL: And who are you talking to? You're the left foot and left leg but who is "you" that needs to help?

CHRISTINE: (laughing) My mother! Oh, that makes a lot of sense.

RANDAL: So do you want mother to come back now?

CHRISTINE: No! (laughter from the group) Never.

RANDAL: So what are you going to do? You've been this help-less foot and you started to call your mother and now you've changed your mind.

CHRISTINE: I'm remembering what she would do a long time ago when I was a baby and wanted to climb the stairs. She would come and pick me up and take me to the top of the stairs. She wouldn't want me to struggle or do it myself.

RANDAL: So now it's time for you to learn to struggle and do it for yourself.

CHRISTINE: (giggling) Yeah, that's right.

RANDAL: Maturation is what Gestalt work is about. The Ge-stalt definition of maturation is to go from environmental support to self-support. Your mother meant well but you learned to look for her help and now it's time for you to do it yourself. It's time to grow up. I'm talking to that part of you that is still back there, that left foot that is struggling and feels paralyzed. I'd like you to imagine now being at the bottom of those steps. It's time for you to go up those steps yourself. Visualize that now. Three, two, one (Randal taps Christine's shoulder), be back there at those steps. All right, you've been just a baby but now you're getting bigger and stronger and you see these steps in front of you. It's time to climb up.

CHRISTINE: It seems easy enough if I'm holding onto the rail.

RANDAL: That's fine. Are you climbing up now, holding onto the rail?

CHRISTINE: Uh huh.

RANDAL: Are you climbing up with both your right foot and your left foot?

CHRISTINE: Uh huh.

RANDAL: How old are you right now as you're doing this?

CHRISTINE: Actually I'm me now, as I am, and I'm pulling myself up the banister. But my legs are going up, too.

RANDAL: So you're using your hands and your legs?

CHRISTINE: Right.

RANDAL: Good. Pull yourself up that bannister. Pull yourself up those steps.

CHRISTINE: Okay. And now I'm at the top.

RANDAL: Good, be at the top. You made it. How do you feel right now?

CHRISTINE: I feel like I'm at the top and it's like at the top of those hurdles I was going over. It's a thin edge and even now I could fall off any time but I feel like it's okay if I fall off. Now that I've gone up the stairs, I can always get up again. I think my fear is something from my mother. She put that inside of me, a fear of falling, a fear of steps, a fear of something.

RANDAL: So where is that fear now, that your mother put in you back then? Is it inside you or is it somewhere else?

CHRISTINE: It's sort of out in the air around me. I can't describe it. It's not so much inside of me, it's gotten outside of me.

RANDAL: It's gotten outside of you. Good. It didn't belong there anymore. Maybe some part belonged there at the time. It was a well-meaning mother trying to help protect her child, but you have grown up and you don't need that. So the fear is around but not inside. Are you aware of it? Are you feeling that fear or a fear like it right now or are you feeling fine?

CHRISTINE: I'm thinking that I didn't know where the fear was coming from and I really didn't even know that it was fear. I thought it was depression and just exhaustion but I'm sure now that it was fear. I'm sure that it was fear of punishment.

RANDAL: Go inside your body. How do you feel now?

CHRISTINE: I'm feeling much better.

RANDAL: Great. You mentioned a few minutes ago about the top of the stairs being like an edge and you could possibly fall. Are you feeling steady up there?

CHRISTINE: Uh huh.

RANDAL: So how does it feel now to be at the top of those steps?

CHRISTINE: Well, it's not really exhilarating. I just think, well, I'm here. I'm not jumping up and down with joy.

RANDAL: So it's not exhilarating but the fact is that you're here. How does that feel?

CHRISTINE: It feels good.

RANDAL: Let it feel good. Go inside your body now and what does your body feel?

CHRISTINE: I really feel tense and I'm trying to get up really fast. I feel very tired.

RANDAL: Where do you feel the tension?

CHRISTINE: Mostly in my shoulders and upper neck and back. It's a muscular tension that I can't relax.

RANDAL: Take responsibility and say "I'm not relaxing, I won't relax."

CHRISTINE: I won't relax.

RANDAL: "I'm tensing myself."

CHRISTINE: I'm tensing myself.

RANDAL: Take this pillow again. Grab this pillow and tense it. That's good. Put all that tension you're feeling into the pillow and say "I'm tensing you."

CHRISTINE: I'm tensing you.

RANDAL: Good. Now breathe as you do it. (Randal takes deep breaths with Christine) Okay, relax. Very good. I'll shake out that pillow here. (Randal holds the pillow to the side and shakes it and Christine giggles) Let go of some of that. Relax. Now get in touch with your body, breathing into your belly. What do you feel in your body right now, and especially those areas that were feeling that tension?

CHRISTINE: It's different. I was able to get rid of a lot of the tension.

RANDAL: The golden rule of Gestalt again. Get that energy out instead of turning it against yourself. I'd like you to bring your mother here to see if there is anything you'd like to say to her. You've made it to the top of these steps. You're on your own now. What would you like to say?

CHRISTINE: I don't want to be a part of you anymore. I was inside you and you wouldn't let me go. I want to be completely separated from you. It's time for you to let me go. Even though I've not seen you for years, you've held me inside of you.

RANDAL: Now switch and be mom.

CHRISTINE: I'm sorry, I wanted you to help me live. (Christine begins to cry) I'm sorry. I have to live my own life... (crying softly)

RANDAL: It's all right to cry. Breathe down into your stomach. Feel that recognition and say that again. "I have to live my own life."

CHRISTINE: I have to live my life by myself.

RANDAL: Be Christine.

CHRISTINE: I feel I'm free from you now. I'm free. And I feel like the hurdle was me trying to get separated from you.

RANDAL: You were still back there crawling like when you were a baby.

CHRISTINE: That's right. (Christine sighs heavily)

RANDAL: Do you know what happens when a baby chick is struggling to get out of an egg and you try to help it by pulling away some of the shell? The effect can limit the chick's ability to grow and develop. There was a part of you that was still back there that hadn't learned to fully crawl, much less do everything you can do. It was a part of you, and that part of you is now learning. Can you say good-bye to your mother now?

CHRISTINE: Uh huh.

RANDAL: Now be your mother one last time. Do you want to say good-bye to Christine?

CHRISTINE: Good-bye. (laughing) Even though it's hard, good-bye. (softly) It's a hard good-bye.

RANDAL: Yes, good-bye. Being born is not easy. Saying good-bye is not easy. But it's a good and healthy step for both of you. Now you are Christine without your mother. Let's look back on that field. Are there still hurdles on that field?

CHRISTINE: They're gone. It's like they've gone down into the ground.

RANDAL: That's interesting. Instead of having to go over the hurdles they've just moved down into the ground. I'd call that a level playing field. (laughter) You're doing great. You now have a nice, smooth field to play in. Go into that field and imagine what position you are in now. Are you lying, sitting, standing, walking, or what?

CHRISTINE: There is something that is very important for me to resolve. I know consciously that when I was being born I almost died because they gave my mother too much ether and then it got into me. She was unconscious and couldn't push and I was also unconscious. There was a critical time that the doctors could not get me out. I was pulled out by forceps and it was a complicated birth. The doctor couldn't get me to breathe for four minutes and thought I would have brain damage. I think it's all mixed up but that process of not being able to get out during child birth and almost dying is part of it, and I'm stuck with being drugged or anesthetized. Something like that.

RANDAL: Have you done ideomotor responses?

CHRISTINE: No.

RANDAL: Okay. I'd like you to put your attention on your right hand. There is a certain finger that is your "yes" finger. Without trying to move it notice if a certain finger begins to move and wiggle.

CHRISTINE: Uh huh. It was this finger. (Christine indicates the index finger on her right hand)

RANDAL: Okay. There is a certain finger that is your "no" finger on your right hand. Notice if a certain finger wants to move. (pause) Think the word "no" until a certain finger begins to twitch and move.

CHRISTINE: My thumb.

RANDAL: Yes, I'm seeing your thumb moving. The question is, Christine, would it be safe and appropriate for you to consciously recall your birth experience?

CHRISTINE: Yes.

RANDAL: I'm asking your subconscious mind but I may be getting a conscious response. Let's ask the fingers without trying to move them and see if a finger wants to move on its own. Keep thinking the question. From your subconscious mind, Christine, is it safe and appropriate for you to go back with your conscious mind and recall any and all aspects of your birth experience at this time?

CHRISTINE: (after a pause) I'm sorry but I can't move my fingers. They won't move.

RANDAL: Okay. I'm going to tap you on your forehead and when I do, your subconscious mind will answer yes or no. Is it safe and appropriate for you to consciously recall your birth experience? Three, two, one. What comes up? Yes or no.

CHRISTINE: No.

RANDAL: All right, that's fine.

CHRISTINE: That's okay, I made the connection.

RANDAL: That's fine. You were bringing the subject up and I was looking at the possibility. You don't need to go back and recall your birth experience to make the breakthroughs that you're making right now. It was just one possibility. I'm noticing your hands and I feel that there is a part of you that is in a process of being reborn. The hands sometimes cramp into a position called tetany during a traumatic birth experience, as the fingers and thumb curl. This is a spontaneous position that your hands have been in for a time now. You're doing great. You've made that connection. What do you feel in your body right now?

CHRISTINE: I feel tingling and I feel like I'm trying to be born. I'm trying to get out. I feel like I have to get out and be alive in this world.

RANDAL: Okay.

CHRISTINE: And I can't die.

RANDAL: We don't have to go back to the birth experience you had, we can do a new birth experience for you. Here is the situation. It's time for you to be born. Get in touch with your breathing. What do you feel in your body right now?

CHRISTINE: I feel like I'm starting to see light and I can't breathe. I want somebody to pull me out.

RANDAL: Well, so far I'm not seeing anybody pulling you out.

CHRISTINE: Uh huh. I know why. I remember I was hurt. (Christine is speaking haltingly) I have this pain in my head. It goes up into my temple...like I'm being stabbed with claws...blinding flash of light...

RANDAL: Is it okay for you to stay with this experience now? I'm asking your subconscious mind.

CHRISTINE: It's okay.

RANDAL: Stay with it. You're going to go through it.

CHRISTINE: My head is feeling like it's being torn off.

RANDAL: Do you want to do it differently this time?

CHRISTINE: No, I know I won't be injured.

RANDAL: Good. Stay with it. You're at the end. This time going through it helps you to purge yourself of that experience. You're getting it out of your system this time. What's happening now?

CHRISTINE: I want to come out...no, I don't.

RANDAL: Do you think you're out now or not?

CHRISTINE: I'm here but I'm inert. I feel like I'm dead...just a blob.

RANDAL: You're beginning to suspect that you're alive.

CHRISTINE: Uh huh.

RANDAL: Stay right here now. What a miraculous experience, birth. It's been difficult, it's been painful, it's been a process of taking a giant step to a new dimension. It's not easy. You may get some help and something may get in the way, but ultimately you've got to do it yourself. You've got to make yourself fly.

CHRISTINE: It's been a test to learn how. I never knew when I was born or if I was born with a lot of pain. I've got to get past the anesthetic.

RANDAL: Uh huh. The anesthetic blocked your consciousness. This time you're being reborn without the anesthetic. That's profoundly different. Right now stay with the experience. This is what you missed and now you've got it. Stay right here in your body. (to the class) For those of you in the back, her arms were curled up under her chin and now they're back down to the floor.

CHRISTINE: I'm okay now.

RANDAL: That's great. What do you feel in your body right now?

CHRISTINE: I feel like I can move. (Christine stretches)

RANDAL: That's right. Stretch those legs out, feel your body moving, feel your arms moving. You can move, you've got a body. You're out of the womb. You're alive. Happy birthday. (laughter) This is one feisty baby! She's already kicking and moving and beginning to sit up! (more laughter as Christine sits up fully) It's only a few minutes and she's sitting up already. All right! We've got a newborn with a full head of hair.

CHRISTINE: It's amazing how I got stuck. I've already lived half my life and I was still stuck.

RANDAL: Yes, we can get stuck in various ways very early, and we don't get through it until we go through it. Many people stay stuck in some ways throughout their lives. What I'd like you to do now is to lie back down. You know that you've sat up and that you can do it. Settle back and stay with your experience. You're in a beautiful and sensitive place right now. You've just been born and you're doing great. (Christine lies back down)

We only use a small percentage of our physical and mental abilities the vast majority of the time. We have capabilities, Christine, beyond our imagination. You've just had an experience that you deserved to have, that had been taken from you. As painful and as scary as it can be, it's a necessary experience for us to have to be full and whole. You've got it back now. You've got your life fully back. You are a sane, healthy, alive, talented, aware, creative, intelligent human being who has accomplished wonderful things, who has gone through many breakthroughs. You have all of that experience in your life, even in spite of having missed this crucial experience. Yet there was a part of you until now that was missing and you've got that part now. Stay with it. Feel it. Feel yourself. Feel your body, your aliveness, that tingling. Be here now. This is a time when you don't need to go anywhere or do anything, there is nobody to please or to satisfy. This is a time that is just for you. This is a very special time because you have just been born. Get in touch with your body and describe to me what you feel in your body right now.

CHRISTINE: I feel opening up. It was like I was in a very tight ball and now I'm opening up and stretching. I feel like I can just evaporate instead of being all tight and yucky.

RANDAL: Feel yourself continuing to open, like a flower opening up, expanding, stretching. You can just lie there completely at ease, completely relaxed, your whole body limp and lazy and loose and free. And even as you do that, you can feel yourself mentally, emotionally, spiritually, even physically, opening, expanding, and evaporating. Spreading your wings, stretching yourself, disappearing into the atmosphere, and yet there is the core of you that is still here.

CHRISTINE: I think I've got to say that now I'm not afraid of the world.

RANDAL: Excellent. Let's move that even another step further. What positive feeling do you feel about the world now?

CHRISTINE: That I'm holding it.

RANDAL: Great. Hold the world.

CHRISTINE: (Christine cups her hands as if holding a sphere over her belly) It seems like I can reach everywhere. I can reach all around it. And it's inside of me. (she moves as if putting the sphere inside her belly)

RANDAL: The world is inside of you now. Christine, I'm going to read to you from a children's book by Chara M. Curtis. It's a book for the child in all of us, called *All I See is a Part of Me*: (reading from the book)

I am a part of all that I see, and all that I see is a part of me...
I used to think that I was small, a little body, that was all.
But then one day I asked the sun, "Who are you?"
He beamed, "We are one."
"But Mr. Sun, how is this true? How can I both be me and you?"
He smiled, "You might ask your sister, Star. She too, is a part of who
you are."

And so I waited until the night, when darkness let me see her light.
"Sister Star, how can it be that I am you and you are me?"

She glowed, "You are larger than you know. You are every place there
is to go. You have a body, this is true, but look at what's inside of you."

I closed my eyes to see within. I saw a light. It made me grin. It re-
minded me of Sister Star. She said, "That light is who you are..." I looked
again at all my light and saw that Sister Star was right. For every question
there could be, the answer is inside of me. All I ever had to do was ask the
part of me that knew.

I wondered as I climbed in bed, does all of me sleep when I rest my
head?

And in the book there's a picture on the wall that says, "Open
your eyes, your dreams are real." (applause and laughter from the
class) Thank you, and thank you, Christine. Isn't this book lovely?

CHRISTINE: It's beautiful. Thank you.

RANDAL: And aren't you lovely? How are you feeling?

CHRISTINE: I feel alive. (laughing) I feel like I finally made it
after all these years. (applause as she sits up)

RANDAL: I'd like you to look around the room at all these beautiful people and make eye contact.

CHRISTINE: It is just incredible. Everybody looks so friendly
and beautiful.

RANDAL: (looking around) Hey, you do. And you. Maybe I was
just born, too. (laughter)

CHRISTINE: You know, I'm right now in transition. I'm right
where I came into the world and it was extremely painful. Maybe it
was so painful I didn't want to be here. I almost died and now (looking around) these people look like the people I wanted to come to.
This is the world I wanted to come into, and it wasn't there. But now
it's here and it's really great.

RANDAL: You've gotten to the real world. You were seeing parts
of the world before but it was within your frame of that experience

that caused you to want to check out, to not want to fully be here. That pain was intermeshed with the vast majority of your experience and now that's gone. Now you can be in the real world and the real world is full of love and magic and miracles, and it's right here.

CHRISTINE: That's really true. I know that now. Thank you.

RANDAL: And I know that you know that much deeper. You might have heard it before and intellectually known and understood it, but you're getting it a lot deeper inside your core, inside your subconscious, inside your heart. I know that. Congratulations. (applause) We'll talk about this experience, but let's have a break first.

RANDAL: (after break) Good job, Christine! Your dream session evolved into a regression, including work on your experience of birth. The dream starts out with the great image of a field with hurdles which are only six inches high and an adult trying to figure out how to get over the hurdles by crawling on the ground. This metaphor was a message about your life and about something that you were doing in your life. I gave you the option to go through the movements of trying to get over the hurdles standing up or lying down. I was glad when you chose to lie down. That way you could more completely actualize the movement and the feeling.

I often have a person report inner physical sensations when there is some emotion or I want to find out what's going on. In this case we did that over and over again.

CHRISTINE: The left side of me being paralyzed had to with the puncture I got from the doctor pulling me out with forceps.

RANDAL: So that feeling of a wound and being clawed had to do with the forceps. The right side of the brain will affect the left side of the body, so the right side was injured. Are you saying that in the birth experience you were temporarily paralyzed?

CHRISTINE: Well, I didn't know that. I just know that now. I was severely damaged on the right side of my head. I had severe bruising and swelling of the head and black eyes for over a month after the delivery. What happened during this hypnosis is that my left side was actually paralyzed.

RANDAL: So the damage to the right side of your brain that you did know about actually caused a temporary semi-paralysis on the left side that you didn't know about until you were spontaneously regressed to that birth experience during this process.

CHRISTINE: It's amazing.

RANDAL: When it was clear that we were going into a regression process I considered taking you to your birth or further into your birth experience. I was seeing that cramping of your fingers and your thumbs that can occur during the birthing process. It's not unusual to get the kind of conflicting signals that you were getting to the question about recalling your birth. You immediately said yes but as I checked further your subconscious said no. Then when I had you keep being aware of your body it seemed that you were already in the birthing process. When I checked again you wanted to go further into it.

CHRISTINE: Intellectually I really wanted to get to the other side because some part of me knew that I wanted to get born. The other thing was that I didn't want to go through all that pain at the same time, so it was like yes, no.

RANDAL: In Gestalt, Perls talks about catastrophic versus anastrophic expectations. This impasse can seem insurmountable. That six inch barrier was a perfect example. "Oh my God, there's a gigantic barrier!"

CHRISTINE: There's another thing. That six inches is about the distance to get outside from the womb. The reason why those barriers were so sharp is because I had those prongs around my head.

RANDAL: So the barriers were an image that came directly from those sharp forceps.

CHRISTINE: They represented a sharpness to me at the edge at the time.

RANDAL: And trying to get over that and beyond the experience of the temporary physical damage and also the emotional trauma of that experience.

CHRISTINE: Yes, it's all there and clear to me now. When my daughter was around three years old, her father and I decided to end our relationship and I began to have flashes of blinding light and severe pain on the side of my head and blacking out. It went on for months. I went to the doctor and the dentist, and they couldn't find a physical reason for the symptoms. I think the ordeal of having to separate from my partner of seven years and my daughter, as we opted for joint custody, re-engaged an unconscious struggle of trying to get separated from my mother during my birth.

RANDAL: And you don't even need to figure it out. Just staying with the process and the awareness of your aliveness, you're going to continue to get more realizations without even trying. Already there are so many things you've communicated that you're aware of. Some minor aspects of the dream may not apply to your birth experience but your dream certainly included the archetypal essence of this imprint. The struggles that came later in your life about not being able to get anywhere or being helped too much, was all enmeshed together.

CHRISTINE: It was all really confusing.

RANDAL: Even before we got to the birth experience there were so many steps that had been taken. For example, when you instilled your tension and paralyzing into the pillow, that was really producing results and teaching you. If we had gotten only up to the point prior to the obvious birth experience and stopped there we would have had a very productive session, and then we went all the way back to the initial sensitizing event.

CLASS MEMBER: As a nurse, I want to point out that as I watched Christine wiggle on the ground I saw the birth process enacted. When infants enter the pelvic basin they are face down. Then they turn to the side to match up their widest diameter to the widest diameter of the pelvis. Then when they come out they come face up.

RANDAL: And that's the exact process she did. In that early stage of the dreamwork, she was actually creating the birth experience as she tried to wiggle forward on the floor.

CHRISTINE: That is so amazing. It was an instinctual thing that I was doing.

RANDAL: Yes, instinctively what you did fit for the dream, but you knew subconsciously that there was something unfinished from that experience, and you found your way back to it.

Q: The breakthroughs were just incredible and what I'm wondering is, is this something that will stay with Christine or is it something that might fade and need a recharge later?

RANDAL: Major steps were taken during this session. In the future there may be something Christine will work on as a result of all she got from this and all she does for herself after this experience. If this was one in a series of private sessions Christine was having with me, a week later she could report what she's gained and what she's discovered, and what feelings have been coming up for her since the dreamwork. I could then support her in her process with post-hypnotic suggestions. That would be valuable, but in the context of this class in which we're all working on ourselves and each other on an ongoing basis, that may not be necessary.

This experience will not fade so that she would need to get reborn again. She has now finally had her birth experience, and she's here. Of course this could lead, sooner or later, toward an opportunity she feels ready to tackle, that she may choose to get support for during sessions.

Not every dream session will work with such profound issues, but if a dream is important enough and vivid enough to remember, already that's significant. Hypnotic dreamwork often has major impact.

Q: I noticed in this session that there were several points at which you could have chosen to complete and you didn't. And even at the very end when she sat up indicating that she was done now, you made the choice to go back and do affirmations with her to counter some of the negative self-talk she had started to get into. You confirmed for her the ways she had been contributing already in life even though she felt she was only half there. Would you say a little more about why that was important to do?

RANDAL: At least the negatives that came up were in the context of past tense, but yes, I wanted to direct her attention toward the many positives and to further take advantage of the opportunities of hypnosis. Gestalt in and of itself is a complete and valuable process, but here we had someone who had just been reborn. She was right there, really sensitive and receptive to suggestion, and it was a fantastic opportunity to give suggestions to anchor that experience further. For example, I wanted to anchor her to that association in her mind that despite everything that had held her back, she had accomplished so much. Christine had sat up but it felt too soon. It was good that she felt finished and complete, but a few minutes right then could be such a precious addition, so I had her lie back down to do some hypnotic work to further integrate and ground her in the experience.

CHRISTINE: And I really appreciate that too, because in my life it's true, as you said, that I've done a lot of things but I never felt any confidence in that. I felt like I just didn't do it good enough and I feel it goes back to being born in a way that was not joyous. I never could be happy about my accomplishments.

RANDAL: You were so woozy when you were born you weren't even sure. "Something is happening. Am I alive? Am I dead? I feel like a blob." You can see how that vague, drugged experience, that dim awareness that kept you from feeling fully alive, could keep you from feeling a sense of accomplishment. When you got to the top of the stairs, for example, you said something like "I'm here, but I'm not exhilarated." That was a metaphor for your life. When you accomplished something you had not felt alive enough to fully appreciate it, and your awareness of that eventually led us to your birth experience. In therapy we deal with what emerges. You stayed with it very well.

Commentary

With delightful synchronicity, the children's book I quoted from had been loaned to me the day before by a student. The book fit so well into Hypnotic Dreamwork's Gestalt orientation that I was considering quoting from it during the seminar that day or during the group hypnosis for the hypnodream. Christine's spontaneous communication about holding the world, then putting it inside of her, led to a perfect place to incorporate the reading.

Another method besides hypnosis that can sometimes strongly effect the subconscious is identification with an authority. Books are a major source for acquiring higher level learning. Reading from a book which the client accepts as authoritative or inspirational can give an added influence to the suggestibility during hypnosis. This is called bibliotherapy, a concept first developed by C. E. Cooke.

Interview One Week Later

RANDAL: We had our session a week ago. Do you have some feedback since that experience?

CHRISTINE: This week I've been able to get tasks completed and that's something new for me. I'm able to get from A to B instead of from A to who knows where. One thing I've had a realization about is that maybe the hematoma inside my head from the forceps healed up, but there was still a psychic scar happening, a wound that hadn't healed up. I had a lot of damage and my eyes were black and blue for about a month and half after I was born. Poor little baby.

RANDAL: We can certainly see from that experience and how much it affected you, that it was a big problem.

CHRISTINE: What it's like is, I'll have a lot of energy to get a project done, a tremendous amount of enthusiasm, and then all of a sudden, somewhere along the line, it's gone! It's dead. So that's a frustration.

RANDAL: Often I have people turn things from past tense into present tense when we're doing hypnosis or dreamwork. In this case let's have you turn present tense into past tense. Can you say what you just said in the past tense and see how that sounds? "Up until now in my life when I used to start something..."

CHRISTINE: Up until I had this regression I would become very excited and enthusiastic and see the whole picture, and then my enthusiasm would fizzle out. I'm not saying it right. I would attempt to complete my initial realization and at some point it would just stop. My enthusiasm and energy would die and then I would feel depressed that I hadn't been able to complete what I had started.

RANDAL: And now you are feeling...

CHRISTINE: Now I really am feeling, and experiencing in this past week, that I'm able to say "I want to do this" and just going ahead and doing it.

RANDAL: That's a big movement you're making.

CHRISTINE: When I was telling my friends about this experience in regression of having my left side feel paralyzed, all of a sudden I had this sensation of healing going on inside my skull. It was tingling and energy coming in and then I realized that I was having a healing there and averting a stroke perhaps, when I'm maybe eighty or eighty-five years old. This healing process here (tapping the right side of her head) was connecting it all up for me. So I'm going to slide right through that one. (laughter)

RANDAL: I like that "slide right through." How's that for a more positive birth experience? (chorus of laughter and "Yeah!" from the class) That birth experience was an imprint for you. You were continuing to live that experience in various ways, especially during major traumas. The memory was in your subconscious mind of that first really tough experience that had been so horrendous. Your dream was just filled with the trauma of your birth, such as the image of crawling over the hurdles, which was like a baby going through the birth canal. You were living your birth experience over again, still attempting to resolve it after all this time. You did a great job. Let's hear it for Christine. (applause)

Letter From Christine

In the two weeks since the hypnotherapy session with you, I am amazed at the way my lifelong thought patterns reveal themselves as ghosts of an experience rather than my life set in stone. I feel I have integrated the paralysis of my left arm and leg, the severe pains I had at the time I separated from my partner, and the stories my mother had told me when I was growing up about my birth.

I believe the physical trauma at my birth caused me to be at risk in my own pregnancy when after 26 hours of Pitocin (a chemical they give mothers because they don't dilate), I still would not dilate. It is my personal belief that I was not wanting to relive my birth (through my daughter's) or at least wanting to protect her from what happened to me. She was a Caesarean baby.

Another symptom I have had throughout my life are dreams of being limp on the left side with a stunted or peg leg. I believe this is all residue from the damage to the right temple area at birth.

One of the most welcome breakthroughs since our session is my present ability to get things done. I have done many things in this life but not without struggle. I have had retarded goals. I have had an underlying fear of going ahead with or completing a project. I feel this directly stems from not having my mother's help during the birth process, feeling that I had to do it all by myself, and then encountering trauma/anoxia/near death. With that in the subconscious, why would I want to do anything at all?

Fear of people has loomed in the background for me. This I attribute to my first encounter with them - not a pleasant beginning. Now this is vanishing. I have had a fear of being annoying to people because I take so long. I don't really take so long, but I believe that babies know what is happening to them and nobody can talk me out of the fact that the emotional feeling I absorbed from the delivery staff was that I was taking too long in my birth. Now the pressure is off, and I find myself taking my own time to do things, not trying to comply with others' time frames. Whew!

I believe a humorous "hangover" from my birth has been my dislike of stop lights and stop signs, or of being tied down with a seat belt in a car. I always looked around for police and if I thought I could get away with not stopping I would. I have had numerous tickets. Of course I would never have put another person's life in jeopardy, but my pocket book has hurt from the numerous tickets I received. I feel this is from not wanting to stop (or be stopped) as I was during my birth.

I see a big difference in myself already. Whereas I have had great difficulty in following directions when driving somewhere, now I find it relatively easy to find my way around in a car. Daily tasks and even life goals such as getting through school do not seem insurmountable. I have spent an inordinate amount of time losing and then hunting for objects such as keys, possibly because of the "unconscious" way I went through life, always in a fog. Now I am able to be conscious of what I am doing and feel more alive and hooked up than I have ever felt before.

As the days go by I look forward to continuing evidence of this freeing from my past. I am so thankful that I have finally come to the place where I can work out this huge block. It is amazing to me how a very difficult birth could follow me my entire life and make my maneuverability through life so difficult. I am really feeling free for the first time, and am without the looming fear of impending doom pervading my every move. Thank you so much!

Chapter 12

Cynthia's Recurring Dream:

Not You, Mother!

CYNTHIA: I realized in keeping a dream journal that I have a recurring dream. And I've done Gestalt work before so I can do it that way.

RANDAL: Uh huh. I'd rather do dream analysis. (laughter from the group) I'm just kidding. This is a recurring dream?

CYNTHIA: Yes. I've just realized it's recurring. I've had at least four versions of it in the past year.

RANDAL: Okay. If you're not sure which version to pick I'd say take the most recent one, unless there is another one that is particularly fascinating.

CYNTHIA: It's pretty simple and I had one the night we were encouraged to remember a dream.

RANDAL: Let's go with that one.

CYNTHIA: In the dream I'm in a group situation, usually with two or more of my close women friends. And they are leaving me out. It's as though they've got some plan or activity that they're going to do together and they don't include me. I ask them why they haven't included me or say that I want to be included and they continue to leave me out or reject me. They're very sad dreams. I wake up upset. And I wake up upset with the women I've dreamt about. (laughter)

RANDAL: And how do they feel? Oh, wait. (more laughter) What are the names of your friends in this recent dream?

CYNTHIA: Barbara and Catherine.

RANDAL: Okay, be Barbara and describe yourself.

CYNTHIA: In the dream or just in real life?

RANDAL: The dream is reality right now.

CYNTHIA: I don't know how to describe myself exactly. My name is Barbara. I'm very focused and...this is hard to do. I can get their attitude towards me but I can't necessarily say much about who they are in themselves yet.

RANDAL: Yes, I know. You've been feeling the dream from your perspective and now I want you to become other characters. At first it's sometimes hard and it may be vague but it will get more real as we work on it.

CYNTHIA: Okay.

RANDAL: Is there anything else you can describe about yourself? In the dream you're going to be doing something. Do you want to talk about that?

CYNTHIA: Well, Catherine and I and some other woman are planning a long dance. (slipping out of the dream) My friend Barbara does night long dances in British Columbia for the solstice and full moons. So they're planning a long dance. (going back into character) I'm planning a long dance with Catherine. And Cindy - that's what they call me - Cindy is over there. She wants to do what we're doing but we don't want her to. She wants to join us.

RANDAL: That's good enough for now. Now be Cindy and describe yourself in this dream.

CYNTHIA: Well, I'm feeling very sad and kind of weak and powerless in relation to these two very strong, sure women. I hate to ask them to include me but I have to because I feel so bad when they leave me out. My feelings are so hurt. And I feel like I'm crawling on the ground. In fact I am crawling on the ground, at least in spirit, asking to be part of what's going on.

RANDAL: I'd like you to get on the ground as if you were crawling right now. (Cynthia looks questionably at the floor) I can hear someone thinking "I'm sure glad I didn't volunteer for this demonstration!" I'll get on the ground with you. (Cynthia and Randal are on their hands and knees) So you feel like you're crawling on the ground. Put Barbara in the chair in front of you there. What do you want to say to her?

CYNTHIA: I can do this better with my eyes closed.

RANDAL: Good. Keep your eyes closed.

CYNTHIA: Barbara, I want you to include me. I want to be part of what you're doing. I want you to love me. I want you to love me as much as you love these other women.

RANDAL: Good.

CYNTHIA: This is about my mother.

RANDAL: Talk to your mother.

CYNTHIA: Do I have to stay on my knees?

RANDAL: You can sit any way you want right now.

CYNTHIA: (Cynthia sits with her legs underneath her and sighs) Maybe it's not my mother. I'll just stay with Cathcrine and Barbara.

RANDAL: Talk to your mother.

CYNTHIA: Okay. I'll talk to my mother, who I'm going to see the day after tomorrow. I want you to pay attention to me and I want you to love me as much as you love yourself. And I want you to...recognize me and see me. (Cynthia's words are halting) I just want to know that I'm important to you...as important as...I don't think it's my sister. Just important. (tears are coming down Cynthia's cheeks and Randal hands her a tissue) But I feel so...just lowly. Worthless when I have to ask. I feel a lot of shame that I want something that I have to ask for. And that other people get without asking.

RANDAL: Good. Now let me help you get up. I'd like you to sit over here and be your mother. (Cynthia sits in the chair she was facing)

CYNTHIA: I thought I was done with this.

RANDAL: You're most of the way there and you're still working on this. You're your mother now. What do you call your daughter? Is your name for her Cynthia or Cindy or what?

CYNTHIA: It depends on whether she's in my good graces or not. She's Cindy and then when I'm angry with her I call her Cynthia.

RANDAL: Okay, so you can call her Cindy or Cynthia now depending. What do you want to say in response to her?

CYNTHIA: I think you should value yourself first. (sigh) And I have no respect for you. No, that's not really what I feel. What I feel is very confused. But I don't like you either when you're crawling and abject and so filled with shame. You're not likable when you're like that.

RANDAL: Tell her what you want from her.

CYNTHIA: I want you to just be strong. I don't want you to look to me to validate your strength.

RANDAL: All right. Switch and be Cindy.

CYNTHIA: But this is an impossible situation because I can't feel strong and healthy and sure of myself unless you recognize that. That's all there is to it.

RANDAL: Switch that to "I won't" instead of "I can't."

CYNTHIA: I won't feel strong and healthy until you recognize me.

RANDAL: Switch and be your mother.

CYNTHIA: Well, it's a standoff because I'm not going to. I'm not going to do that until you do it for yourself. I'm not going to give that to you. I won't do it.

RANDAL: Switch and be Cindy.

CYNTHIA: Well, I'm at least as strong as you are in everything but this. This is my last dependency. (Cynthia sobs quietly)

RANDAL: Go inside your body. What do you feel?

CYNTHIA: I just feel hurt. And I feel frustrated because I've done so much and come so far and I'm just stuck here with her.

RANDAL: "...with you."

CYNTHIA: I'm stuck here with you.

RANDAL: What do you feel inside your body?

CYNTHIA: (Cynthia sighs a couple of times as she cries and Randal hands her a tissue) I feel very powerless.

RANDAL: Where do you feel powerless?

CYNTHIA: I feel like the whole front of my body is unprotected. It feels very vulnerable.

RANDAL: How does it feel vulnerable? Can you describe it any further?

CYNTHIA: It feels vulnerable because I want to be loved.

RANDAL: Let's do this one more time. Stay here and say "I want you to love me."

CYNTHIA: I know she loves me, though. That's not what it's about.

RANDAL: So tell her what you want one more time.

CYNTHIA: I want you to recognize me as a strong person. I want you to see who I am... (Cynthia pauses and cries softly) I've worked so hard to become... (Randal gives Cynthia another tissue)

RANDAL: Good. Switch and be mom. Or do you call her mother?

CYNTHIA: Mother mostly.

RANDAL: Be mother. What do you say?

CYNTHIA: I'm afraid of you.

RANDAL: Okay. You haven't shared that, at least not in this process. Tell her what you're afraid of.

CYNTHIA: I'm afraid of you being more than I am. I'm afraid of you going beyond me.

RANDAL: You've acknowledged your fear that Cindy might go beyond you. Now can you tell her something you want from her?

CYNTHIA: From Cindy?

RANDAL: Yes.

CYNTHIA: I want you to stay small.

RANDAL: Now switch and be Cindy.

CYNTHIA: Well I won't. I can't. I am who I am.

RANDAL: Stay with "I won't." It's more powerful when you say that. You're taking responsibility.

CYNTHIA: I won't.

RANDAL: Instead of staying small, tell her what you're doing right here and now.

CYNTHIA: I'm saying who I am and I'm not small. I'm not small at all.

RANDAL: Stand up and tell her that.

CYNTHIA: (Cynthia stands up) I'm not small, mother.

RANDAL: Good. Say it in a positive way. Tell her how good you are now.

CYNTHIA: I've worked very hard to heal myself and to grow and I've done a lot. I'm quite proud of myself for what I've done.

RANDAL: Good. Give her another example of some of these positive qualities. For example, "One of the things I'm doing is..."

CYNTHIA: There are lots of things really. One thing is I've been able to help a large number of people.

RANDAL: Very good. Now switch and be mother.

CYNTHIA: Where did she go? (the class laughs)

RANDAL: Actually, you may have to look up a little to see Cindy right now. She's standing but she can sit down for a moment and you can talk directly to her.

CYNTHIA: (sigh) Well, it scares me because I'm afraid to be left behind.

RANDAL: Say "You scare me. I'm afraid you're leaving me behind."

CYNTHIA: You scare me. I'm afraid you're leaving me behind. I'm afraid that you've found another mother. That's all.

RANDAL: See, the table is turning here. Switch. You can stand up or sit down, whatever you want to do, and be Cindy.

CYNTHIA: I'd rather sit. Well, I'd be glad to take you with me if you want to come. I'd be glad to include you if you want to be included.

RANDAL: All right. Switch.

CYNTHIA: Well, I'm not sure I'm strong enough. I don't think I can do it.

RANDAL: Good. Now switch. (to class) Notice the integration, the kind of dance that's happening right now. Okay, Cindy.

CYNTHIA: Well, it's up to you. It's your choice. I hope that you choose to come but I doubt that you will.

RANDAL: Switch.

CYNTHIA: (sighs) Now I feel confused.

RANDAL: Stay with the confusion. It will sort itself out.

CYNTHIA: My confusion is that I really do want your help but the way I try to get it is in other ways. I don't want help for what you can help me with. (to Randal) I need to go over there for a minute. (Cynthia switches chairs and becomes Cindy) Well, my fear is the way you're going to ask me for my help is physically, rather than asking me for the kind of help I can really give you. That you're going to become physically in need of me but not admitting that there are things I could help you with that would be really meaningful in terms of your death.

RANDAL: Very good. Switch.

CYNTHIA: Whenever I get over here I just don't know if I have the strength. It would take so much strength.

RANDAL: What would take so much strength?

CYNTHIA: It would take so much strength to really face myself.

RANDAL: So do you have the strength to face yourself? As mother.

CYNTHIA: Yes, I do.

RANDAL: Good. Then use that strength. Gather up that strength and face yourself right now.

CYNTHIA: I'm not sure how to do that.

RANDAL: Some part of you knows how to do it. Go inside your body. What do you feel right now?

CYNTHIA: Afraid.

RANDAL: Where do you feel afraid?

CYNTHIA: I feel pounding in my chest and a feeling of being ungrounded and out of my body.

RANDAL: Okay, take this pillow and do to this pillow what's happening in your chest. (Randal is holding a pillow in front of Cynthia)

CYNTHIA: It's not a violent pounding. It's just thump, thump. (Cynthia pounds rhythmically with her right fist against the pillow)

RANDAL: Now keep doing that and what do you feel?

CYNTHIA: I'm still afraid.

RANDAL: Keep pounding and make it harder now. (Cynthia pounds harder but still rhythmically) All right. Now relax. Go in your body. Do you feel the same or different?

CYNTHIA: It's a little bit different.

RANDAL: What do you feel in you chest right now?

CYNTHIA: Well, the right side feels like it's moving. I can feel the movement.

RANDAL: Do you feel the pounding in your chest?

CYNTHIA: Not so much.

RANDAL: Do you feel more grounded or less grounded?

CYNTHIA: More grounded. It feels like an impasse.

RANDAL: Yes, but you're in the middle of it and working on it. Stay with it. What do you want to say to your daughter?

CYNTHIA: Well, in fact, if I can tell the truth, I do admire you. I respect you and I couldn't do what you've done, I don't think, given the circumstances of my life.

RANDAL: Good for you. Now switch.

CYNTHIA: I understand. I'm just sorry. I wish you well.

RANDAL: When you say you're sorry, what are you sorry about?

CYNTHIA: Well, I'm sorry that you can't and I do understand how hard it would be for you.

RANDAL: She can't go along with you, you mean?

CYNTHIA: Yes.

RANDAL: But can you accept that she's not going along with you? That she won't?

CYNTHIA: Yes, I can.

RANDAL: How does it feel to hear her tell you that she actually does admire you?

CYNTHIA: Good.

RANDAL: So tell her that.

CYNTHIA: It feels good for me to hear that you see me and that you recognize me for what I've done.

RANDAL: Good. Tell her something you like about her.

CYNTHIA: Oh, I like lots of things about you. I like your love of music and I love your piano playing.

RANDAL: Switch and be mother.

CYNTHIA: Well, there are lots of things I like about you, too. We love each other. That's true.

RANDAL: Come over here. Can you now say good-bye to your mother?

CYNTHIA: There's one more thing I have to say over there.

RANDAL: Please do.

CYNTHIA: (Cynthia changes chairs) I know that we're going to get to try this again.

RANDAL: How about saying, "I know we're going to get to do this again." Being together again, is that what you're referring to?

CYNTHIA: Uh huh.

RANDAL: Be a little more positive.

CYNTHIA: I know we'll get to do this again and it'll be different.

RANDAL: Very good. Switch. (Cynthia sobs and cries quietly for a minute) Breathe down into your stomach and feel your feelings.

CYNTHIA: I'm very glad. I love you very much.

RANDAL: Keep breathing.

CYNTHIA: I feel done.

RANDAL: Okay, say good-bye to your mother.

CYNTHIA: (laughing) I'm going to see her the day after tomorrow. Bye mother. I wish you well.

RANDAL: Switch and say good-bye to your daughter.

CYNTHIA: Good-bye.

RANDAL: Come over here and be Cindy. (Randal moves behind Cynthia and puts his hands on her shoulders) Take a deep breath and go way down. As I push down on your shoulders you go even deeper. Take another deep breath and as you exhale send a wave of relaxation down your body. I'm going to gently rock your head. (he massages the back of her neck with one hand while holding her forehead and making slight rotations with his other hand) As I do feel a wave of relaxation taking you deeper, deeper, deeper. Way down. That's good. Deeper with every easy breath that you take. Feel your grounding cord going right down to the center of the earth. Feel white light showering down on you. Open up your heart and be aware of what your mother just told you. You were aware of her love but she also really does admire a lot of things about you. She was even wondering whether she could keep up. Take that in.

You're a grown-up now, an adult, mature woman who is a powerful healer. Your mother does respect you and what you have done. Saying good-bye to her has set her free and set you free. When you see your mother you can love her for who she is. You don't need her. You can enjoy being together sometimes. And recognize that whatever way she is being outwardly, deep down she really does admire you. You're a strong, healthy adult. She's not in this world to live up to your expectations and you're not in this world to live up to hers. You're doing your thing and she's doing her thing and that's fine.

You have within you tremendous strength and you have a lot of love and respect for yourself. I'm going to give you a pillow now and what I'd like you to do is hold this girl who needed approval from her parents. Tell her you're her mommy now. Tell that girl that she is great just the way she is.

CYNTHIA: You're wonderful just the way you are.

RANDAL: Now be the girl. You're being held by this beautiful mother who not only loves and appreciates you but wants to tell you, and who is very open. Be that girl and feel the mother within, totally loving you for who you are. Take it in. "As I child I saw through a glass darkly. As an adult I let go of childhood things." You are now an adult but we all carry a child within. You have a beautiful, lovable girl who is exuberant, playful and creative. That is an important part of you. Part of the reason you are such a powerful healer is that she is full of wonder and joy. She has a lot of insight because of her awareness of the world around her. You tap into that little girl within you when you do your healing work with people. You're a powerful woman. You've got the power of the girl within, you've got your higher self, you have tremendous wisdom that you tap into. The more you give, the more you receive. You are very powerful in working with people and you are also very powerful in working with yourself. What you are finding easier and more natural to do now, is to heal yourself. "Healer heal thyself." And give a lot of love and attention and affection to that girl within you. She deserves it. Let her know over and over again that you're proud of her, that she's doing great.

CYNTHIA: She has a name.

RANDAL: What's her name?

CYNTHIA: Cynthia Ann.

RANDAL: Is there anything you'd like to say to Cynthia Ann? You don't have to. (Cynthia shakes her head) That's fine. Now breathe down into your belly. Is there anything further you'd like to say before I bring you out of hypnosis? (Cynthia shakes her head) Okay. See yourself on the top of a mountain and there are people below. They're listening in rapt attention as you speak. You can see yourself walking down to the people and not saying a word. You're just feeling each other's energy. They're taking in your energy and your wisdom and your love and they're gaining so much just by being with you. Nothing even needs to be said. You're a natural leader, a natural inspiration. I'm going to let you count silently to yourself. You can count from one to five to bring yourself up out of hypnosis. (after a pause Cynthia opens her eyes and stretches) Good. (Randal hands Cynthia another tissue)

(to class) We started out with Cynthia's dream and were doing a Gestalt dialogue between herself and one of the characters when Cynthia spontaneously said, "This is about my mother." I asked her to begin to talk to her mother, which was obviously a significant issue, and then we went with what came up. Even though we didn't stay within the direct context of the dream, the core theme of the dream led Cynthia to the issue with her mother.

The darkest hour is so often just before the dawn. Cynthia made the comment, "This is it! This is the stuck place." Then she broke right through it and you saw how quickly she came together. The integration was very interesting. Here was Cindy, who was powerless and afraid and needed the approval of the mother, and here was the mother doing the same thing in her own way. Dealing with issues of power and respect, each side had its own top dog and under dog, but then with the integration came spontaneous acknowledgment and appreciation. That's ultimately where you hope the therapy will lead. I didn't tell her what to say, she came up with it on her own and that's what you want to do in Gestalt work. The two sides went back and forth without much compromise at first, but typically people begin to work through it. Cynthia was in a highly emotional state and very receptive at that point, and also feeling very frustrated. When a person is feeling that frustration, that impasse, if you stay with it the integration often begins.

Q: Cynthia was already in hypnosis before you did the deepening. What was the purpose of the deepening?

RANDAL: Yes, dreamwork and Gestalt dialogue tends to put people in hypnosis. I was deepening the state to further increase her suggestibility and also signaling her that now this was a time to be passive. She had been very active and this was a time to become receptive.

Commentary

In both this session and the previous session with Christine, the dreamer moved out of the immediate dream imagery into a dialogue with her mother. One difference is that Cynthia stayed within that dialogue, whereas Christine's dialogue eventually developed to a specific significant early childhood memory that led into regression.

Chapter 13

Nina's Fairy Tale Dream:
Saving Her Russian Village

RANDAL: We have time now for a brief dream demonstration. Who would like to volunteer?

NINA: My dream isn't very recent.

RANDAL: How long ago was it?

NINA: Two months ago.

RANDAL: That's fine. A dream is often relevant if it was within the last few months, especially if you're still fascinated by it.

NINA: I would like to find out more about it.

RANDAL: Okay, come up here and tell the dream in the present tense as if it's happening now.

NINA: In this dream I am a young man. I'm in a settlement. It's not very real, it's more like a fairy tale. The people living there are terrified that a bunch of buffaloes are going to run through that place. And these buffaloes are eating human beings. They are terrible. They are so huge and hairy and there are so many of them. Everybody is panicked and leaving town. Somebody told us that if you can stand still, absolutely frozen, buffalo will never touch you. But if you move just a little bit, the buffalo will eat you up immediately. Everybody is trying to figure out how they can stand still. It's scary. And nobody is sure if they can stand completely motionless. So it was like a terrible challenge and that was horrifying too.

RANDAL: "I am horrified."

NINA: I am horrified too. I start to think about my relatives and that's going to be the scary part of it. I think, "If the buffalo are going to swallow me, okay, but if they are going to swallow somebody

I know and love in front of me, I won't be able to stand it." All of a sudden I realize that everybody is looking for a solution in their own way and I would like to come up with a more general solution. I'm a hero in this fairy tale so I decide to say to the people that I've got a solution. I tell them, "The buffalo are afraid of fire. Let's create a whole ring of fire to surround the city. The buffalo will never come." The people seem to be agreeable at first but they say, "No, fire is very dangerous for us. It is going to burn the whole city." But though I know the fire won't burn the city, I admit they can be afraid of fire as much as they are afraid of buffalo. So I tell them that we can create a second ring with water, so there will be two rings. Actually that's the end of the dream. It is very unusual for me to have this kind of a dream.

RANDAL: Well, it's a powerful and detailed dream. If this is a wish fulfillment dream, you have a completion. You wake up with a sense of, "Oh, that's the solution," and everybody's happy with it. If it is a frustration dream it is unfinished. There may be some concern about, "Oh, we have to hurry!" or "Will this really work?" Both wish fulfillment and frustration dreams can be healing in their own way. Is it your feeling that you have a sense of completion when you wake up?

NINA: Yes. It was a great feeling when I woke up to know that I can create this kind of solution. Not only for me but for a whole group of people. To know that I have everything necessary to create this kind of change. It was a surprise.

RANDAL: Good. You immigrated here from Russia several years ago. Did this settlement seem to be in a Russian setting?

NINA: It seems like this could have been long ago in Russia. But of course there aren't any buffalo there.

RANDAL: Okay. Be this human-eating buffalo and describe yourself.

NINA: (pause) I feel like I'm an element. I have no conscience and there is no difference for me in what I'm eating or what I'm destroying or creating. I'm just under the law of the universe.

RANDAL: And how does that feel? Do you like it or not?

NINA: I have no feelings.

RANDAL: What is that experience for you of having no feelings? Can you describe it? Can you give it any adjectives?

NINA: Yes. It's interesting. I am like the air. I just am. I exist and nothing has any meaning more than just existence. It is just this way and there cannot be any judgment about it. It is as it is.

RANDAL: (Randal moves in front of Nina and holds the index and middle finger of his right hand out) Now look out here at my two fingers. Watch my two fingertips. Watch them circling around as they move closer and closer toward your face. (Randal is moving his hand in small circles as it approaches Nina's eyes) Feel your eyelids getting heavier and heavier, heavier and heavier. Keep following these circular movements of my fingers as they move down in front of your face until your eyelids close down. Now feel your eyelids relaxing completely. Take a deep breath, fill up your lungs... and exhale, feeling yourself going deeper.

Feel yourself go deeper with every breath. I'm going to be lifting up your hands now and helping you stretch out your arms and hands (Randal guides Nina's hands straight out with the elbows locked) I'm helping you squeeze the palms of your hands together, interlocking your fingers. Squeeze the palms of your hands together. You can hold your arms up now. I'd like you to imagine that your arms are becoming like one solid trunk of a tree, as if they are together onc tree trunk. As I help you squeeze your hands more and more tightly together your hands are becoming stuck together. As I take my hands away your arms stay together, part of the same tree trunk. (Randal presses Nina's interlocked fingers and then lets go) I'm going to count from five down to one. With each number that I count your hands squeeze more and more tightly together. At the count of one try to pull your hands apart. The harder you try the tighter they squeeze together and the deeper into hypnosis you go. Five, stuck together, four, sealing together, three, your hands are stuck tighter and tighter together. Two, on the next number I count the harder you try to pull your hands apart the tighter they squeeze and the deeper into hypnosis you go. Number one, try to pull your hands apart but they're stuck tightly together until I touch your hands, and when I touch your hands you will be able to easily separate your hands and your hands and arms will relax completely. Now I'll touch your hands. (Randal touches Nina's hands and they fall to her lap) As I push down on your shoulders feel the tension leaving your shoulders. As I stroke your arms once, moving down your arms with my hands, feel the tension draining out of your shoulders, arms and hands, and feel yourself go much deeper.

Now go to the feeling just before the end of the dream, when the whole town is terrified and in a panic. Get the feeling of observing that. You are taking charge when nobody else is taking charge. The reality hits you that as hard as it would be for yourself, it would be even worse to see anything happen to your relatives that you love so much. Such special feelings from and for them. And while others are panicking and trying to figure out how to escape you come up with a solution - fire. And you realize that people are just as afraid of fire as they are of the buffalo, so you come up with another creative solution - having a ring of water between the town and the ring of fire.

You have saved the town. You've come up with solutions that work. You are a healer. Feel an expansiveness with each inhale of oxygen. With each exhale just let go of any cares or tensions. With each inhalation you are breathing in a sense of pride, a wonderful sense of accomplishment. People really love and respect you for saving the town. And you can visualize now, that people are going right to work and setting up this ring of fire, and they're setting up a moat. Everybody is working and they're doing it very fast. They found water to circle the town and now they're about to light the fire. Maybe they can see the buffalo way in the distance, maybe not. But they are on time. People are there waiting to light the fire.

It's a good feeling to know that this is inside of you. You've saved the town. You've come up with that solution through your life's experience. "I am a part of all that I have met, yet all experience is an arch where through glows that on traveled world whose margin fades forever as I move." That's from James Joyce. You are taking all of your life experiences and moving forward, finding solutions for yourself and others. The dream of the hero is a dream of a healer. You use your creative instincts for your own benefit and for the benefit of others. When you are working as a therapist you use your own inner resources and you magnify them out.

You will continue to get more and more enjoyment and wisdom and a glowing sense of achievement from this dream. You can radiate feelings of success in so many ways as you continue to gain control in your life. All those exciting shifts that are happening, that you are creating and using to your advantage in your life - that you are healthy, that you are a non–smoker, that you are becoming a hypnotherapist.

I'm going to count from one to five. With each number that I count you become more and more alert, awake and aware. At the count of five you open your eyes. (Randal counts, giving suggestions between numbers. After a pause Nina opens her eyes)

NINA: Thank you, Randal. (Nina and Randal hug) That was great. Especially about bringing the therapist together with that dream.

RANDAL: So it fit for you?

NINA: Yes, very much. Now it's making a lot more sense.

RANDAL: You look great.

NINA: Thank you. You made me bloom.

RANDAL: That's what you did in the dream. You blossomed.

NINA: Somehow I sense that it is a very significant dream for me. It's very validating. And then you emphasized it and helped me to own it.

RANDAL: Yes. And you already began to do that when you did your dream work. In your dream you really were a hero.

NINA: No, no. That was the wrong word.

RANDAL: I want to be very clear that you were a hero in the dream and therefore you are a hero. This is an experience of you finding solutions in your life. You are at a point in which you're taking charge and initiative. You're finding solutions to things and I have a sense that part of it could be that you are moving forward from your other job and getting more into your hypnotherapy.

NINA: Yes, it's all together. It's amazing you still remember about my quitting the job and quitting smoking. Everything fell into place.

RANDAL: I remembered that back when I helped you quit smoking you were going through a lot of changes. You've had more challenges over the past month, such as the experience of someone stealing all of your credit cards and using them. Yet I'm sure as you continue to work with your dream, it will be an example of how you can continue to find a way to make things work out.

NINA: You've helped me to realize something. I'm actually handling this particular situation very differently than I've ever done before.

RANDAL: Yes. You were learning to turn this tragedy into an opportunity for growth and realization, for going on to the next level.

NINA: Like the buffalo. It just is. I have this situation. There is no judgment. There is no fear about it. I'm just having this situation.

RANDAL: Yes. You becoming the buffalo was great. It was a very accepting, "be here now" process. Other persons may have gotten into the drama of it, or developed it as something negative, but you just let it go through you. It was an experience of just being "like an element".

NINA: It was a learning experience for me, too, when I was trying to be a buffalo. I was a buffalo.

RANDAL: I felt that you had gotten a sense of completion and I moved straight from there into post-hypnotic suggestions. Otherwise I might have had you become different characters like the townspeople and yourself, or the fire and the water. With wish fulfillment dreams like this, there doesn't have to necessarily be something to work out, just a chance to much more deeply own feelings such as appreciation, accomplishment and success. Your breathing, voice, face and so forth showed signs of light hypnosis, although you began to move more deeply as you became the buffalo. I sensed that was quite a profound experience for you, so I immediately deepened the state at that point. A lot was gained from doing the hypnosis, which is not something that is done in traditional Gestalt work. Are there any questions for me or for Nina?

Q: (to Nina) It seemed like when you were the buffalo you didn't feel any fear, but from the outside as the ego, it was a terrifying force.

NINA: I was surprised. I expected to find anger or some kind of emotion but I didn't find any. Randal was trying to help me find out if it felt bad or good, but I couldn't judge it. Now I can use it in my life experience, as I'm doing with the credit cards.

RANDAL: You've owned the ability to do that. The buffalo was a good metaphor. It didn't mean to hurt anybody, it was just being itself. That is an example of the integration that takes place in dreamwork. You tapped into a very special ability. I asked and you stated, "I just am." I wanted to see you become the buffalo but I had no idea what the experience would be. It's not about expectancies. "Wait a minute. How can you feel nothing? You're that big buffalo eating people!" That's not a judgment for anyone to make. I want to re-main supportive. That's better than neutral. In Gestalt work I rec-ommend being supportive of each character. Not in the sense of help-ing out or of trying to find the solution, but with detached compas-sion, encouraging each character to express and actualize itself.

Commentary

My announced intention was to demonstrate a brief session. Even so, I spontaneously moved toward hypnotic suggestion especially quickly. One of the reasons was Nina's great sense of satisfaction at the conclusion of this dream. With her ethereal, transcendental ex-perience of being the buffalo, I intuitively felt like evolving her ex-perience immediately into hypnotic suggestion at that time.

Any form of this work can be very effective. In many cases, valu-able progress or results can be accomplished even when there is lim-ited time during a therapy session to work with a dream. The thera-pist may do a little added hypnosis at or near the end of the dream-work, or, as in this case, emphasize suggestion. Trust your intuition.

Chapter 14

Liz's Dream and Regression:

The Assassin and Victim Number Six

LIZ: I had an assassin dream recently. Actually this is my third assassin dream.

RANDAL: This issue is obviously very important to your subconscious.

LIZ: It has several episodes.

RANDAL: Did all of this take place the same night?

LIZ: Yes.

RANDAL: Go ahead and say what you remember in the present tense.

LIZ: All right. In the first stage I suddenly come to consciousness in the dream and I'm driving the car. I feel really shocked because it's night time and I've been driving unconscious. My husband, who usually is the driver at night, is asleep in the back seat. I wake him up and ask him when he turned it over to me. Then we make a rest stop because I don't feel totally safe to drive. We stop for coffee at a kind of old school complex that has a restaurant in it. We're drinking our coffee and the restaurant owner's son is sitting next to me. He talks about a water shortage and says they can't boil hot dogs and make cokes because of that. This doesn't impact me all that much because I know there is generally a water shortage and I don't drink cokes or eat hot dogs very often anyway, but he says it affects the others.

The next scene is in the gymnasium of this same old school. There's a walkway around and I'm on the upper level with a group of people. There is an assassin nearby with a gun and I get the distinct impression that he is just doing random shooting. I don't feel particularly threatened, which is odd, but I sneak out on a cross walk and go down the hall into another room. There are several of us in what looks like a choir room, although there is no indication of music. I'm busy trying to put wooden wedges in the door and one of the wedges is broken when I finally get it in. A woman walks in the other door and says, "You believe in taking chances, don't you?" That scene ends and again there's no panic, but we're just barricading ourselves against possible shooting.

Oh, I skipped one scene. Before we got to the room, when I walked past the cross walk, I looked down in the gym and saw the assassin writing a number on a black board... (pause) It was seven, and the assumption was he was chalking up his seventh victim. So after the room episode I'm with another woman. We're in a bus and she is the driver. We're driving down the road getting away from the school. There are people walking down the road ahead of us, nobody in a panic. Two well-dressed women don't get out of the way of the bus and we have to push them out of the way. Then I find myself outside the bus and I realize that the woman inside is a professional driver and somehow that seems significant.

Then the assassin comes up and he seems to be treating me in a rather friendly fashion, surprisingly normal, and he says, "How did you come to play the piano?" And I do a big double take and go back in my mind and try to answer that question honestly, because I do play the piano. That's a big thing in my life. I describe to him that when I was a little girl I was taken to a neighbor's house to try their piano and when we got one I sat down and picked out "Silent Night" with three fingers.

In the next scene I realize the assassin is in a position he can't get himself out of without going to prison and he doesn't want to go to prison. I become a therapist and I ask him, "How can I make you comfortable?" or "How can we resolve this without further violence?" The interaction is a little vague but there is a lake there and the resolution is that he walks into the lake and doesn't come out again.

RANDAL: Are you with him when he does this?

LIZ: I'm watching from the shore.

RANDAL: Is this something he announces he's going to do or he just does?

LIZ: It's a little fuzzy at that point. (pause) He just does it. Evidently we have gone through some sort of dialogue and that is the resolution he chooses. So that is the end of the assassin. And I wake up naturally.

RANDAL: How do you feel as you wake up?

LIZ: Well, like it was an important thing. Surprised that I was doing therapy, that I was in that particular state of mind. And I would have to say relieved.

RANDAL: Is there a sense of completion?

LIZ: Resolve.

RANDAL: Yes, a major resolution.

LIZ: Resolve without violence.

RANDAL: Uh huh. While there were aspects of frustration, you found a solution. You didn't wake up because you had an impasse, you woke up because the dream had some resolution. That's significant. Start with, "I am an assassin" and describe yourself.

LIZ: I am an assassin. I am a rather small man. Light brown hair, combed in a smooth fashion. I am sniping to make people uncomfortable. I have a weapon that kills them. I don't have a strong emotional sense of violence, more of goading. I'm wearing nondescript, light blue garments. Not threatening, but I have people totally at bay.

RANDAL: In your dream do you actually see any of the victims who have been shot?

LIZ: No.

RANDAL: Even though there's no actual sight of the victims in the dream, I'd like you to switch places and become one of the persons who has gotten shot by the assassin and talk to the assassin.

LIZ: (Liz switches chairs) I guess the one before number seven is the only one I have any link to.

RANDAL: So be victim number six.

LIZ: Number six?

RANDAL: Yes.

LIZ: (pause) I have been blown away in the middle of my life and I resent it.

RANDAL: Say, "I resent you." You're talking to the assassin.

LIZ: I resent you blowing me away. The timing was all wrong.

RANDAL: Okay. Switch and be the assassin.

LIZ: (Liz switches chairs) It was your time. I chose it for my own reasons.

RANDAL: Okay. Switch. (to the class) It's important to be neutral through this.

LIZ: For you or for me?

RANDAL: I'm sorry. For me. I'm telling the group right now that I'm being neutral, encouraging each of you to communicate in the best way you can. Okay? He just said it was your time. He chose your time.

LIZ: But I'm only six. (Liz gasps and starts to cry) I can allow that or I can stop.

RANDAL: Stay with your feelings. Breathe into your stomach. That's good, Liz. (Liz continues crying) But you're only six. (Randal gives a tissue to Liz)

LIZ: Boy, there's a lot of emotion but I don't have any focus.

RANDAL: Do you have any feeling for where that comes from when you say you're only six and you break into tears?

LIZ: Right in here (tapping her chest).

RANDAL: When you say you're only six, are you talking about victim number six, age six, or what?

LIZ: I'm talking about age six and my heart hurts, although it's not on the left side. (Liz motions to the center of her chest)

RANDAL: It's right there in the center. I'd like you to lie on the floor. (Liz lies on the floor and pillows are put under her head and knees) Liz, focus on this area in your chest. Say that again, "I'm only six."

LIZ: I'm only six. (gasps again and cries)

RANDAL: Okay, become six years old. (Liz sobs) You're doing fine, Liz. Stay with the feeling. Something happens when you're six years old. What happens? I'm going to count from five down to one and at the count of one some word that has to do with it will come clear. Five, four, three, two, one. (Randal taps Liz on the forehead and her body spasms) What is it? What happens when you're six years old?

LIZ: It's punishment.

RANDAL: Are you getting punished? (Liz nods and sobs) How are you getting punished?

LIZ: Two times are coming together. The first one was when my mother had a switch and switched me on the legs. It really hurt me. I'm not sure about the age.

RANDAL: So maybe it was six, maybe not.

LIZ: The other one was six, I know.

RANDAL: Okay. What's this other one?

LIZ: It was one of the first days of school.

RANDAL: Present tense. It's one of the first days of school.

LIZ: It's the first day of school and the teacher said not to color any further than the calf and I colored farther because I love to color and she took me up in front of the class and switched me. I was very shy. (cries) She publicly paddled me.

RANDAL: This was the second time you got switched?

LIZ: The first one was when my mother switched me and it really hurt my heart.

RANDAL: Let's go to the first time. Feel that experience and feel that really hurting your heart.

LIZ: And my legs.

RANDAL: Yes, and your legs. Feel that. How old are you, just off the top of your head?

LIZ: Three. (sobs)

RANDAL: Keep breathing. Now stop the feeling. She's stopped switching you. What do you want to say to her?

LIZ: I hate you.

RANDAL: Good. Tell her that again.

LIZ: I hate you. You don't like me.

RANDAL: When I touch your left shoulder I want you to be your mother. What does your mother say in response? (Randal touches Liz's shoulder)

LIZ: But you did what I didn't want you to do. You're not me. I want you to be me.

RANDAL: Now be Liz. What's your name when you're three years old?

LIZ: Elizabeth.

RANDAL: Be Elizabeth. You heard what your mother just said.

LIZ: I'm me. I'm not you. I'm me! I'm me! (sobbing)

RANDAL: Good. Say that again.

LIZ: I'm me!

RANDAL: Tell her what you want from her.

LIZ: I want you to love me. I want you to like me. You don't.

RANDAL: "I want you to accept me as me."

LIZ: I want you to accept me as me.

RANDAL: All right. Now be mother again. What does she say?

LIZ: I can't.

RANDAL: Instead of saying "I can't," say "I won't."

LIZ: I won't.

RANDAL: And elaborate a little.

LIZ: I won't because I need you to be me. I need you to be the little girl that I wasn't allowed to be. I was my father's son.

RANDAL: Uh huh. Switch and be Elizabeth.

LIZ: It's not fair.

RANDAL: Say "You're not fair."

LIZ: You're not fair. You're not the person I thought you were going to be. (sobs) You're not the mother I picked for this life.

RANDAL: Stay with your feelings.

LIZ: How did I get into this? I don't want to be here. I want to go home!

RANDAL: Be your mother. What does she say?

LIZ: I'm here to train you, my dear.

RANDAL: She says you're not the mother she picked. What do you want to say to that?

LIZ: I stepped in. I pushed her back and I took her place.

RANDAL: Now be Elizabeth.

LIZ: How could you do such a thing? What have you got against me?

RANDAL: Be your mother.

LIZ: I hate you.

RANDAL: Are you talking to your mother or is your mother talking to Elizabeth?

LIZ: My mother is talking.

RANDAL: You say, "I hate you." Is there anything else you want to say to Elizabeth?

LIZ: I've hated you for eons. I'm jealous of who you are. (sobs) I'm enraged. Now you're my child and I'm supposed to take care of you.

RANDAL: Now be Elizabeth.

LIZ: I am who I am and you are who you are and we're stuck together. Maybe this time we can work it out. (sobs)

RANDAL: Go into your body. What do you feel in your body?

LIZ: My hands are really feeling odd and tingling. Like they want to move.

RANDAL: Let your hands move any way they want to move. What else do you feel in your body?

LIZ: (Liz is moving her hands all around, making fists then straightening her fingers) I've got a flow of liquid in my throat. (clears her throat) I think maybe I've been drowned sometime. My ankles are odd. They feel like they're tingling.

RANDAL: Stay with your physical feelings. Stay in touch with your body. Your ankles feel odd.

LIZ: Like they had a noose around them. Like I'm hanging upside down in the water. (sobs) I can't identify the emotion. Not rage, not fear. (pause) Longing. It's longing.

RANDAL: Show me your "yes" finger on your left or right hand. (Liz raises her right index finger.) Okay. Show me your "no" finger. (Liz raises her right thumb) Okay. I'm going to do ideomotor responses with you now, Liz. This experience, whether it's exactly this way or something like this, you feel like you're in the water and you have a noose around your ankles...

LIZ: And my neck.

RANDAL: And your neck. The question is, is it safe and appropriate for you to go back to recall this experience now with your conscious mind? (as Liz's right index finger rises her whole body spasms) The answer is yes. The next question, is it safe and appropriate for you to be open to your feelings as you recall this experience with your conscious mind? (Liz's body spasms again as her right index finger rises) Yes. I'm going to count from five down to one. At the count of one you go back to this experience. Experience this now more thoroughly, more vividly. It's coming clearer to you. Five, four, three, two, one. (Randal taps Liz's forehead with his finger) In this experience now. Get a feeling for it. (Liz's hands float up and stay suspended in the air)

LIZ: It's floating. My hands are floating above the water. I'm not sure whether I'm being born or whether I'm in the lake. My hands are funny. (Liz's fingers are contorting and her thumbs are pulled in)

RANDAL: Yes. Just let your hands do what they want to do. This may be a birth experience or it may be another experience. Let's ask your fingers. Your fingers can stay in the position they are. Your subconscious mind knows exactly what's going on. Is this an experience of being born? (Liz's body spasms) I don't know the answer to that, only your subconscious mind knows. (Liz's hands jerk into the air and then down to rest on her stomach) Your "yes" finger was above your other fingers but I am not certain of your answer so I'm going to ask you again. Is this experience that you're having now, at least in part, an experience of being born? (Liz's little finger lifts) I'm getting a little finger response. There may be something more or different or in addition.

LIZ: I'm in a different state now. It's like I'm coming into a body for the first time or into a fetus. I'm floating. (Liz's fingers move and her hands raise up again)

RANDAL: Stay with it. You're doing fine.

LIZ: It feels like space instead of water now. I'm afraid.

RANDAL: I want you to know it's going to be okay this time. You're going to go through it. Of course you're afraid at first. This is something very new and special. Stay with it.

LIZ: My hands are tingling.

RANDAL: Yes. Tingle your hands.

LIZ: I feel my elbows.

RANDAL: Yes.

LIZ: I feel my forearms.

RANDAL: Stay with it. You're learning a great deal right now.

LIZ: I tingle in the throat and in the front of my body and the small of my back.

RANDAL: I'd like you to make it more active. Rather than say "I tingle" say "I'm tingling" those areas. "I'm tingling my throat, I'm tingling my back."

LIZ: I'm energizing.

RANDAL: Yes

LIZ: I'm energizing. (sobbing) Air! I like it. (calms down a little) I feel my leg. It moves.

RANDAL: Good. Stay completely in your body and discover all of this.

LIZ: I've got tears on my face. Eons of tears. (crying)

RANDAL: And those tears can come out. It's okay to cry.

LIZ: My throat has been blocked.

RANDAL: It's okay to release your throat. (Liz clears her throat) Take some deep breaths and as you exhale let out any sounds that want to come out.

LIZ: There was a little voice in my dream this week. Just a little voice and it felt like it was coming from down here (touching her abdomen). It didn't feel like that but it told me later.

RANDAL: It's coming from down there. Let that voice come out. (Liz cries) That's good. It's good to cry. Let those eons of tears out. It's so good to get it all out.

LIZ: (in a big voice) And I always know who I am.

RANDAL: Good. Stay with the feelings. Let that voice from down in your gut come out. All that blocking, all those eons. Let it come out. (Liz starts to make noises) That's good.

LIZ: (loudly) Ahhhhhhh!

RANDAL: Good. Do that again. (in unison with Liz) Ahhhhhhh!

LIZ: (sobs) I have voices all over.

RANDAL: Let all the voices come out, Liz. From your mouth, from your eyes, from your hands, from your whole body. Let your body express itself in whatever way it wants to. Keep breathing down into your gut and feel those feelings. Feel so alive. Feel more alive than you've ever felt. That's good. (Liz puts her hands on her abdomen) Totally feel your body.

LIZ: What is all of this? There's a mass. It doesn't all belong to me.

RANDAL: Describe that mass. What is it's size, it's shape? Is it moving or is it still?

LIZ: It's fibrous. It's dark. It's shapeless. It's like tangled threads of yarn. It's what I used to talk about when I told my mother my tummy hurts. It's a dark mass.

RANDAL: Become that dark mass now. Let it become your whole body.

LIZ: Can you take me deeper?

RANDAL: Take yourself deeper. Right now.

LIZ: (Liz begins to roll around wildly with her hands reaching up in all directions) I want out! I want out! I'm trapped!

RANDAL: That's it. Stay with the feelings. You can get out.

LIZ: (rolls off of the mat and stops face up with arms outstretched) I've forgotten who I am.

RANDAL: Just be yourself. Focus on your breathing. Go into your body now. What do you feel?

LIZ: I'm below the surface of the water. My legs are tingling. My palms are tingling. I feel lighter and I feel supported.

RANDAL: Good. Feel supported.

LIZ: I feel supported by water.

RANDAL: Let the water support you.

LIZ: And underneath by earth. My hands want something.

RANDAL: All right. Let your hands do whatever they want to do, whether they just stay there or move. (Liz's arms reach up and then collapse down as she rolls onto her side, sobbing) Stay with the feeling. What do your hands want?

LIZ: They want to hold onto someone who loves me.

RANDAL: Okay. Let's find your real mother. She's here. (Randal places a large pillow on Liz's stomach and positions her hands on either side) Can you find your real mother here? Do you want to talk to her? Or you can just be here with her.

LIZ: What a relief.

RANDAL: Yes. Be here now. Your real mother is back. Feel that totally loving mother that was pushed away before. She's back for good. Let her in. (Liz lets go of the pillow and places her arms out at her sides) That's right, just receive now. (Liz puts one hand back on the pillow and Randal strokes it) Would you like to say something to your real, loving mother?

LIZ: It's been so lonely.

RANDAL: "I've been so lonely."

LIZ: I've been so lonely. You haven't been in my world. Will you be in my world please?

RANDAL: Now be her. What does she say?

LIZ: She says she's here. Not in body.

RANDAL: Okay, be Liz and tell her if there's something further that you want from her.

LIZ: I would like a sense of your presence with me so I can feel cherished all the time. I would like you to be the comfort in my stomach to replace that ugly mass.

RANDAL: Be her. What does she say?

LIZ: I will be a ball of energy in your stomach that you can access whenever you want.

RANDAL: Okay. (Randal removes the pillow) Now let her come in. (Liz makes movements with her hands above her stomach) Help her to come in. A beautiful, radiant ball of energy replacing that mass. Letting the mass dissolve away so the ball of energy is replacing it. (Liz lets her arms relax down to the floor) Good.

LIZ: My face feels lighter.

RANDAL: Get in touch with your stomach. What does it feel like in your stomach now?

LIZ: Much lighter.

RANDAL: Good. Know that that ball of energy is growing stronger and more loving and radiant and clear. (Liz puts her hand on her chest) What are you feeling in your chest?

LIZ: I still need something. My heart still needs healing.

RANDAL: Go to your heart and describe the feeling in your heart right now.

LIZ: It's changing. I need to learn how to be in a body and separate from everything else and it's hard. (cries) But I'll do it.

RANDAL: How can you make it easy for you to be in your body?

LIZ: I would like a little bit of everything to be with me in my heart.

RANDAL: Would that be good for you, to have a little bit of everything?

LIZ: That would be just right.

RANDAL: How can you get a little bit of everything to be in there with you in your heart?

LIZ: I'll ask for it...and everyone. And maybe open a little tiny channel.

RANDAL: Is that little tiny channel opening now? Does that give you enough of everyone in your heart?

LIZ: I think maybe it's the beginning of the process.

RANDAL: Is that little tiny channel gradually getting bigger?

LIZ: It's calling attention to the tightness between my shoulder blades that I've had with me forever.

RANDAL: Describe that tightness between your shoulder blades.

LIZ: It's like I've been stabbed in the back and betrayed and I can't count on life.

RANDAL: Well, it's time to stab back. (Randal picks up a different pillow) Let's take your hand and put a knife in it. (picks up Liz's right hand) Okay, there's a knife in your hand. This is a different pillow.

LIZ: (laughing) Not mother, please!

RANDAL: No, not her. Okay, stab it. (Liz stabs at the pillow with her right hand) Use the other hand too.

LIZ: (Liz hits with both hands) Oh, that feels so marvelous.

RANDAL: Good. Hit it. Do it. (Liz hits again)

LIZ: Oh yes, yes, yes. Once was enough. That was a good one.

RANDAL: Good. The rest was just to know you can do this with a pillow again if you ever need to get it out of you. Isn't that great? Feel your feelings. Feel your body.

LIZ: Everything is in transit.

RANDAL: You're very alive.

LIZ: Yes! Shooting off energy everywhere.

RANDAL: Good. Let it go. You've got tremendous energy within you. You've got all of your own energy and you've got the energy of your real mother there.

LIZ: I don't know if this is many lives or whether it's a metaphor, but it feels great.

RANDAL: It is at least all the incredible range of aspects of what you've experienced and who you are in this life.

LIZ: Different dimensions.

RANDAL: Different dimensions and all of the above. Spiritually, physically, the whole history of the universe is there with you.

LIZ: It sure is. And I feel like the universe right now.

RANDAL: Good. Be the universe.

LIZ: What I would like most in all the world is a drink of water.

RANDAL: All right. Somebody is getting it for you right now. (Liz sits up)

LIZ: I'm exhausted. Talk about taking care of everything at once. (Liz is given a glass of water) For some reason my hands feel a little bit weak.

RANDAL: Your hands have just gotten rid of a lot of energy.

LIZ: Back on earth.

RANDAL: Stay in your body. You're doing great.

LIZ: That's been a hard one for me. That's one of my life's tasks.

RANDAL: It's been hard and you've just done some miraculous things. You may be amazed at how easy it can become.

LIZ: I like that. Strangely enough, my maiden name, in its original language, meant "taking a body".

RANDAL: I'd like you to lie back down here. Do you want to take another sip of water first?

LIZ: Please. (Liz lies down after a drink)

RANDAL: Take your time now. You've just experienced so much. You have all the time in the world.

LIZ: It's amazing to feel comfortable.

RANDAL: You may be surprised at how easy it can be to feel comfortable. And to know that the goal is not that we will feel comfortable all of the time because we won't, but when you start to feel some discomfort, Liz, you can do something about it. You have so many more resources to use now, so much more power and energy. And you're letting go of old stuff you took on that wasn't yours. You're releasing that negative energy from your stomach and chest and putting good energy into those areas. You had that for eons, all that time, and it took one blow of your hand and it was gone. Do you realize how powerful you are?

LIZ: I look forward to finding out.

RANDAL: You are finding out and you look forward to finding out again and again.

LIZ: In real life.

RANDAL: This is real life. That's all you have to do, Liz. You've just done it and you can do it over and over again, like the snap of my fingers. (snaps fingers) Just like that. You can just banish it. You can have a negative feeling or a frustration or feel stuck and just like that, you get it out of your system. You know deep down inside what to do and you've been doing it all along. Your energy keeps evolving. You become that energy and let it out. There are many ways to do that and you don't have to figure out how. You just do it at the time. You are more powerful than you knew and you are getting more powerful every day. Life is a process and you keep evolving, you keep changing moment by moment. That's all good. When feelings that are uncomfortable come up you become those feelings and let them go, just like that.

LIZ: I've stayed away from negative feelings for so long and that's not the trick.

RANDAL: That's not the trick because you've tried to avoid them, and that hasn't worked. What does work is having the feeling and realizing, "I can do this. It's not going to kill me or hurt me. I can feel this feeling." And as soon as you do that you move on. You may move on by doing something physical or by communicating something to someone. By shifting your body or your mind, you shift your feelings. You go there with the feeling, allow yourself to become it, and it's gone.

LIZ: That's a wonderful tool. I just did that with a little headache. I just went into it and it's gone.

RANDAL: Just now?

LIZ: Yes.

RANDAL: See how powerful you are?

LIZ: I have to practice.

RANDAL: Instead of avoiding it you become it and you can practice this over and over. Practice makes perfect. Each time you do that you get better at it. You find more and more constructive and creative ways to let everything work out.

LIZ: What a tool. Okay.

RANDAL: That's great. Take your time. You don't have to say anything more. I'd like you to relax now, Liz. Let me get you a pillow and you can rest your leg back down. (Liz nods and Randal tucks a pillow under her knees) Let's support you with your mother here.

LIZ: I like that.

RANDAL: (shaking the other pillow off to the side) We'll clear the energy out, just like it went through the pillow. It's down deep into mother earth now. She can help it transform.

LIZ: I'll be a mother lover now.

RANDAL: Good. And you can especially love the mother within you. Both this mother in here (putting his hand over Liz's abdomen) or this mother in here (putting his hand over Liz's heart). The various mothers within you. And Liz, you have been wonderful and you are becoming even more wonderful. You've been going through so much and you don't have to do anything more now. This incredible process just keeps evolving but also part of this process is to just relax and not have to do anything or go anywhere. Little things can happen and shift and move and that's fine, but right now I'd like you to focus on letting your breathing be slow and steady. Feel your center and imagine you've got a grounding cord from the base of your spine right down to the center of the earth. And you can feel that floating feeling, being supported by water at times, and at other times you can be supported by ground.

LIZ: Don't forget air.

RANDAL: Yes, you can breathe in and be supported and floated in air and you can be supported by spiritual energy. You can be supported by love. You can be supported by your friends. I'd like you to notice that connection, that channel to your heart now, and feel that it's getting bigger and more flexible. You're taking in the good, loving energy from everybody in this room.

LIZ: I may cry.

RANDAL: That's fine. Those eons of tears that you had. There will be many times when you feel like crying and many times they will be tears of joy. Any kind of tears is fine. It's good to get them out. If anybody would like to say anything to Liz right now, please go ahead.

MANY CLASS MEMBERS: Welcome back, Liz.

LIZ: Thank you.

CLASS MEMBER: Liz, I felt the spirit of your mother and that she's with you always from now on.

LIZ: Thank you for that. It's hard to trust, you know.

RANDAL: Say "It's becoming easier to trust."

LIZ: It's becoming easier to trust.

CLASS MEMBER: I'll bet when you meditate she'll be there. She'll always be present. She'll probably be your guardian angel.

RANDAL: That's beautiful. Thank you very much.

CLASS MEMBER: In our session this morning, Liz, you talked about a feeling of hunger.

LIZ: That's right. Right here (touching her stomach).

RANDAL: You're not going to have that kind of hunger anymore. From now on if you get hungry it'll be a physical hunger for sustenance rather than hunger for love.

LIZ: How about that. Well, I may call mother first.

RANDAL: Yes. And that may be just what you're looking for at that point. She'll be here whenever you want.

MARLEEN: (kneeling beside Liz to hug her) You know what? The therapist in you did this all. Remember when you started with the dream? The therapist already figured it all out, how it was going to heal. Now you can follow it through.

LIZ: Oh, that's funny. You mean I set this all up?

MARLEEN: Yes, and you can go inside right now and play the piano.

LIZ: Uh oh. (cries)

MARLEEN: Play for little Liz. The most beautiful song you can think of. (Liz becomes calmer)

LIZ: Actually, what I want is an instrument that's not created yet.

RANDAL: Create it and play it.

LIZ: Actually it's me and I am creating it. I just made that link. (Marleen hugs her again and leaves)

CLASS MEMBER: Liz, what you just said is "The instrument is me and I'm playing it." That's so good to hear.

RANDAL: Thank you. (to Liz) How do you feel?

LIZ: I'm convalescing. (laughter)

RANDAL: How does your body feel right now?

LIZ: Really energized. I've got a lot of tingling in it but it feels good. Thank you. It took a lot of trust in everybody here to do something like that.

RANDAL: And thank you. That's an acknowledgment from you for the whole group. I appreciate your willingness to feel the intimacy of the group. You stayed with your feelings and had the courage to move from one strange feeling to the next, dealing with your greatest fears and desires and issues. You will discover that this is affecting you in all aspects of your life. This is just the beginning. (applause)

RANDAL: (after a break) When I do dreamwork it's not unusual for a session to turn into a regression. In a way, as I've said, a dream is a kind of regression. But Liz left the reality of the dream to regress to specific associated experiences from her childhood, and all that that entailed. Do you remember how the dream started? Liz was driving unconsciously. Liz is not driving unconsciously anymore.

One of the interesting things that happened during the regression is that Liz got a sense that her mother wasn't the one she had picked. She felt there was another person that should have been her mother and this one was dumping a lot of herself on Liz. But if we accept that we choose our parents, then we can accept more responsibility to make active change. I feel that there was an inner wisdom, a higher self in Liz, that even then knew, "Hey, I don't deserve this. Why is my mother doing this to me? This is not the mother I deserve." Sometimes I will integrate an ideal or inner mother when I'm doing the dialogue. I didn't do that initially with Liz because I wanted to stay with the Gestalt process, to help her to mobilize her own resources as a child.

I really felt for Liz, the little three year old that had to deal with a very demanding mother. The tendency can be to want to come to the rescue, but it's better to encourage a person to come to his or her own rescue. You'd be surprised how powerful a child can be and when you think about what this three year old was realizing, she was very powerful. Before I brought in this other part of her to support the child, I wanted to give the child a chance to go further to work it out.

During Gestalt regression you can dialogue between persons or parts of yourself. I felt there was so much happening inside of her during the dialogue with her mother that I repeatedly asked Liz to go inside, and tremendous energy came up. Initially I was expecting to use this energy as a way for her to find more resources in her dialogue with her mother. For example, if she was tensing a certain part of her body, she could take the pillow that was her mother and tense the pillow. In therapy you take the energy you've turned in against yourself and get that energy out without hurting anybody. In this case her energy led us away from the dialogue with the biological mother and into various transformative processes, and one of the results was that we eventually brought in an ideal mother.

Liz talked about eons of tears that she'd been holding back. She didn't say lifetimes, but some people might consider this to be a series of lives. First and foremost, it was her experience of this life. We may also consider additional possibilities such as what Jung referred to as the collective unconscious, tapping into the awareness and experience of humanity. Another theoretical possibility could have to do with cellular memory. What matters is that in the here and now she began to release tears that she'd been holding back for a long time.

By going with the flow, the experience evolved beyond the interaction with the mother. I encouraged Liz to keep working with that mass in her stomach rather than trying to avoid it. (to Liz) It was beautiful to see how powerful you were when you became that twisting mass of chords and threads. As soon as you let your body become it, you writhed out of it and dispersed it, just like that. It can be as simple as a few physical movements.

At the end of the session I encouraged Liz to recognize what she is doing and how easy it is to make a shift. She made some miraculous changes and helping her recognize that she was making those changes and encouraging her to keep making them was important reframing.

LIZ: When you had me lie down on the floor, Randal, I felt you grounding yourself. I felt that first deep breath and that was important to me because I knew that you were going to stay separate, so I was able to trust myself.

RANDAL: Thank you. Detached compassion is so important. The best way that I can be supportive of you is to trust you, to know that you have your own resources. At a certain point I did do ideomotor questioning regarding whether it was safe for you to go further into your emotions. If it happens spontaneously I don't always do that, but you were getting into such strong feelings that I wanted to double check.

LIZ: I wasn't sure what those answers were going to be.

RANDAL: They came on their own very quickly. Some of your strong emotions seemed to come out of the blue and this was a safe place for you to be able to work with that. By the way, did you go and look in the mirror like I asked you to at the break? You look beautiful.

LIZ: I did. My eyes were all puffy and I couldn't see myself looking beautiful at all.

RANDAL: How many here can see her looking beautiful? (loud applause)

LIZ: Thank you all.

RANDAL: Thank you. You had the courage to trust the moment, which is exactly what Gestalt is about. Whatever emerges is appropriate. If a person starts to resist and says, "I can't remember what you just said," I can go with the resistance. It's a win win situation. No matter what comes up, we can use it as an opportunity. Whenever someone opens up in class, it tends to bring us closer together and helps to create an energy in which miracles happen.

Chapter 15

Jim's Dream:

The Crashing Waves on the Computer Screen

JIM: I'm sitting on the floor with another person. We're facing a man in a suit who is on a swivel chair. He reminds me of the father of one of my good friends in high school. He's got a wonderful device, something like a laptop computer. We've come to ask him for advice and he's giving us examples of times when you might go to someone for advice. He's smiling just to make us comfortable, and he says, "Say, for instance, you had trouble reading, that you didn't like to read books because to you they were long and detailed and tedious and boring. What you might do is find people who like to read books and talk to them and find out what their experience is and what they get out of it. What they do when they read, why it makes them happy, how they learned it, things like that. Or say you wanted to learn chess, you might go to a chess master. You'd ask him how he learned chess, what he likes about chess, what he's thinking about when he's doing chess, and if he uses a chess computer." Then at that point his little lap top computer started turning into a chess computer. Pieces started moving around on it and he said, "And you might ask if the way they learned to play chess is still relevant today because so much is changing." Then he turned around again and fooled with his...

RANDAL: "He turns around again and is now fooling with his..."

JIM: He's fooling with his laptop computer, so he's not facing us for a second. Then he turns it back around and there's a whole bunch of pictures on it. There are maybe five different pictures about post-age stamp size and they're moving. They were grouped so that they were sort of related...

RANDAL: "They're grouped so they're related..."

JIM: There are four groups of related scenes in the different corners. I think one of them is a city scene and one is some sort of in-door scene. Then there is one that's like a prairie, sort of like around here in the summer, with mostly dry grass and a few trees. Then on the lower right are scenes with the beach and woods with streams. Everything there has a lot of water in it. At this point he's not really saying anything, but I'm feeling very attracted toward the water scenes. He turns again, fiddles with his lap top, and when he turns back it's one of the water scenes blown up big. I feel great about that. I really identify with the water and the power of the waves coming in. Then the man says something like, "There's a lot of creativity needed in corporations." That's all the fragment I remember. My alarm clock rang shortly thereafter. I remember thinking about that and then coming awake.

RANDAL: The point of waking up is very important when it's a last escape during an impasse. Or awakening can occur at the conclusion of a wish fulfillment dream. Of course if the waking up is as a result of something external such as an alarm clock or a loud noise, then it doesn't have the significance of an impasse.

JIM: I'm very curious to continue that dream. It was getting interesting.

RANDAL: All right. I would like you to become this laptop computer. Say "I am a laptop computer" and describe what you look like and feel like.

JIM: I'm feeling that I have access to a bunch of different things - scenes or realities even. And I guess that I can display them to people. I enjoy that.

RANDAL: Good. Are there any other ways you can describe yourself ?

JIM: I'm connected to a lot of different things. I get the sense that I serve a lot of different people that way, too. Anybody can tap into this thing. It's like a network.

RANDAL: You're part of a network, is that what you're saying?

JIM: Yes.

RANDAL: So you are a very powerful computer.

JIM: (laughing) I guess so.

RANDAL: You can have many different scenes coming on at any one time, for example, and you can access various powerful connections. Do you feel you fulfill your function very well?

JIM: Yes, generally.

RANDAL: Good. Now I'd like you to become that scene you were so drawn to. Become that water scene that ends up on the entire screen of the computer. Describe yourself.

JIM: There are waves coming in. It's like I'm by the rocks and there's a lot of motion of water coming against and sometimes over the rocks and then flowing back out. There's a sense of drama and power to it. It's very blue.

RANDAL: Identify with that. Say "I have a sense of drama and power." This is you now. You're not looking at this, you're becoming this.

JIM: I'm internalizing this right now. I'm trying to be the water and see how that is and I don't really know how to describe it yet. It's definitely a nice feeling.

RANDAL: Good. In fact don't say anything yet. Become the water. From the outside you were really identifying with this water. Become the powerful waves, rolling in and out and crashing on the rocks and so forth. (Jim giggles and uses his arms to imitate a wave) Great. My next step was to have you gesture and you're already doing it spontaneously. Gesture some more. (Jim continues to gesture and makes some sounds) Good. Make sounds. Really get into it now. (Jim is giggling and making sounds as he gestures) How does that feel?

JIM: Good.

RANDAL: Describe yourself from the inside. You are this process. You are these waves.

JIM: I move things around, get them wet. I go out and then I come back and swirl around. I generally stir things up - little pebbles on the beach, sand, kind of mix things up. Then I'll sort of spit off bits of myself and the bits will merge back in, little fragments of foam floating off, spraying off, and then coming back in.

RANDAL: So you enjoy doing that? Being that?

JIM: Yes.

Randal: Now I'd like you to be one of those little pebbles that is being strewn around by the waves. (Jim giggles again)

JIM: Going for a ride!

RANDAL: Experience what it feels like to go for that ride as a pebble. A wave is coming in and crashing and what's happening?

JIM: I'm sort of spinning around, getting a little dizzy. I feel okay about it though because I'm a hard little pebble. It's not going to hurt me. I'll come down somewhere else and it'll do it again. (Jim makes a wave sound)

RANDAL: Did you enjoy it?

JIM: Yeah.

RANDAL: Kind of fun?

JIM: Yeah. It feels like a roller coaster.

RANDAL: Now I'd like you to be - what would you call him? The teacher or the expert?

JIM: Let's call him Mr. Asher.

RANDAL: Mr. Asher. Is that your friend's father?

JIM: Yes.

RANDAL: So describe who you are and what you do.

JIM: I'm aware of these two people on the floor and I'm trying to show them something interesting that will guide them where they want to go. Something that will excite them. I'm moving kind of quickly. I'm aware of myself but I'm just focusing on what I'm doing.

RANDAL: Do you feel good about who you are and what you're doing?

JIM: Yes.

RANDAL: All right. How do you feel as Jim in this dream? Are you finding it quite interesting? Are you getting what you came here for?

JIM: It's interesting. I think I was looking mostly for what to do next as a career. So far it seems helpful in the abstract but I don't feel like I've made up my mind or anything. I do feel like it's given me some new angles on myself.

RANDAL: So you feel that there is still a ways to go but in some abstract way it is leading you where you want to go? (Jim nods) Most dreams involve elements of frustration. Here we have a wish fulfillment dream in which things are working pretty much in harmony. I usually develop dialogue during dreamwork but I'd like to do something different here. Jim, look out here at my little finger and follow my finger as I move it toward your face. I'm continuing to move it to where my hand is above your head. I want you to keep looking at my little finger right up here so that you're almost looking straight up. Now I want you to keep your eyeballs rolled up but close your eyelids down so your eyeballs are rolled up behind your closed eyes. Now I want you to try to open your eyes when I snap my fingers at the count of one, but you'll find your eyelids are locked tightly closed. Three, two, one (Randal snaps his fingers), go ahead and try to open them but the harder you try the tighter they lock and seal. When I touch your right shoulder relax your eyeballs behind your closed eyes, keep your eyes closed, and feel yourself going deeper. Take a nice deep breath and as you exhale, send a wave of relaxation down your body.

Now I would like you, in your mind, to go to the beach. You're not just seeing the beach on your computer screen, but actually going to a beautiful beach. Find yourself on a lovely sandy beach with the waves rolling in and rolling back out again. It's a beautiful day. The sun is shining and warming your body. The air is fresh and clean and clear. The air smells so good, such clean fresh air. Sunlight is sparkling on the water. As you continue to watch the waves rolling in and rolling back out, it's taking you deeper. And you continue going deeper with every easy, deep breath that you take.

Jim, I want you to signal with your left hand. Show me your "yes" finger. (Jim's index finger rises) It's your index finger. Now show me your "no" finger. (Jim's middle finger rises) Your middle finger.

Now I'd like you to get back to the feeling of being the powerful waves, moving around and kicking things up. All the different aspects of being very active and moving things around. As soon as you can get that feeling signal with your "yes" finger. (Jim's finger moves) Good. Stay with that feeling. Get into that feeling more as I push down on your shoulders. Become the free, powerful waves. You're moving around and thrashing up these pebbles. People find you fascinating. Jim was watching the image of you on the computer screen and he was so happy when the image got blown up so that he could see you more clearly. You like to be seen and to express yourself with all of that creative force and beauty. You have that constant movement that keeps going around and around, that is a freedom of expression, a joyful feeling, a creativity. It is the essence of you. And parts of you can go off and they come back again. You can strew things around and give them adventures. All you have to do is just be yourself. Feel that your movements are responding to others around you, to the sun and the moon and to gravity. You can even rise up against gravity because you are that powerful. When you come into the shore you lift up and come crashing down and then you lift up again. You are eternal. You are continuous. You are deep.

And Jim, you are taking on these qualities and becoming these qualities in many creative ways in your life. That spontaneity, that movement, that freedom, that flexibility, that energy. There is another word that is a positive word that has to do with being the waves. That word is going to come to your mind when I count from three down to one. A positive word, an energy about those waves. Three, two, on the next number you're going to say a word that has to do with being these waves. One. What word pops up?

JIM: Whoosh.

RANDAL: Whoosh? (Randal gets up and circles around Jim making the sound several times as Jim giggles) Whooooshhhh. Feel that freedom. Whooooshhhh. The freedom of being a wave, of doing what you want to do. Some days you'll get really big and expressive. Other times you might be more calm. And now experience being the computer, being state of the art, powerful, having tremendous sources of information at your disposal. You have tremendous knowledge in your subconscious mind that has access to the collective consciousness. And you use that energy. You use it when you do hypnotherapy, and you use it to help yourself move forward in your life in many creative ways. What a wonderful balance between these two, the crashing waves and the computer. You have the freedom and movement of the waves, and the organization of the computer that has access to many forms of information, and that can turn that information into vivid imagery that can be quite fascinating.

People that come to see you when you are being a therapist may only use one small aspect of you and yet that can be so valuable. You have so much to offer and so much to give. You've got all this software and you're connected to a network of other computers. You can download tremendous sources of information. That is another powerful part of who you are. You've got great graphics and vivid imagery that you can show people, that you can use to communicate with. You're on the cutting edge and you're in excellent working order. Just feel yourself each day, Jim, tapping into the tremendous power of the computer that is a part of you. And also the power of the waves. What a nice complement between those two. You've got the one that is the storehouse of knowledge with tremendous accessibility, and the other that is playful. Each day you are finding different ways to be one or the other, or to integrate the two to develop greater joy and awareness and creativity within yourself; in your personal life, in the work that you do, in class, all of these different ways.

Before I bring you out of the hypnosis, is there anything that you would like to ask or to say at this time? You can signal yes or no with your finger signals. (pause, then Jim signals no) Okay. You're going to continue to get more insight and enjoyment from this process. Some of that will not be discovered intellectually, but rather by certain ways of being. You may also find that if a continuation of this dream is valuable for you at this time, that you will develop that. If there is some particular place your subconscious mind wants to go further with this, your subconscious mind will do that, and will give you a signal to help you remember. And maybe the continuation of this will be very easily and appropriately expressed and experienced in your daily life rather than in your dreams, or in both. In a moment I'm going to count from one to five. At the count of five you are fully alert, awake and aware. (Randal counts, giving suggestions between numbers, and Jim opens his eyes) Welcome back.

JIM: Hello. (Randal and Jim hug)

RANDAL: Is there anything you would like to say about how it felt to be the computer or how it felt to be the waves?

JIM: I really enjoyed being both.

RANDAL: They certainly complemented each other.

JIM: (laughing) I was so glad you asked about the pebbles point of view.

RANDAL: As a pebble, getting tossed around by the waves might be great. "I'd be bored if I was just sitting there all the time. I'm not getting hurt or anything." When I asked you to become the pebble I didn't assume there would be conflict. Your response could have been positive or negative. It's not for me to try to figure out what it's going to be, it's for me to just have you become that and see where it goes. If the pebble's response had been something like "Stop pushing me around!" then we would have developed a dialogue. But we could have done a dialogue even with a positive response such as you had. For example, the rock might have said, "Thanks for the ride. It was really great," and that's useful, too. It just didn't seem necessary. You were doing a good job. Most things were going well, and in some cases especially interesting, such as you saying, "Oh, look at this. Not only can I see that scene but it's blown up and I can see it on the whole screen." Most dreams will be frustrating in some way, but this was something without any real conflict. During therapy with a wish fulfillment dream I tend to focus less on dialogue. If dialogue happens it will emphasize appreciation. There are other things I could have done with this. I could have had you become the swivel chair, some of the other scenes on the computer, or some aspect of the computer such as the screen. And didn't you say you were there with someone?

JIM: The other person was actually kind of shadowy.

RANDAL: So that was kind of vague. I went with what seemed to have more of the juice, such as the picture that eventually got blown up on the screen. I had you become five different characters. I was prepared at any point to turn it into a dialogue but it felt sufficient to have you just be each character. I got a little creative at one point, whooshing around there.

JIM: (laughing) That was really fun!

RANDAL: There are different ways we learn and different ways we experience things and it can be fun to be a wave. When you were describing the incoming and outgoing waves and using your hands it was beautiful. You really became those waves. I loved how you used that "whoosh" sound and all the little things that were going on. I could almost see the frothy motion.

JIM: Yes, it was great.

RANDAL: Any other thoughts you'd like to share?

JIM: It's definitely giving me a lot to think about.

RANDAL: You don't necessarily need to do that much think-ing about it, but rather when you have time today or later tonight, meditate on it and just identify. Become the computer, and another time become the waves and find different ways in which you may be integrating those two experiences.

JIM: Actually, that would be a fascinating dialogue.

RANDAL: And that's an example. You can have a dialogue be-tween those two on your own later. (to the class) I did just a couple of minutes of deepening after Jim had become different parts of the dream because he was already in hypnosis. One sign of hypnosis can be a spontaneous redness occurring in the whites of a person's eyes and I'm noticing that with Jim now. This is not something you would normally expect as a result of such a short process. This is a sign of having gone at least into a medium depth of hypnosis. Let's give a hand to Jim. (applause) Are there any questions?

Q: You gave Jim the instruction to recount the dream as though it was happening. And many people will do what Jim did, which is to speak sometimes in the present and slip back into the past. If you're going to have hypnotic influence, do you have to keep the person in the present?

RANDAL: Yes, to get the greatest likelihood of hypnotic response. But sometimes people can stay with the past tense and still get a strong response. It's generally best to keep bringing your client back to the present.

JIM: You also had to get me to go into becoming the wave, rather than just watching the wave.

RANDAL: Yes, at the time you were rather detached, like some-one looking at the computer rather than becoming the computer. In this case I wanted you to actually become that very scene, not just the picture of it.

Interview One Week Later

RANDAL: Do you have any thoughts or realizations since our session? Any way in which some aspect of your life feels different since that time?

JIM: I feel great. That feeling of being a wave has stuck with me. I've been stirring things up just for the heck of it.

RANDAL: Keep identifying with the waves. What is it to be a wave? Continue being a wave in your life. My sense is that this playful and spontaneous part of you is saying, "Let's stir things up. Let's have some fun!"

Chapter 16

Karen's Dream:
The Golden Child in the Moving Painting

KAREN: I have a dream that is a significant one but there's very little conversation. It looks like a painting and it's my family.

RANDAL: There's hardly any dialogue?

KAREN: Yes. It looked like a classic Italian painting and in view was my family and myself as a very small child. I was this wonderful golden child, like perfection. Then there was myself at an older part of my life.

RANDAL: In the same painting?

KAREN: Yes, and there was some movement in the painting. After I woke up I had some gut level feelings about characters like my mother and my father, but nothing about me.

RANDAL: Did you have this dream in recent months?

KAREN: Yes. I've had about five of this type of dream where I wake up and recall the dream in the middle of the night. Usually I get some kind of information, but I couldn't figure this one out.

RANDAL: This time don't even try. Just become it and you'll get it on a deep level. When you say you've had this type of dream, what do you mean?

KAREN: What's similar is that it's in the middle of the night and I wake up and sit straight up in bed. Then I remember the dream and I solve a problem or get some understanding from a gut level.

RANDAL: So what's recurring is not a particular dream that's similar to other dreams, but that several times you've had a powerful dream in the middle of the night and your intuition or gut feeling is that it has some important information to it. Other times you've gotten at least a major part of that information easily and quickly and this time you did not get that.

KAREN: Exactly.

RANDAL: I'd like you to describe this dream from beginning to end. I realize there may be little motion but if there is some, describe it as you are going along. Describe the painting and the different parts of it. I'd like you to vividly picture it as you do it.

KAREN: All right. I see a painting of classical Italian style. I can tell because there's a building to the left of the painting with columns that are that style. It's set in a garden and my father is standing there, but he doesn't look like my real dad.

RANDAL: The father is standing there in the painting?

KAREN: The whole family is in the painting. I'm beginning to describe from the right hand side now. He is standing there and my mother is standing next to him. In the center of the scene is a wonderful golden child. She's probably about three or four. She has curly hair and she almost seems to glow. She's like total perfection. Golden curls and happy. Behind her is me and... I get that that's me, that I'm also there as a nurse or maid in the painting. My mother leaves to go shopping, then my father walks past me as the nurse. I get the feeling as he's walking past that there's some kind of attraction between us. Maybe not attraction, but a power struggle. I'm not sure what it is. That's all the movement that I see.

RANDAL: Does this movement take place all within the painting?

KAREN: That's confusing because I see the painting and I have a feeling of the movement.

RANDAL: Is there something in this dream besides the painting?

KAREN: In the beginning I was looking at the painting and then I'm inside the painting. It's like I've walked inside this perfect picture.

RANDAL: So the rest of it is within this painting and even though it's a painting, there is some movement. What's the last thing you remember? Is it the feeling of attraction or some power struggle between yourself as the nurse and the person who is your father as he is walking by you? Or do you remember some other aspect of the painting after that?

KAREN: No, that's the last thing.

RANDAL: Okay. Go into the painting in a different way now in which the whole thing is you. Say, "I am a painting" and then describe the special qualities about yourself.

KAREN: Okay. I am a classic Italian painting, probably from the eighteenth century. I have a very ornate frame. I'm a good piece of art and I'm a perfect picture of a family. But underneath it's not the perfect picture. It appears to be...

RANDAL: "I appear to be..."

KAREN: ...a painting of an Italian family standing in the garden. But actually there are other things going on in this painting.

RANDAL: "Other things going on within me."

KAREN: There are other things going on beneath the surface or inside me.

RANDAL: All right. Now I'd like you to be the golden child and describe yourself.

KAREN: I'm like pure white. I'm perfect. I'm loved and I'm loving. I don't seem to have any flaws. I love life. I'm totally in awe of everything around me. Perfection.

RANDAL: Good. How does that feel?

KAREN: It feels wonderful.

RANDAL: Say "I feel wonderful."

KAREN: I feel wonderful.

RANDAL: Now describe yourself, Karen, as the caretaker.

KAREN: I'm sad. I'm a servant. I'm not loved. I'm barely appreciated. I don't feel very much in my body. I don't feel I belong anywhere. I don't belong in this family and I don't seem to have one of my own.

RANDAL: And how does that feel?

KAREN: Sad.

RANDAL: Yes. Now be the father and describe yourself.

KAREN: I'm stern. I'm powerful but not in a good way. I like to control people. I do that by playing people off each other. I'm very strong. I'm pretty much completely self–contained. I don't really care that much about other people, except how they assist me.

RANDAL: You're the caretaker now. (Randal places a chair in front of Karen) I'd like you to picture the father in this other chair and say whatever you would like to say to him.

KAREN: You don't care about me. (Karen's eyes begin to water) You barely tolerate me. You make me very sad.

RANDAL: Switch and become him. Say whatever you would like to say to her.

KAREN: You're pathetic. You should get control of your emotions. What am I to do with you? I can't control you when you're like this.

RANDAL: Okay, switch and respond to what he just said.

KAREN: I think you're pathetic. (Karen's voice becomes emotional) You're cold, you're calculating. You don't care about people. You don't love anybody. I hate you.

RANDAL: Now switch and become him. You're doing very well.

KAREN: Well, I still think you're pathetic but I am listening to you a little bit. I don't think I'm cold but yes, I am calculating. I need to be. I need to control this family. This is my job. You better get it straight and get in line or get out.

RANDAL: Okay, switch.

KAREN: I don't want to leave. (more emphatically) I don't want to leave. Okay, I'll do what you say.

RANDAL: Tell him something you want from him.

KAREN: I want you to accept me for me. I don't want to be directed all the time.

RANDAL: Good. Switch.

KAREN: Okay, so what do you want to do? You can do anything you want as long as you take care of the baby and my wife and myself. You have to take care of us. You have to keep things running in the family. You have to keep everything organized. As long as you do that, I don't care what else you do. I don't have any emotion about it. But I don't like you sniveling and crying.

RANDAL: Switch.

KAREN: I have nothing to say to that. (Karen cries) I feel like your servant.

RANDAL: Go inside yourself and feel what you feel like inside.

KAREN: What I didn't say is I feel like your servant and I'm supposed to be your daughter.

RANDAL: And tell him how that feels.

KAREN: It feels awful. It feels sad and it makes me feel very unimportant.

RANDAL: Then say that again. "I feel like I'm your servant and I'm supposed to be your daughter."

KAREN: I feel like your servant and I'm supposed to be your daughter. I'm supposed to be your family.

RANDAL: Switch.

KAREN: Well, you're not my family. You're the help. You're like the family, we include you in everything, but you're not really in the family. What am I supposed to say to you? I don't want emotion. I just want you to do what you're supposed to. Take care of your job. I don't want personal feelings involved here.

RANDAL: All right, switch. There is some disagreement here. He's saying, "You're not the family. You're the hired help here. You're the person who's here to help us." So what do you want to say to that?

KAREN: I am your family! I'm your daughter. I'm your servant, but I'm part of the family. I'm confused about that.

RANDAL: That's okay. Stay with the confusion. Confusion will eventually sort itself out.

KAREN: I feel like you include me in everything, you treat me like I'm part of the family, and then there's no discerning point but I'm excluded because I'm not your family. I'm just someone out here. I don't know how you feel about me.

RANDAL: Stay with this feeling now. There's an impasse here. "You're not my family. You're not my daughter," and "I am your daughter." Go inside. Close your eyes. You feel that you're his daughter and that you're part of the family but you're not accepted that way. How does that feel?

KAREN: Crushing.

RANDAL: And how do you feel when you say crushing? What part of your body feels what? (Karen's head leans forward and she slumps down in her chair) That's good, the way you're slumping now. Feel that crushing feeling. Get into it even more and feel the feeling of being crushed. Where in your body do you feel it?

KAREN: I feel it in my stomach and it feels like fear and maybe anger.

RANDAL: Describe the size, the shape, the movement if there's movement.

KAREN: It's round and I feel as if I want to scream.

RANDAL: You're welcome to scream if that's what you feel like. You say it's round. Is it moving or is it just staying there? (Karen begins to curl up) Become the ball. Your whole body is now this ball. (Karen moves around, drawing her hands into her chest) That's good. (Her arms and legs start making circular movements) Okay, there's a revolving, circular energy. Now can you put the energy into this pillow? (Randal holds out a pillow and Karen grabs it) That's good. (She starts to hit it on her lap and Randal puts it on the chair in front of her) Let's start hitting it on here. Start pounding down on it and say "I hate you."

KAREN: (Karen pounds very hard with both fists and shouts) I hate you! I hate you! I hate you!

RANDAL: Good.

KAREN: (Karen pounds it once more) I hate you!

RANDAL: Good. Now go inside your body. What do you feel? Do you feel the same energy or is it different?

KAREN: It's different.

RANDAL: You've gotten a lot out of your system. What do you feel now?

KAREN: I still feel a round shape but it's not seething and writhing and doing what it was and it's not black. It was black.

RANDAL: Is there a color to it now?

KAREN: Yes, it's a light blue.

RANDAL: Good. You're releasing that energy out of your system instead of internalizing it. Does anybody come to your mind when you're saying "I hate you" and you're getting that energy out?

KAREN: Obviously my father.

RANDAL: When you say your father, are you talking about your father in the painting?

KAREN: In the painting only because in real life I love my father.

RANDAL: So there's no other direct connection that you're experiencing. That's fine.

KAREN: I don't like my mother very much.

RANDAL: This might or might not have something to do with your mother. The father in this painting, in this dream, is the manifestation of that energy that sometimes comes up in your life. Switch and become the father and see what he has to say.

KAREN: Well, how was that for you? I think that people who are emotional are weak. They make themselves open for people to take advantage of.

RANDAL: Personalize that. Say "I think you're weak and you make yourself open."

KAREN: I think you're weak when you're emotional. You make it even easier for me to control you. It's pathetic.

RANDAL: "You're pathetic."

KAREN: You're pathetic. You don't even see how it works. When you're like that, you're like a bowl of jello. Anyone can mold you. You're very easily manipulated and I think that's weak.

RANDAL: Good. Now switch. (Randal addresses the class) It's very important to give each side total space to say whatever it wants to say. These are all important parts that need to be honored within Karen. And they're finding ways of expressing and evolving as we go along here.

KAREN: You make me feel so unimportant. You make me feel so small and so insignificant.

RANDAL: When you say, "You make me feel.." you are being a victim of what he makes you do. I'd like you to take responsibility and say, "When you say this to me I feel..." That way you are creating this feeling as a response.

KAREN: When you say that, I feel small and insignificant and weak and unable to take care of myself. I feel totally incapable of achieving any kind of success in life, any kind of self–satisfaction.

RANDAL: What I'd like you to do now is take further responsibility and say, "When I feel this way I won't take responsibility..." Say something in that way and notice how it feels.

KAREN: When I feel weak and insignificant and small, I don't want to take care of myself, I don't want to achieve anything, I don't want to be a success. I don't want to do anything.

RANDAL: Good. Tell him what you want from him.

KAREN: I want your respect. I want your love if you can give me any but I don't think you can. But I want your respect so that I can go on with my life. I want to be able to feel good about myself and I need to know that you respect me to be able to do that.

RANDAL: Okay, switch.

KAREN: So I respect you. Actually I guess I'm not being very loving. I do love you, I just find it very difficult.

RANDAL: Reverse that last sentence. Say, "I find it difficult to love you but I do love you."

KAREN: I find it difficult to love you but I do love you. I think I'm pretty hard on you. I don't give you much of a chance or even a break now and then. And I don't understand why I feel that way about you. I just seem to reject you, to put you outside of the family. And I guess I'm sorry for that.

RANDAL: Make that statement a little bit stronger. "I am sorry for that."

KAREN: I am sorry for that. I am. And I do love you.

RANDAL: Great. Now switch.

KAREN: I needed to hear that. I still don't know if you respect me, but to know that you love me makes me feel better. (to Randal) I seem to be jumping out of it right now.

RANDAL: I noticed a shift take place just then. You've really come a long way. I think we're moving toward a completion now. You said, "I still don't know if you respect me but I appreciate the fact that you love me." Okay, let's see what he says to that.

KAREN: I actually do respect you. I think it's more like I don't respect myself for the way I've treated you. Yes, that's it. It's almost like I'm afraid of you. I'm afraid that you're actually stronger than I am and if I give you any kind of encouragement you might take over. I mean be more powerful than I am.

RANDAL: Good. Let's switch.

KAREN: I have no need to be more powerful than you are. I have my own inner strength. I don't need to control other people. It's not something I want to do ever. I appreciate that you do love me. I don't have any sense that I could ever overpower you or want to control you.

RANDAL: Good, switch.

KAREN: I know you'd want to control me if you got a chance to. (shaking her head) Where did that come from?

RANDAL: It's interesting how this is developing. What was the last thing you said?

KAREN: I don't remember.

RANDAL: You feel that she really would try to control you.

KAREN: You would try to control me if you got a chance to. That's my fear.

RANDAL: Let's see what she says to that. There could be something there or he could be projecting, so look inside yourself and find the truth about that.

KAREN: I would try to control you if it came up.

RANDAL: Tell him how you would like to control him.

KAREN: I'd like to control you so that I could get some feeling of love when I needed it and respect and support.

RANDAL: Okay. (Randal points to the opposite chair and Karen switches)

KAREN: He's saying "Well, I support you." I'm jumping out from it.

RANDAL: But stay with it a moment longer. You're doing fine.

KAREN: I love you, I respect you, and I support you. I don't know about the issue of control. I feel that if I love people they can control me.

RANDAL: Okay, let's switch one more time.

KAREN: I guess that's true. If you love people they can control you.

RANDAL: Let's wrap this up now. How do you feel about what he said, "I love you, I do respect you." We're getting into more subtle things about control, but do you get that?

KAREN: Actually I felt a softening of that character. An opening of the heart.

RANDAL: Yes. Do you realize how powerful you are? How dramatically this character changed? I think some of your jumping out is that there is so much integration that you're becoming almost the same character now.

KAREN: Yes, I started to get confused about which one I am.

RANDAL: That's great. What do you want to thank him for? Give him some appreciation.

KAREN: Thank you for being so powerful and strong and protective. I never looked at it that way.

RANDAL: "I never looked at you that way."

KAREN: I never looked at you that way.

RANDAL: Excellent. Now switch and take that in. And give some appreciation of her.

KAREN: Thank you for that. Sometimes I feel like I'm just a controlling asshole. Thank you for giving me love and gentleness and kindness and appreciating me.

RANDAL: Good. (Randal motions to the other chair and Karen switches) Close your eyes and focus on your breathing. Let your breathing be slow and steady and deep and continuous. I'm going to push down on your shoulders. Take a nice deep breath and fill up your lungs and on the exhale send a wave of relaxation down your body. (Randal pushes down on the exhale)

Now I'm going to place your thumb and index finger of your right hand together. I'd like you to imagine I've placed some powerful epoxy glue on your thumb and your forefinger that is hardening until your finger and your thumb are now stuck together. I'm going to count from three down to one. At the count of one you'll try to pull your finger and your thumb apart but the harder you try the tighter they squeeze together and the deeper into hypnosis you go. (Randal's hands are holding Karen's thumb and finger together) As I take my fingers away now your fingers are becoming tighter and tighter together. Three, tighter and tighter together. Two, stuck together. One, go ahead and try but the harder you try, the tighter your finger and thumb squeeze together and the further into hypnosis you go. Now when I snap my fingers you'll find it's as if the epoxy glue is instantly dissolved. You'll be able to separate your finger and thumb and go much deeper. Three, two, one (Randal snaps his fingers), feel yourself going deeper. That's good. Way down, and the deeper you go the more easily you can hear and act on my suggestions.

Karen, you just did a wonderful job of integrating different parts of yourself. Those parts came together from two extremes within you, so that you can appreciate both your inner strength and your emotions. On one side is the authority and on the other side is that part that wants love and affection and approval. These parts of you are now becoming more integrated in your life. So become a painting that has more and more movement and aliveness. You are a beautiful painting, with powerful, creative strokes. And yet you are much more than that because the painting is only the beginning. There are many beautiful aspects of you and these aspects are moving with greater fluidity and greater creativity.

Deep within you there is Karen, the golden child, who is feeling wonderful and happy and joyous. People really appreciate you and respect you and love you. You are the apple of their eyes. And you can appreciate the love and affection and approval that is around you in your life – in your classes, in your work, and in your friendships. In your life in general you are opening up more of this love, affection, approval, respect, and honor. Your joyous presence radiates this golden light and people feel drawn to you and your loving energy. You are delighted in being who you are. And this golden child is only one aspect of the beautiful person that you are. There is so much more to you.

What you are doing automatically, just in the process of life itself, is becoming more accepting and loving toward yourself. You are creating more balance between the part of you that needs to discipline yourself and develop structure, and other parts of you that want to play and be creative and feel your emotions. You're finding that life is a joyous dance that is becoming more fascinating and satisfying as your life develops.

Now at the count of five you are fully alert, awake and aware. (Randal counts, giving suggestions for becoming fully aware between numbers, and Karen opens her eyes)

KAREN: Thank you.

RANDAL: Good job. (Karen and Randal hug) Karen did a fine job of staying with her feelings. Something was going on between the caretaker and the father and the first thing Karen said as the caretaker was "I'm so unhappy." It seemed logical to go to where these two figures were having difficulties and have them dialogue with each other. Some of you may have identified more with the emotional maid than the strict father, but each character had a story and each one had extremes that needed the power and energy of the other one to be able to manifest itself more completely. She eventually became so connected with those two parts coming together that she jumped out of it a few times. When two parts begin to fully integrate it may become difficult to have a dialogue because the same person is talking, or even the same aspect of the person.

If the relationship between the caretaker and the father had been quickly resolved, I could have checked the relationship between the caretaker and the golden child to see if it was positive and nurturing. Perhaps the golden child could have helped the caretaker to feel more appreciated and loved if that was still necessary.

Sometimes people get a dramatic insight beyond getting in touch with different aspects of themselves and the way they respond inwardly and in the world. After she hit the pillow I asked her who she was talking to. There had been some very strong emotion coming up and sometimes the object becomes another person who is a current relationship or an unfinished relationship from the past. If that happens then there is the potential at that point to move into a regression. Is there anything you'd like to add, Karen?

KAREN: I feel very peaceful. I really tried to stay away from analyzing any of it. I was aware of that state of total perfection and balance. That's how I feel.

RANDAL: Great. It looks like the golden child in you is beginning to enjoy herself more.

Postscript: Karen Writes Four Years Later

My dreamwork experience was very helpful in integrating and giving recognition to a judgemental, cold and calculating part (the father figure) of myself. It gave me a lot of inner peace to recognize that as just another "part" of my personality, and to love and accept it. I am very happy to have experienced that session with you. I have done more work integrating the two figures of myself in the dream.

Chapter 17

Hypnodreams

Eliciting a Hypnodream

If a person recalls a fairly recent dream, I will work with that. But a hypnodream can also effectively take us to direct subconscious connections to issues.

An elicited hypnodream is a "dream" that takes place as a result of a suggestion during hypnosis. The entire dream is started and developed by the dreamer with no suggestion of any specific imagery from the therapist. The deeper a person is in hypnosis, the more similar a hypnodream will be to a normal dream. If this is done during an individual session, the hypnotist may request the subject to speak aloud to describe the dream as it is occurring. In lighter states this may be somewhat distracting to some, but it works fine for most people. If necessary, the hypnodream can be done silently, and then the hypnotherapist can receive an account at the conclusion and commence dreamwork.

After the dreamer has described or recounted the hypnodream, the same rules for hypnotic Gestalt dreamwork apply, with one exception. Instead of doing the dreamwork in the traditional Gestalt position of sitting and switching chairs I will have the person stay in the same position, usually reclining or resting back in a comfortable chair and switch characters by means of a signal, such as a touch on the shoulder. Physically switching is generally not significantly disruptive during traditional Gestalt dreamwork, but with the relaxation and passivity resulting from a hypnotic induction in effect, it would be an unnecessary distraction. Also, some persons find that after a formal induction they can more easily accept the instant switch to become a different character without the simultaneous physical switch.

The hypnodream is experienced silently by participants if done in a group setting. After the hypnodream during group hypnosis is complete, participants can be encouraged to go through their dreams again, only making it more positive this time. Obviously, there are fewer kinds of possibilities for therapy while a group hypnosis is in progress than there are during an individual session. After bringing the group out of hypnosis, the hypnotherapist may work with a volunteer who would like some follow-up dreamwork, as was done with Tom in Chapter 19.

Hypnodreams are more likely than regular dreams to be wish fulfillment dreams, especially for persons in lighter states of hypnosis. For many people, the hypnodream will go smoothly or will have a few temporary annoyances that the dreamer quickly and easily overcomes. However, many persons will encounter the frustration levels typical of most dreams. The hypnodream of Delores in the next chapter includes some challenges for which she fairly rapidly found creative solutions. The hypnodream that led to Tom's therapy had become a major frustration dream. As with regular dreams, any kind of hypnodream gives an opportunity for valuable dreamwork, including one with no frustration elements at all.

In addition, as the client develops the various characters and interactions during dreamwork this can in some cases lead to a continuation of the dream itself, thus becoming a hypnodream. This occurs with Patrick in Chapter 7 and Jan in Chapter 20. Patrick's dreamwork spontaneously evolves into a continuation of his original dream, whereas the evolution of Jan's dream is initiated from suggestion by the therapist. As with the elicited hypnodream which is formed prior to dreamwork, the imagery of a hypnodream that occurs during dreamwork is entirely created by the dreamer.

Guided Hypnodreams

Another form of hypnodream involves the guidance of a group or individual with the imagery of a suggested dream. This can lend itself particularly well to group participation. The hypnotist is essentially encouraging the group or individual toward wish fulfillment dreams, and it is important that any of the guided suggestions be focused on positive visualizations. If someone spontaneously develops a negative association, that can be worked with during dreamwork if necessary. However, I believe it is not appropriate for the therapist to attempt to initiate frustration elements. The subconscious mind can learn, reframe, and gain much from being encouraged to focus on a series of positive images. The value can be in the process itself, in creating and experiencing good feelings, confidence, discovery and positive mental expectancy.

Hypnodream metaphors can be beneficial in many ways, such as giving the dreamer symbolic growth experiences. Remember that our dreams are metaphors for our experience of ourselves and the world. The subconscious mind often thinks in metaphors. The following imagery is an example of a guided individual or group hypnodream which can be suggested after a hypnotic induction.

Imagine a meadow covered with flowers and thick with blades of wild green grass. Young seedlings line the edges and lead into a grove of stately, older trees. Now imagine that you're a caterpillar and for some time you've been in this field, facing the elements, eating and growing, and now some part of your being senses that something wonderful is about to happen. You've been preparing for a kind of transformation, an expansion, and you're looking for a special place, a home, to withdraw and prepare. You're ready to shed your outer skeleton, something you've done several times before as a caterpillar, but this time you will grow beyond your present form in a way you've never done before.

Finding a safe resting place, a sturdy branch in a nearby tree, you attach yourself securely with silk threads, hanging upside down. As your transformation begins you tap into a source of tremendous wisdom and power within you, and find, incredibly, that you are able to form a chrysalis around you, a shiny green protection. Beneath the chrysalis, the circular ridges that were once the skeleton of the caterpillar are becoming smooth and soft, and you are turning into a jelly that contains all the cells needed to build a butterfly.

You can completely let go now, trusting the process, trusting your own life force. You rest comfortably, even as you gradually transform with each passing minute. There is no name at this time for the evolving gelatinous form which is you. The protective chrysalis around you has become very smooth, grayish in color. As the process continues, the outer color changes to a shiny, translucent blue. The pattern of your newly forming wings is just becoming visible from the outside. Your chrysalis continues to change, becoming even more transparent and clear.

It's almost time to emerge. You can feel the energy flowing into your mid section and head, getting ready to burst forth from the chrysalis. Taking a deep breath, feeling the expansion, you begin to break free. Once out of the chrysalis you pause for several minutes as your wings gradually dry. As blood pumps into your wings, they begin to unfold. You are a brilliantly colored monarch butterfly, and you adjust your position to stand upright on the remains of the chrysalis as you spread your beautiful orange wings.

You are ready now to fly for the first time. You pause for a moment with wings uplifted, bathed in glittering light as the sun filters through the tops of surrounding trees, scattering a kaleidoscope of patterns onto surrounding leaves. You have emerged from the chrysalis and you see the world with new eyes. You can see ranges of colors beyond the spectrum of ordinary vision. As you look out at the colorful meadow it gives you a sense of pleasure you haven't experienced before. You breathe in and the aromatic blend of wild flowers gives you new strength and vitality. When you are ready you lift off, feeling the exhilarating sensation of freedom and expansion.

Feel the joy of your first flight. Discover your new found lightness. You now fly to a beautiful yellow flower and land with surprising ease. You enjoy the pungent aroma. Now you lift off again, soaring to new heights, your wings instinctively fluttering, carrying you higher.

The difference between guided imagery (or fantasy or visualization) and a guided hypnodream is in the suggestion of a dream. The subconscious mind will often conjure up more dreamlike images, identifications and experiences when a dream is suggested than when it is not.

Dream researchers Cavallero and Natale have documented that people who were asked to make up a "dream" while awake produced accounts that could not be differentiated by experts from accounts of actual nighttime dreams, although the subjective experience of such a made-up dream would not compare to the real thing. Through an elicited or guided hypnodream, however, many dreamers can create experiences and associations within their subconscious minds that feel very similar to sleeping dreams.

CHAPTER 18

Delores' Hypnodream:

The Soaring Bicycle Ride to the Golden Planet

The following hypnodream is developed in session with much of the therapy taking place as it unfolds. Over the course of her verbalization during the hypnodream, the various steps of hypnotic dreamwork are periodically interwoven, with the exception that there is no Gestalt dialogue in the traditional sense.

RANDAL: (after a hypnotic induction) In a moment, I'll count from five down to one. At the count of one you begin to have a dream, easily noticing whatever images come up, and this further deepens your hypnotic state. Your dream is about anything your subconscious wants to dream about. You can easily verbalize as you enter this dream. In fact, describing your dream aloud and giving an ongoing account makes the experience that much more vivid for you and takes you even deeper. Here we go now. Five, four, three, you are beginning to experience a dream. Two, on the next number I'll tap you lightly on your forehead, and you can easily describe your dream as it develops. One. (Randal taps her on her forehead)

DELORES: I'm on a bicycle.

RANDAL: Are you riding this bicycle or are you just sitting on it?

DELORES: I'm just sitting.

RANDAL: Okay, look around you. What do you see?

DELORES: Lots of trees.

RANDAL: Anything else?

DELORES: Houses.

RANDAL: Anything else?

DELORES: It's a red bicycle.

RANDAL: How does it feel to be sitting on this bicycle?

DELORES: I'm still looking.

RANDAL: You're looking at the bicycle right now?

DELORES: Uh huh. I'm afraid to get on it but I want to.

RANDAL: Okay. You can do one of three things. You can get on it, you could not get on it, or you can stand there and think about it. Whatever you want to do. (pause)

DELORES: I'm still deciding.

RANDAL: That's okay.

DELORES: Now I'll get on it.

RANDAL: Now that you're on it are you sitting on it or are you going somewhere?

DELORES: Not yet.

RANDAL: Fine. Just be there sitting on the bike. How does it feel?

DELORES: It feels high off the ground.

RANDAL: Does it feel too high or just high?

DELORES: It's too high but that's the way it's supposed to be, so I have my foot on the curb. I'm pushing off and I don't know which direction to go. I think I'll go straight ahead.

RANDAL: Okay.

DELORES: I like the feeling of the wind. (pause) I'm coming to an intersection. Now I have to decide which way to go again. I've got to go left.

RANDAL: All right.

DELORES: (pause) I come to another intersection but this time I know which way I want to go. I'm going to go around the corner and down the street that has cobblestones along the side and the center is paved. And I watch the trees. It's a sunny day.

RANDAL: Uh huh.

DELORES: I'm looking at it and it feels like unchartered territory. I'm afraid to go ahead but I want to. It looks black and dark. (Delores' voice quivers and she starts to cry) I'm looking for sunshine and I see a glimmer. But the dark is still there down on the ground. The dark is getting smaller. It's beginning to shrink. It hurts in here (tapping her chest).

RANDAL: Yes.

DELORES: And I see blue sky but the dark is really dark. The dark is coming down and getting small and there is more blue sky and sunshine and a rainbow. As soon as the dark gets a little lower I can continue on. I have to wait for it.

RANDAL: Uh huh.

DELORES: It's about two feet high. (pause) It's about one foot high. (pause) It's about six inches. (pause) And now it's flattened out and it's even with the pavement so I can ride over it.

RANDAL: Good.

DELORES: It feels really funny. (crying and smiling) The front of my bicycle is leaving the ground.

RANDAL: Beautiful. Feel your excitement. (Randal gently touches a tissue to the sides of her eyes to keep the water from running down her cheeks. This process of tearing and using tissues continues through the entire hypnodream)

DELORES: Light, blue puffy clouds. Now it's really smooth and nice. I don't have to worry about falling off or falling down.

RANDAL: Great.

DELORES: I'm really soaring.

RANDAL: Feel yourself soaring. Feel the freedom of that exhilaration.

DELORES: It does feel so free.

RANDAL: Take your time and savor it. You don't have to talk, just feel the wind blowing against you and know that you don't have to worry about anything. You're just soaring along. How wonderful it feels.

DELORES: There is something round out there.

RANDAL: Something round?

DELORES: Something like a planet.

RANDAL: How do you feel when you look at it?

DELORES: Like it's inviting. It has an aura around it – a nice golden-colored aura.

RANDAL: Beautiful. Are you getting closer to it now?

DELORES: No, it seems to be the same size. I want to go to it but it seems far away.

RANDAL: How does it feel to be looking at it from this distance? Do you feel that inviting feeling or is it different?

DELORES: There is some resistance but it's pulling me.

RANDAL: Feel that pull. The planet is a long ways away so it may take a little while to get there. I'm going to tap you on the forehead and when I do, time speeds up hundreds of times faster so you can go there very quickly. Five, four, three, two, one. (Randal taps Delores on the forehead) Feel time speeding up now. You can signal with a finger on your right hand when you're just about to get there. (after a pause Delores signals with a finger) Good. Now time is slowing back down to normal and you're almost to the planet. Are you about to land or are you still flying toward it?

DELORES: Still going toward it.

RANDAL: Okay. Does it appear much bigger now?

DELORES: Uh huh. And it's very warm and inviting, really golden, and there are some sort of forms on it.

RANDAL: You can already see them or you just sense them?

DELORES: I can see them.

RANDAL: Okay, you're getting real close now.

DELORES: There are mountains, but the mountains have angular edges.

RANDAL: Are you still on your bicycle?

DELORES: No, I think it disappeared.

RANDAL: Are you just there in your body?

DELORES: There are wings underneath part of me.

RANDAL: Oh, so you have wings. Feel the wings now taking you down toward the planet. Are you still in the air?

DELORES: I'm hovering.

RANDAL: Look down below you and see what you see as you hover.

DELORES: It's beautiful. The rivers look like crystals and the crystals are flowing. They're all shimmering like long narrow beads of crystal and they reach all the way down to the ground. They're solid in form rather than being beads. It's like they're made of shining metal. And there are things that look like flowers but they are gems – colored gems. And I'm looking for people but I don't see any.

RANDAL: Are you still hovering?

DELORES: I'm floating but I'm very close to it. I just don't have my feet down.

RANDAL: You may not need to come right to this planet. At least not for now. Just feel yourself floating and looking around. What do you see? Are you still looking for people or are you looking at other things?

DELORES: I'm looking for life forms of some kind. (pause) It looks like a form described in a book I read about a long time ago. Rounded, soft–bodied beings, sort of like little dough men. And I see one of them that looks friendly but they don't have any features. There are only shapes there, like a head and arms and legs and a torso, but there are no faces. No facial expressions at all, but they feel friendly. And now I see lots of them. It's like they're all coming out from someplace way off in the distance. I don't know where. And they're all coming closer. And now they're all around me and they feel like positive energy. They tell me everything is okay.

RANDAL: Do you want to ask them anything?

DELORES: What is it like living here?

RANDAL: Are they all responding or does someone respond to you?

DELORES: They don't talk but they communicate.

RANDAL: Telepathically?

DELORES: Uh huh. (Delores begins crying) They said it's all peace and it's all beautiful and everything is integrated. Everything is one and whole.

RANDAL: That's beautiful.

DELORES: And I just meld in with them.

RANDAL: Wonderful.

DELORES: I'm disappearing as a form. I'm going with them and it's as though they all become one form too. I'm one with them and they're one with me and there is no distinction between entities. We're floating and just being in that state. And I feel a soreness here (motioning to the area of her heart), sort of a hurt. An ache.

RANDAL: Sort of a heartache?

DELORES: Uh huh. I said sort of an ache but it is a heartache.

RANDAL: What is your heartache telling you?

DELORES: That I'm at one with everyone and everything and that's the way it is and the way it's supposed to be. And that I must never cause separateness or division. That I must be connected and at one because that's the end destiny and in order to get there I have to be that way, and that causes feelings of completeness, wholeness, unity and enlightenment.

RANDAL: How does it feel to hear your heart saying these things?

DELORES: It feels like what I want to hear and know and what I need to hear and know.

RANDAL: How does your heart feel now?

DELORES: Big and red and alive, and like that's the way it's supposed to be.

RANDAL: Feel that big, red, alive, powerful heart that you have. The loving heart.

DELORES: It's bigger than anything else. It's bigger than my head.

RANDAL: Good, make it bigger than everything else.

DELORES: And it's soft and malleable.

RANDAL: Good.

DELORES: And I'd like to go inside it.

RANDAL: Go inside it.

DELORES: It has an opening right where the two curves come together at the top. It's an opening for people to come in. (Delores cries softly) I'm inside but I want other people in here too.

RANDAL: Good, who do you want to let in?

DELORES: Everybody.

RANDAL: Everybody you know or everybody?

DELORES: Everybody.

RANDAL: Okay, let everybody in now. Big heart, huh?

DELORES: Uh huh.

RANDAL: Good. Is everybody going in now?

DELORES: Uh huh.

RANDAL: Is it getting even bigger?

DELORES: There is plenty of room.

RANDAL: You've got everybody else's heart in there too. That makes more room, doesn't it? Is that the way it works?

DELORES: Uh huh.

RANDAL: What a big heart you have.

DELORES: It feels wonderful.

RANDAL: Beautiful.

DELORES: I want to be sure Theresa and Ann and Linda are in there.

RANDAL: Okay, bring in Theresa and Ann and Linda. Do you find them in there among those billions of people?

DELORES: Uh huh.

RANDAL: Good. Feel how good that feels to have them in your heart. (pause) How does it feel to be that heart?

DELORES: It feels good.

RANDAL: You're giving unconditional love?

DELORES: Uh huh.

RANDAL: Can you receive unconditional love?

DELORES: I have some fear of being rejected.

RANDAL: So whose heart would you like to go into? Do you feel like you're in their hearts now by having them in your heart?

Delores: Not quite. (pause) I'm concerned about Ann – about getting connected with her in her heart.

RANDAL: Okay. It may be sufficient just to say what you did. Can you do something right now, with all the power of your big heart?

Delores: I can beam out but she has to receive. It's up to her.

RANDAL: Beam out and see what she does. Is she open to receiving from you?

DELORES: Yes, she definitely is. That feels good.

RANDAL: It's good for you to put out your feelings, Delores. You have a lot of insight and you have a lot of love. That's healing for others and it's healing for you to be able to do that.

DELORES: Yes, I feel that the cord is connected – from my heart to their hearts.

RANDAL: Good, all three of them. Do you feel their love for you?

DELORES: Uh huh.

RANDAL: Can you take that in?

DELORES: Uh huh.

RANDAL: Good, I can feel that too. Is there anybody else that you feel you particularly want to connect your heart with?

DELORES: Yes, with David and Dan and Tom.

RANDAL: Okay, connect your heart with them. How does that feel? Do you feel it going both ways with each of them?

DELORES: I feel it going out.

RANDAL: Okay, let's take them one at a time. Let's go with David first. Feel the love from your heart going to his heart. Can you feel that?

DELORES: Uh huh.

RANDAL: Good. Can you feel it coming from him to you?

DELORES: Uh huh.

RANDAL: Good, enjoy that. (pause) Okay, now Dan. Do you feel your heart going to his heart?

DELORES: Yes.

RANDAL: Do you feel it coming from him?

DELORES: Yes.

RANDAL: Good. Now Tom. Can you feel your heart going to his?

DELORES: Uh huh.

RANDAL: Do you feel it coming back from him?

DELORES: Uh huh.

RANDAL: Good.

DELORES: Especially from him. Big heart!

RANDAL: Take it all in. It goes both ways, you know. Feel it on a deep, deep level. Even deeper than before. It's so easy.

DELORES: It feels so peaceful.

RANDAL: Good, experience that peacefulness, Delores. Take it in. It's okay. You don't have to do anything right now or try to do anything. It's okay for you to receive, to accept this peace. Feel it deep down. Feel it for its own sake and its own healing of you. You deserve that.

DELORES: The connectedness feels so good.

RANDAL: Yes, feel the connectedness. Know that that's one great gift you have – the ability to connect with people deeply and beautifully. You'll naturally be a healer and love it because you gain so much when you help to heal people and you also let people heal you. You let them into your heart. Reach out to those that you really care for. On some level you can love everyone unconditionally with that huge heart of yours. And you also can tap into your intuition and know that there are times with some people that it's important to back off, that they might not be ready for that connection or you might not be ready for a connection with them. Is that true on some level?

DELORES: I think so.

RANDAL: You can be wide open on a certain level to everybody all the time and also be sensitive to not take on negative energy from someone else. Do you understand what I'm saying?

DELORES: I do. I think I need to dwell on that and understand it better.

RANDAL: Yes, that's the other side of the coin. Everything we've been doing is valid and important. You have all those powers. And to be your most powerful toward yourself and others, there are also times when you have to back off from other people's negative energy. Just let them have that space and let go.

DELORES: Uh huh.

RANDAL: And you continue to understand on a deeper level as that process goes on in your subconscious mind. It will go on today, tonight when you sleep and dream, and tomorrow. What you're tapping into is your higher self. We all have a higher self. We're all one. You can tap into that with everyone and yet with some people the best thing you can do is just back off, and that's okay. You've heard the saying, "God grant me the serenity to accept the things I cannot change, the courage to change the things I can, and the wisdom to know the difference."

DELORES: Uh huh.

RANDAL: Does that fit for you?

DELORES: Yes. Will you say it once more?

RANDAL: You say it after me. "God grant me the serenity to accept the things I cannot change..."

DELORES: God grant me the serenity to accept the things I cannot change.

RANDAL: "....the courage to change the things I can..."

DELORES: The courage to change the things I can.

RANDAL: "...and the wisdom to know the difference."

DELORES: And the wisdom to know the difference.

RANDAL: Let it sink in. (pause) You've got a beautiful heart, Delores. You're doing wonderful things to heal the world. I know how deeply you care about these things. Know that you're doing more than you consciously realize, and you're going to continue to do even more. As you give of your special gifts and your special love, you're also taking time to receive and time to rest. Sometimes you can relax and enjoy playing, being light and free, soaring on your wings. It's good for you to do that, too. There is a time for everything. A time for waking and a time for sleeping, a time for giving and a time for receiving, a time for playing and a time for working. Ironically, as you let go of the need to always be giving, you find that when you give you are that much more powerful as a result. That's part of life – contact and withdrawal.

DELORES: While God is granting, there is one other thing I'd like – a good sense of humor.

RANDAL: A good sense of humor – absolutely! We all need that. I'll bet you have a good sense of humor.

DELORES: I love to laugh.

RANDAL: That's important. Laughing is a very important form of play. To see the irony, the humor in things, is a profound wisdom. Go inside your body now. How does it feel?

DELORES: It feels numb except for my heart.

RANDAL: Numbness through almost all of your body is a sign of medium-deep hypnosis. And what does your heart feel?

DELORES: Very full and alive.

RANDAL: Feel that big, full, alive heart. Your awareness of the rest of your body will come back very quickly when you come back from hypnosis. You deserve that big, full heart. It heals you. You naturally heal others too, just by being yourself. Isn't that nice how that works? Sometimes we heal just by letting go of issues. If you find yourself worrying about something, sometimes the best thing you can do is to just let it go. Give yourself a break. Your subconscious mind can work on it if it is important, and if there is something you can do, it will come to you later.

DELORES: I feel connected to your heart too, Randal.

RANDAL: And I feel connected to yours, Delores. We have a good, strong connection. Thank you.

DELORES: Thank you.

RANDAL: Good, feel that connection going back and forth. Take it in and let that connection go both ways.

DELORES: We're all laughing.

RANDAL: Oh yeah? Good. Can you feel that connection with everyone in the room?

DELORES: Uh huh.

RANDAL: I'm going to throw in everybody in the world too.

DELORES: I love it.

RANDAL: Can you feel it right now?

DELORES: Uh huh.

RANDAL: Over five billion connections.

DELORES: There are a lot of big hearts out there.

RANDAL: Yes there are. You have an especially strong connection with those hearts that are really big.

DELORES: Yes, the connection runs both ways all right.

RANDAL: Yes, it's got to run both ways equally. There are moments when you're going to allow yourself to just receive. Many moments, many times, when you can savor the love from somebody else. Just take it in. It's good to receive.

Commentary

Hypnodreams within individual therapy sessions typically begin with the hypnosis induction, followed by the hypnodream (which, as in this case, I usually have the client verbalize as it is occurring), followed by the hypnotic dreamwork steps I have delineated at the conclusion of Chapter Two.

Much of Delores' therapy takes place during, rather than after, the development of the hypnodream, which gradually evolves at the end to a combination of a dialogue between her and myself and hypnotic suggestions. Although there is not a standard Gestalt dialogue, at various times Delores spontaneously reports a telepathic communication with the forms she encounters and with her heart, describing what is said to her, rather than becoming that form or the heart. Part of the reason for not having Delores become the other part and dialogue was that her hypnodream was still in progress and developing so well (including her spontaneously finding creative solutions to any problems that arose). I wanted her to keep any dialogue minimal and continue the flow of the hypnodream while it was in progress. Since she had come so far and reached such a beautiful conclusion, no further dialogue was needed at the end of the hypnodream.

Postscript: Delores Writes Nine Years Later

Thanks very much for the copy of my hypnodream. I loved reading it and it is very timely. I have been working on keeping my heart open, especially combining that with being a better business person regarding my hypnotherapy practice. It's rather related to balancing the left and right brain and still keeping the heart connection. It is coming together!

The hypnodream I experienced from our session in 1988 is still impacting my life. The message from my subconscious to open my heart to all, and your positive affirmations regarding my healing abilities, assist me in meeting my clients with confidence, compassion, and unconditional love. Thank you for the original experience and for this opportunity to review my dream. It was wonderful to "hear" those positive, loving affirmations that you gave me during the session again.

Chapter 19

The Evolution Of Tom's Hypnodream into Regression:

The Drowning Woman

RANDAL: (following a group hypnodream session and a report of an unfinished process from Tom) Yes, we can work with your hypnodream, Tom. Have a seat and describe the dream you just had.

TOM: Okay. Mary and I are in Mexico and I'm teaching her to not be afraid of the water. She had a bad experience when she was a child and this has been going on for months. We start by just sitting in the sand on the beach and letting the water lap against her legs and getting her used to the warmth and the sun. We're wearing T–shirts. I finally get her to where she will wade out into the water and let the sand squish up between her toes and feel the sun on her body. Then slowly, it takes months to get to this point, she will let herself float with me holding her.

RANDAL: And this is the dream you are repeating right now?

TOM: Yes. So now we flash forward and right below the villas there are a lot of rocks and it's very dramatic because all the fish come in. It's like a huge aquarium. We finally get her to the point where she will put on a face mask and fins, and holding onto my T–shirt, she will float out by the rocks. We see the fish, have a wonderful time, and boom! Super-imposed on top of this is a little one year old black baby in a dark red lace bonnet, booties and dress. Right on top of this scene. It won't go away. And we're floating by the rocks, not getting too close because they are coral and they'll cut you up like shredded lettuce. I keep thinking and trying to say, "Mary, stay away from the rocks!" but she goes to the rocks. I keep trying to pull her away and the T–shirt keeps stretching longer and longer and finally it rips. Into the rocks goes Mary and that's when I wake up.

RANDAL: Okay, be Mary at the end of the scene going into the rocks. Let's just jump right into it.

TOM: Sure. (Tom leans back in his chair and closes his eyes) Can't figure out the black baby on top of the scene.

RANDAL: We'll find out about that, too. But now be Mary going into the rocks. How does that feel?

TOM: I'm having trouble breathing. A combination of delight and fear. Refracted light. Light-headed. Can't seem to control the anxiety. Pulling harder on Tom's T–shirt.

RANDAL: How do you feel inside as this is happening?

TOM: A lot of fear in my stomach.

RANDAL: And what is that fear? Is it a sensation or a movement or what?

TOM: Paralyzing.

RANDAL: So say, "I am paralyzing myself."

TOM: (pause, then softly) I am paralyzing myself.

RANDAL: Feel that. Now when I touch your shoulder I would like you to describe yourself as the rock. (Tom's face looks intense) Just a minute. What's going on with you right now, Tom? What are you feeling?

TOM: A lot of flashes. Panic. Fear.

RANDAL: Stay with that panic and fear. I'm going to count from five down to one. At the count of one you're going to go back to some time when you felt panic and fear. I'd like you to show me your "yes" finger right now. (Tom's right index finger rises) Show me your "no" finger. (Tom's right thumb rises) Okay, relax your fingers. Let your subconscious be your guide. Tom, is it safe and appropriate for you to go back and recall a time when you felt the same kind of panic and fear? (Tom's index finger rises) And is it okay as you go back to this time and recall it, to be open to your feelings? (Tom's index finger rises) All right. I'm going to count from ten down to one. I want you to stay with the feeling of fear and panic. You're going to go to an earlier time when you felt these feelings. Ten, nine, going back in time. Eight, seven, six, five, four, three, two, one. You're right there. Where are you? Is it night time or day time? Pick one.

TOM: Day time.

RANDAL: Are you alone or with others?

TOM: Alone.

RANDAL: Are you under thirty years old? Yes or no.

TOM: Yes.

RANDAL: Are you under fifteen years old?

TOM: Yes.

RANDAL: Are you under five years old? (Tom's thumb rises) How old are you? (Tom holds up six fingers) Six years old. Are you outside? (Tom's index finger rises) Yes. You're six years old, you're alone outside, and it's daytime. What's happening? Describe the scene.

TOM: Beach.

RANDAL: Are you on the beach? (Tom's thumb rises) Are you near a beach? (Tom's index finger rises) Okay, you're near a beach. You say you are alone. Do you see anybody at all or nobody?

TOM: Water.

RANDAL: Just water. How do you feel when you are looking at that water?

TOM: Scared.

RANDAL: What is it about the water that is scaring you?

TOM: Black.

RANDAL: Where does that come from?

TOM: All around.

RANDAL: You mean you see black and you associate that with the water? Or what?

TOM: Father.

RANDAL: What is it about your father that has to do with this water?

TOM: On the beach. He's watching. I don't understand.

RANDAL: Since you don't understand, do you feel bothered that he's way off on the beach?

TOM: I'm scared.

RANDAL: What is it about this water that is scaring you? Does it have to do with your father?

TOM: Cramps.

RANDAL: Cramps from being in the water? Were you just swimming in this water by yourself? (Tom's face is intense but there is no response) Did you get frightened because you were swimming and you got cramps? Or what? (no response) All right. So feel your experience. Be back in your body. Have your cramps gone away or do you still feel them?

TOM: Some.

RANDAL: So if you were going to say something to the water, what would you say?

TOM: Go away.

RANDAL: All right. I'd like you to switch now. (Randal touches Tom's shoulder to encourage him to switch to the opposite chair but Tom has trouble moving) You can stay right there. You're quite deep now. Just feel yourself go deeper. (Randal moves behind Tom and puts his hands on Tom's shoulders) When I push down on your shoulders just feel yourself go deeper. This time when I touch your left shoulder you're going to switch and be the water. Become the water when I touch your left shoulder and say whatever you have to say to Bob. What's your name when you're six years old?

TOM: Tommy.

RANDAL: Okay, talk to Tommy, water, when I touch you on the shoulder. Three, two, one. He says he's scared of you and he wants you to go away. (Randal touches Tom's shoulder) What do you say to him?

TOM: Relax. Float.

RANDAL: All right. When I touch your shoulder again, switch and be Tommy. (Randal touches Tom's shoulder) What do you want to say to the water?

TOM: (long pause and sigh) Trouble opening my mouth.

RANDAL: You mean now in this process or trouble at that time?

TOM: Now.

RANDAL: All right. We can do more work right now with dialogue than we can with finger signals so I encourage you to find that it will be easy enough for you to say certain key words. You're doing very well. You can express yourself. That's good.

TOM: Fighting the water. Panic. Can't catch my breath. Swallowing a lot of sea water. Father watching.

RANDAL: I see. How do you feel about your father watching?

TOM: I don't understand.

RANDAL: You don't understand why he's not helping?

TOM: Yes.

RANDAL: All right. Put your father there in front of you. When I touch your left shoulder switch and be your father. (Randal touches Tom's shoulder) What does your father say?

TOM: This is how you learn to swim.

RANDAL: Switch and be Tommy.

TOM: I can't stand up over my head.

RANDAL: And what does your father say?

TOM: That's the idea.

RANDAL: What do you say to that, Tommy?

TOM: Hold me! Grab me! Save me!

RANDAL: Did your father put you in this situation to try to force you to learn to swim?

TOM: Yes.

RANDAL: So you're asking him to save you. What does your father say in response to that?

TOM: No.

RANDAL: So what happens next in this scene?

TOM: I grab him.

RANDAL: You grab him. And what happens when you grab him?

TOM: He pushes me away.

RANDAL: How do you feel about that?

TOM: Mad.

RANDAL: Okay, tell your father off now. What do you want to say to him?

TOM: (pause) Can't.

RANDAL: Well, maybe you won't, but you could say something to him. Here's the scene now. You fought your way out of the water. You're off on the beach now and you have adult Tom with you to talk to your father. You have full grown, mature Tom with you so you don't have to be afraid. Tom's here to protect Tommy. You can be there with Tom talking to your father. What do you want to say?

TOM: Why? Why?

RANDAL: And what does your father say in response?

TOM: That's the way I learned.

RANDAL: Switch and be Tommy. What do you want to say to your father about that?

TOM: Doesn't have to be like that.

RANDAL: Now switch and be the father. Your son just had a very difficult time with that and he said it doesn't have to be that hard way. Be Dad and talk to Tommy. What do you want to say?

TOM: Disgusted.

RANDAL: Disgusted. You are disgusted with...?

TOM: Tommy.

RANDAL: Respond to your father.

TOM: Why?

RANDAL: And what does your father say?

TOM: Walks away.

RANDAL: Switch and be Tommy again. Instead of asking why, make a statement to your father. Tell him how you feel about his attitude and how he's calling what you're saying disgusting. Tell him so he can hear you, even if he's trying to walk away.

TOM: The sun is very hot. Getting burned.

RANDAL: Getting burned out here on the beach?

TOM: Uh huh.

RANDAL: Tell your father how you feel about that.

TOM: I can't.

RANDAL: You're here with Tom and it's very important for you to stand up for yourself. Your father just criticized you. It's time for you to criticize him back. Speak up to your father now. You can do it. As a six year old what do you call him? Dad, daddy, father or what?

TOM: Bill.

RANDAL: All right, talk to Bill now. I can help you, too. Tom is here and we're going to have this talk with Bill. We tell him, "Hey, you have to come back here. Your son has something important to say to you." We're here to help you and to protect you. You can say anything you want to Bill. You can say it in a whisper or you can say it loudly, but tell him what's wrong with his attitude and how he's treating you.

TOM: It was totally unnecessary to have done that.

RANDAL: What does he say?

TOM: He hits me.

RANDAL: How do you respond to that?

TOM: Try hitting back.

RANDAL: All right. (Randal gets a pillow and holds it up) Here he is right in front of you. Go ahead and hit him back. (Tom punches the pillow) That's good. Hit him again. (Tom punches the pillow again) Say "I hate you!" (no response) Go on, say it. I hate you! (tears come down Tom's face) What do you feel?

TOM: Black.

RANDAL: Do you see black or feel blackness or what? Go inside your body. Black is fine but just see if there is anything else, too.

TOM: Red.

RANDAL: Okay. Is that what you're seeing or is that what you're feeling?

TOM: All of it. (tears flow)

RANDAL: Feel your feelings. It's okay to cry. It's okay to be angry. The important thing for you, Tommy, and you, Tom, is that you express whatever you feel now. Get it out there where it belongs. How did that feel to hit your father? Did that feel good or did that not feel good?

TOM: Bad.

RANDAL: What is it about it that felt bad?

TOM: It's not right.

RANDAL: It doesn't feel right. Well, he's a lot bigger and he was hitting you.

TOM: Still not right.

RANDAL: So what do you want to tell your father now?

TOM: Let's don't be together anymore.

RANDAL: All right. What does your father say to that?

TOM: Okay.

RANDAL: All right. Be Tommy again. Does that feel right for you?

TOM: Yes.

RANDAL: Good. You know, Tommy, you've been living with this for a long time. We sometimes keep experiences from early childhood all the way to our adult lives. You've been keeping the energy of this father that you don't need any more. So how do you want to say good-bye to your father? Maybe you've already said good-bye. Do you feel like he's gone now? Has he disappeared or walked away?

TOM: Yes.

RANDAL: Can you imagine having a father that was more caring and loving than that? Can you imagine what he would be like and what he would look like? Imagine that right now. If you could pick a father, anyone in the world, who would it be? It could be someone you've seen before or that you've never seen. It could be a famous person, a historical person, an old friend, or some stranger. (Tom is smiling) You're starting to get an image? Good. You're smiling about it. Tell me something about your new-found father.

TOM: John Wayne.

RANDAL: John Wayne! (audience joins in laughter) All right. A strong, tough, real man, but a man with a heart, too, huh?

TOM: (Tom is grinning) Yeah.

RANDAL: Good. It sounds like a man who could protect you rather than having to be protected from your father. Imagine being there with this nice, tough cowboy, John Wayne. He can show you how to be a man just by being himself without having to put you through ordeals. Just let him be himself and let him have a great time being a loving daddy to you. You've got this wonderful version of John Wayne to be with you whenever you want. That's for the child part of you, for your inner child. This charismatic, strong father is able to handle tough situations and is also supportive of your feelings.

TOM: What is this black baby doing here?

RANDAL: Well, well, well. (laughter from audience) We've gone from the dream to some associated regression work. Let's go to the dream again. Now we're back to the black baby. Become that little baby and describe yourself.

TOM: A little black baby with booties and black, kinky hair. Very black. It's a girl baby.

RANDAL: Okay, that's you, all right? (laughter from audience) Yes. Surprised yourself, didn't you? And you have this bonnet, you said. A white bonnet?

RANDAL: Oh, you sound adorable. (more laughter)

TOM: Booties, crocheted lace.

RANDAL: And are you just floating there? Are you in some kind of basket or container, or are you holding onto someone or what?

TOM: Just kind of floating out there. Floating around.

RANDAL: And you're big, is that right?

TOM: Huge!

RANDAL: Huge! A giant little baby. (laughing) Okay. But a little newborn.

TOM: No! About a year old.

RANDAL: About a year.

TOM: Pink ribbons holding on my booties.

RANDAL: Okay, how does it feel to be this baby? Do you like it? Are you happy? (Tom looks happy and playful and is squirming and reaching down to his foot) Good. Do you want to talk to these ribbons? What would you like to say to these cute little ribbons?

TOM: (giggles) Pull the bow undone. Pull the bow. (Tom is kicking his foot and laughing)

RANDAL: You undid the bow. Are you kicking it off your footsie there? All right. Is that a fun thing to do? If your bootie could talk to you what would your bootie say?

TOM: It's over there.

RANDAL: It's over there. Become the cute little bootie. Are you dark red like the other parts? (Tom giggles and nods) With pink laces. How do you feel just lying there?

TOM: Sitting up.

RANDAL: Okay. Just feel what it's like to be this one year-old gigantic black baby.

TOM: Sitting on the porch. White porch swing. (pause) Tray in front of me on the swing. Somebody is sitting next to me pushing the swing.

RANDAL: Does that feel good to you? (Tom giggles) Just take that experience in. Feel what it feels like to have everything taken care of for you. You're someone very special. Are the people rocking you giants also? Or are you very big for a baby compared to them? (Tom doesn't appear to be listening. He is giggling and squirming and reaching down to his other foot and kicking it. The audience is laughing.) Are you kicking off your other bootie?

TOM: Uh huh. (Tom is leaning back and beaming)

RANDAL: All right! You're really relaxing. Enjoy it. Just kick back and be this giant baby. (Tom's hands are fiddling around his neck) Okay, it looks like you're loosening your bonnet, huh? (Randal and the audience are laughing at Tom's antics) Totally indulge in this experience. Love it. Just take it in. Just being cared for and rocked and being able to be so utterly relaxed.

TOM: Going to sleep.

RANDAL: So you're just relaxing on this swing. I'd like you to focus on your breathing and slow your breathing down. Allow yourself to become very passive now and I'm going to talk to you. You feel your whole body becoming totally loose and limp. (Randal moves behind Tom) As I rub your shoulders you feel yourself go deeper and deeper relaxed. That's good. When I drop your left hand just let it drop to your lap and go much deeper. When I drop your right hand feel yourself go much deeper. Go way down.

All right, Tom, we're back here in 1994 but you can keep the image of having your new John Wayne father, of having a new kind of relationship with this loving, supportive, big, strong man that can take care of the part of you that is a boy. You can also continue to enjoy and grow from the experience of being this beautiful baby, receiving really good care. You deserve to have this good care. How good it feels to just relax. Just kick off your booties and loosen your bonnet and feel yourself getting rocked. How utterly sweet it is. Deep down inside you're beginning to recognize more that you deserve and enjoy having situations in which you're taken care of. You find ways to take care of yourself and ways to be receptive to nurturance. You're creating a more nurturing and accepting environment in your own life.

TOM: Fire.

RANDAL: You're seeing fire now?

TOM: Yes.

RANDAL: Which part of you is seeing this fire? How old are you?

TOM: Baby.

RANDAL: Are you the black baby or yourself as a baby?

TOM: Black baby.

RANDAL: Finger signal yes or no, is this experience of being a baby a symbolic part of Tom? (Tom's thumb rises) The answer is no. Is this experience a dream or fantasy? (Tom's thumb rises) The answer is no. Are you recalling something you read or heard? (Tom's thumb rises) No. Is this an experience of someone's life? (Tom's index finger rises) The answer is yes. Is this a memory from the collective unconscious? (Tom's thumb rises) No. Do you experience being this baby as a past life of Tom's? (pause, then Tom's index finger rises) Yes. What happens in this past life regarding this fire and the baby? When I touch you on the forehead at the count of one, you can describe what happens, if anything. Three, two, one. (Randal taps Tom's forehead) What happens about this fire? Do you stay protected from it? (long pause) Do you get hurt in this fire? (Tom's index finger rises) The answer is yes. Do you live through this fire? (Tom's thumb rises) The answer is no.

You don't need to go back and recall this fire any more vividly than what you just felt here. You know what happened. The crucial question is, is there something that Tom has carried over from that awful trauma that is in some way blocking him in his current life? Yes or no. (Tom's index finger rises) The answer is yes. I want you to analyze that experience with your subconscious mind now and when you get a realization with your conscious mind, signal with your "yes" finger. (Tom's index finger rises) All right, when I touch you on your forehead you'll be able to speak and say something about how this has been affecting you in your life up to this point. Three, two, one. (Randal taps Tom's forehead) Go ahead.

TOM: Fear. Trap.

RANDAL: Feeling fearful and trapped at various times in your life?

TOM: Unable to do anything about the situation. (deep sigh)

RANDAL: Is there a situation in your life now in which you feel fearful, trapped and unable to do anything?

TOM: Not anymore.

RANDAL: This is something that right now you are not feeling but you have felt in your life at some time.

TOM: Lots of white light.

RANDAL: I would like you to bring the baby here. (Randal hands Tom a pillow) Here's the baby that had that terrible experience. I'd like you to talk to her. What would you like to say to her?

TOM: It was meant to be. Life. Death. Cycle.

RANDAL: Switch and what does she say?

TOM: Why?

RANDAL: Be Tom and talk to her.

TOM: (sigh) Learning experience.

RANDAL: Do you want to tell her whether she goes beyond that and is able to gain in some way from this as a learning experience? Is that correct or not?

TOM: (sadly) No, she's gone.

RANDAL: She's gone. Keep breathing and feel your feelings. Say good-bye to her.

TOM: Just white light.

RANDAL: Just white light. Okay, so she's passed on after that experience and gone to the light. Now that she's gone to the light does she have a greater wisdom about this experience that's been so painful or not?

TOM: Just a baby.

RANDAL: What can you send to her in the light? What can you say to her? Is there anything, even though she's gone and she's up in the light? Can you still reach her?

TOM: Peace.

RANDAL: Life isn't always fair. Somehow it helps to know that we can make the most of things and turn challenges into advantages. And she can go on and live in another life at another time and can gain from this very unfair experience. Over time she begins to get certain wisdom from her experiences that, among other things, helps her to live life more fully and creatively, with more aliveness and enjoyment. You have another life later that becomes Tom. And that life can be filled with a lot of wonder and experience. Tom still had memories of certain traumas from the past, including this little girl who had this terrible experience of being trapped and helpless. And at times Tom felt trapped and helpless, unable to do anything about the situation and feeling fearful. One of the times he felt that way was when his father threw him in the water and wouldn't help him out. That brought back the memory of being that adorable little baby.

Life was unfair for young Tom then, just as it was unfair before. But Tommy grew up, developed, learned, expanded, used his life's experience, sense of humor, insight, therapy, joy, love, work, friends, family, and all of these different assets and allies to continue to move forward and to let go of misconceptions that came from these difficulties from the past. And Tom, you are continuing to recognize all of the abundance that is in your life right now. So when or if you begin to feel in some way trapped or fearful, you can find various positive, alternative ways to be much more in control than you were in those former experiences, which are continuing to fade away and go to the light.

Time is healing and you are healing and moving forward just by becoming aware of such an experience, seeing it, and then letting go of it. It can be a magnificent letting go. You may be amazed at how good you feel. If you are in a situation in the future in which you might have previously felt trapped, you find that you have many more alternatives than you had at other times when you truly were trapped. Now you don't have to be. Now you use all of your life's experiences to rise above each situation and find creative solutions. You recognize that most situations have various positive possibilities.

See that beautiful little girl and send her light now. She is healing. See her as healing. Take that six year old boy who is right here with you and send him healing. Give that boy a good hug and let him know it's all going to be okay, that he'll never have to deal with such an experience again because you take good care of him. You can let him go at his own pace, a lot more gently. You understand that he can learn in more gentle ways. And he is learning very well, in the loving environment that he deserves. I'd like you to practice some self–hypnosis, Tom, in the days and weeks ahead, and become this boy going out and having adventures with John Wayne. Having a fun time with a loving man who is going to show you around the world but take care of you, recognizing that you're just a boy and that you deserve to be treated gently. You'll come along in your own time.

Good job, Tom. Soon I'll begin to help you return to your full conscious awareness. First, is there anything else you want to say or ask me before I bring you out of the hypnosis?

TOM: Why is it necessary to have bad things happen?

RANDAL: Everybody in the room can identify with having been a victim to unfair circumstances. Certain situations occur for us at all ages that don't seem fair. Sometimes they're caused by people or sometimes by a natural calamity. The American visionary, Peace Pilgrim, often spoke of having a healthy attitude about difficulties. In *Peace Pilgrim's Wisdom*, a book of her insights compiled by Cheryl Canfield, she says, "If only you could see the whole picture, if you knew the whole story, you would realize that no problem ever comes to you that does not have a purpose in your life, that cannot contribute to your inner growth." Difficulties can be turned into something positive if we see them as opportunities to learn and grow. In addition, we can find wonderful, joyful experiences in life. Even when bad things happen there is often still a lot to be grateful for. Evolution is happening, and some things are better than fair. We are fortunate today in many ways compared to what life used to be like. We have many conveniences and opportunities, and much technology and entertainment that was unheard of a few generations ago.

TOM: And faster.

RANDAL: Yes, the evolution is happening faster. Now I'm going to count from one to five and with each number that I count you will become more and more alert, awake, and aware. Also you' will continue to receive more and more insights that are peaceful and enlightening for you, helping you to be more accepting of life and recognizing that with each difficult situation that comes up, there are various opportunities both within that situation and otherwise. A kind of lightening, freeing, uplifting experience is happening within you. Some of that is beyond your conscious mind, just a certain peace and tranquility within that is having a greater affect on your life. Getting ready now. (Randal counts, giving suggestions between numbers) Open your eyes. Take a deep breath. (Tom is quite deep and not moving) Coming back. Take your time. Coming back, number five. Fully alert. (big sigh, eyes open, Tom laughs) Welcome back.

TOM: Thank you, Randal. Thank you everybody. (applause)

RANDAL: Well, that regression to the experience of the boy was important and then there was the black baby.

TOM: That image wouldn't go away.

RANDAL: There was a similar experience of the baby and the boy. You were doing reasonably well, then suddenly your father threw you in the water and triggered what may be a previous experience.

TOM: Well, that was how they used to learn how to swim. They would just throw you in the water.

RANDAL: There are better ways to teach you.

TOM: There sure are. My frustration probably goes back to that genetic base and the environment.

RANDAL: It was interesting that you hesitated when I asked you if this was a past life of yours because other possibilities could have included a metaphor, or theoretically, a collective unconscious memory or cellular memory, rather than an actual past life of that person.

TOM: I would say it was cellular memory.

RANDAL: Did you get a sense of what century it was or what continent?

TOM: Yes, I would say it was the South and lightening struck the house. In the panic and confusion the baby got burned to death. Bad way to go. All that lace and stuff went really fast. Beautiful baby.

RANDAL: Well, isn't it good to know that in spite of such great traumas, people can go on and go to the light and possibly beyond.

TOM: Right! Thank you. Wow! (applause)

RANDAL: (after a break) Let's review this. We started out with a group hypnodream and demonstrated that a hypnodream can be very effective for creating a "dream" for someone who has no recent dream recall. In the dream, Tom was working with Mary, teaching her to swim and not be afraid of the water. Meanwhile, during the hypnodream, there was the image of the baby that just seemed to be there. Some hypnodreams are somewhat more logical, closer to everyday life than normal dreams, but here was an example of something clear out of the blue. I had a choice of whether to go first with the baby or the swimming scene. After describing the dream, I had Tom become the character of Mary, and he spontaneously went quite deep into hypnosis.

When he began responding so emotionally to the swimming scene, that seemed to be triggering an earlier experience. After he signaled with ideomotor responses that it was safe to go back and recall an earlier experience, I used the affect bridge and he went to the trauma at age six with his father. I usually find when doing Gestalt dialogue that there is enough reasonableness from the other character for some integration to take place, but apparently not in this case. They ultimately went their separate ways, so we created an ideal father. It was a John Wayne figure, who would be a very good and supportive father for Tommy, a father who would be masculine and also loving.

I was giving some positive suggestions about him and his ideal father, and suddenly he recalled the baby again. Obviously this was important, but it would be inappropriate to assume that some tragedy had happened. I just had him become the baby. At first it looked as if the baby was simply hanging out, happily kicking her shoes off and so forth. It could have been an archetypal image in which, as the six year old having fun and then suddenly being thrown into the water, he identified the experience as being like this beautiful baby that is in bliss and suddenly experiences tragedy. I don't expect what comes up to be positive or negative, I just go with the flow and discover where the energy leads us.

I asked how it felt to be this baby and it seemed to be very good, so I gave more positive suggestions for integration of the great feeling of enjoyment. Then suddenly the word "fire" came out. His ideomotor responses first suggested the possibility of a past life memory, but just as a dream can be a metaphor for our lives, an apparent past life memory could be a metaphor from the subconscious mind. Even though Robert hesitantly called the memory of the baby and the fire a past life memory at first, his intuition later was that this was a cellular memory. Whether it was a metaphor, a cellular memory, the collective unconscious, a past life or whatever, the therapy we did is the same and just as relevant. Tom got in touch with issues that have periodically come up for him, of being afraid or feeling trapped and unable to do anything. Whatever else it might be, the image was at least symbolic because his experience of that sudden terrifying fire was similar to his experience of almost drowning. Metaphor is the language of the subconscious. What matters is that he had an experience at some point in his life that was emotionally like the trauma of this baby. That was his existential experience.

Then we moved on to hypno-analysis to check the relevance of that experience to current expectancy in his life. This leads to hypnotic re-education. Just becoming aware of an experience and feeling it can be a very positive step in letting go. After major trauma, it is common for people to keep subconsciously expecting the same kind of experience that they earlier felt overwhelmed by. A person who has had an experience of being trapped or helpless at a young age needs to learn that now, as an adult, he doesn't have to expect life to continue to be like that. Tom came up with some questions and realizations, and I gave him some ideas to help him understand and cope. I gave more suggestions for further realizations to continue, including realizations about letting go, moving on in life, and all kinds of warm fuzzies. (laughter from the group)

I checked to see if he felt finished and he asked, "Why do bad things happen?" I did further reframing, elaborating on how we use difficulties to create opportunities.

Okay, Tom, come on up here. Anything you'd like to say to the group?

TOM: The white light was blinding beyond words. It was very intense.

RANDAL: When the baby died?

TOM: Yes. And there was a strong identification, for lack of a better way to put it. What brought me to hypnotherapy originally, about a year and a half ago, is that I'd had three heart attacks and died three different times. And no white light, no angels, no out–of–body experience. I was disappointed. (laughter from the group)

RANDAL: If you're going to go to the trouble of dying you should at least get some white light experiences like those you have read about!

TOM: Yes! I was taking a lot of medication and was looking for a vehicle to get off the medication and calm down and that's what brought me here. I wanted to learn self–hypnosis as a way to calm down without the medication, and get through things without the violent tendencies which obviously come from my past. And I needed a little more understanding and sympathy for myself. This has helped immensely.

In the experience just now I had the sense that you were getting ready to bring me up and I was trying to come up but I couldn't. This black baby was floating over here and would not go away. I couldn't seem to say anything to you like, "Wait a minute" or something, but it started with that hypnodream.

RANDAL: You hadn't remembered any dreams, as you told the class earlier, and then this hypnodream brought you right into that specific experience. Sometimes a very brief hypnodream, just a few minutes, can bring you in touch with some part of you that is unfinished, as we saw here.

This regression was thorough enough that you may not need further regression on this issue. In the weeks ahead, Tom, anchor this session with some positive hypnotic suggestions in session or in self-hypnosis, for such issues as trusting life, trusting your experiences, expecting the positive as opposed to the negative. The negative is being trapped, being out of control. The positive is feeling in control, trusting life to work out and good things to come your way. Give yourself positive suggestions as a habit. You might create a tape for yourself and play that tape every day, or do self–hypnosis each night when you go to bed. Focus on the positive, on good mental expectancy, as well as the image of this powerful, positive John Wayne figure.

TOM: This dream was a real surprise to me. A black baby of all things! I'm from way down South and we're reared with a strong, macho male image. You don't break through that easily and it tips the scales. The tip is violence. You try so hard to keep a lid on that violence because once it tips to the other side it's just black rage.

RANDAL: When you were doing the dialogue with your father, your father hit you and you wanted to hit him back. You did that. Then you used your free will and didn't want to do that anymore. You decided to let go of the relationship. Even though we're dealing with you as a six year old, you get to rewrite the script. The first thing we do is try to rewrite the script within. If that doesn't work directly, you have the ability to create a new father. This time that was your choice. You did a good job creating him, and I'm glad for you.

TOM: Yes, me too. I think he was just the product of his environment. He was the product of the way he was brought up. He didn't know any better. He was doing it the way it was done to him. Hopefully, we're moving to a greater level of sensitivity.

Q: I can see how wonderfully this worked out but I'm a little confused because you said in the beginning, "Don't take sides." In the part with the father it seemed to me that you were.

RANDAL: During dreamwork I don't take sides. First I will take one side and help the person experience and express some feeling, then I'll go to the other side and do the same thing. In Gestalt regression that is usually the case also. The key is that often something has been imploded and taken in. Even though you're talking to the parent, you may also be talking to the parent inside of the person, the father within, and for that reason I usually avoid taking sides. Usually the person is able to mobilize his own resources, and both sides begin to listen, compromise, and integrate.

But there are times during regression dialogue when there is a parent or a bully or a teacher, etc., who is exceptionally uncompromising. During the dialogue, I may create some detachment. Instead of becoming the other side, I say, "Now, what does the other side say?" Even if the issue is with a stranger I will still often initially do the traditional Gestalt dialogue, because it is possible that some energy from the stranger was imploded. At other times I may not have the person identify with the stranger. If we're doing a traditional Gestalt dialogue in regression and the topdog continues to be completely harsh and uncompromising, I may allow or encourage a letting go. I wasn't taking sides at first when I had Tom express himself to his father but soon after that I did, when he and his father decided to separate.

Q: I recall that you used stronger language than he was willing to use.

RANDAL: At one point I told Tom to tell his father "I hate you" because that was what he was obviously feeling. He did not repeat the words, but the awareness got him further in touch with his feelings, which was good. I then encouraged his expression of those feelings.

TOM: I was really blocked. I think one of the things that was fascinating to me on the inside of this experience was when you had me be my father. He totally couldn't understand the panic or fear I felt. It just didn't register. To him it was disgusting. Why can't my son swim? Why is he panicking? It helps me understand him better. He's gone now but it's part of the big picture, this switching back and forth.

RANDAL: At various points we could all see Tom's struggle as he tried to get in touch with something. Sometimes during Gestalt dialogue the parent starts with something like, "Hey, come on! What's the big deal?" And after you go back and forth a few times the parent usually starts to get it. Often what makes the parent start to get it is that this other side does find a way to assert itself more strongly. So when I say I don't take sides, I mean I take both sides. I give each side a chance to express itself instead of holding back. Now suppose I came back to the father and he was trying to compromise. I'll do what I can to have the father get in touch with his feelings, whether his feelings are positive or negative. If he says, "Wait, there you go again. You're always telling me what I should do. I went through hell when I was a kid." Well, great. Then I encourage the father to say that. I encourage each side to be expressive, rather than trying to get them to compromise with each other.

Usually compromise and understanding eventually happens during the process, occurring spontaneously. It's more powerful to let the parts within discover their ability to compromise.

Q: Were you looking at Tom's experience of the baby as symbolic rather than an actual past life experience?

RANDAL: Is a dream an actual experience? While it is occurring a dream is absolutely real. When a person in hypnosis has a vivid, emotional visualization without that having been suggested, I accept that as the individual's existential process. If the imagery seems to be a possible past life regression, I work with that in the same way I would work with a dream or an age regression. Whether there is such a thing as reincarnation and the memory is an actual past life memory or not, is irrelevant to the process. I accept whatever associated memories or visualizations that come up as valid subconscious messages, meaningful in the therapeutic context. Whether or not it is a metaphor, it is the reality of the person's subjective experience of life.

Commentary

Adult Tom was brought to the beach scene to give Tommy added support when he became afraid to speak to his father. There was the potential of bringing adult Tom into the dialogue if necessary but Tommy began communicating his feelings well again at that point, in part by just having Tom there with him. Dialogues between parent, child and adult are Transactional Analysis techniques.

The method of having the client visualize an ideal parent to give further support to the inner child was used with Liz's regression in Chapter 14 as well as with Tom. However, issues in regression between parent and child do not usually need to lead to an ideal parent visualization. For example, the work started from Christine's and Cynthia's dreams in Chapters 11 and 12 did not necessitate development of an idealized parent because Christine's mother was a reasonable figure and Cynthia's mother eventually developed receptive and reasonable communication.

Chapter 20

Jan's Dream:

Journey to the Sacred Mountain

JAN: (telling her dream) I'm seated by the side of a large fireplace with two other people. One whole wall of the room is a window that looks out onto a mountain. The mountain is like something you'd expect to see on Mars or some arid planet. I lived in New Mexico for a time and this looks similar to some of the deeply textured rock structures there. The mountain itself is a rock formation. Even though it's far away I can really see and sense its different textures and caverns.

One of the people with me is a man and one is a woman. The woman is a friend of mine whose clarity and outspokenness I respect. I enjoy listening to her and I'd like to get to a point where I have that clarity as quickly as she does. The man is a friend who does vision quests. He's not the man I know, although it's his energy. Physically he looks like a male part of myself.

The sun is coming up over the mountain even though everything is light already, and it feels cozy and good. The room is big and open with white or beige carpeting. I look out of the window and the sun is just cresting the mountain top. We decide that we're going to go to the mountain and I find myself near the back of an old buttercup yellow Volkswagen van. My woman friend is toward the front of the van and the man comes back and gives me a very erotic kiss, then walks to the front. I know that I'm preparing to go to the top of the mountain.

I have one of those chocolate brown cigarettes near my mouth and this little two inch high being...you know how a bird of prey puts its wings up when it's in the process of clamping onto something? Well, this little being comes and its talons go around my cigarette. Then it makes a buzzing noise and lifts the cigarette away from my mouth. (Jan quit smoking during the semester she has been in this class - she the class are laughing)

In the interim there is a hawk flying overhead. I've often laid on mountaintops or hillsides and looked up at a hawk. They're almost transparent against the blue sky with the sun going through their feathers. It's like having access to another dimension. So the hawk is flying above me and I realize that I'm now prepared to do whatever I need to, in preparation for this climb up the mountain. Then the hawk flies right through me, between my heart and throat chakras. I see energy lines around my body in an arc and the hawk is flying around my upper chakras. I feel my body moving slightly. I don't feel the movement so much as I sense it. Something is shifting and I feel as if I'm being rearranged. I thank the hawk and I feel really good about what I've experienced and then I awaken.

RANDAL: Wow!

JAN: I don't usually have dreams about hawks. And there was this great little being about two inches high, a little hawk that just buzzed the cigarette right away from me.

RANDAL: The little being was a hawk as well. I'd like you to be this two inch being. (laughter from class and Jan) Let's get right into it.

JAN: Okay. I'm coming down and approaching this person and my talons grip onto the cigarette, but my wings are up like this. (Jan demonstrates with her arms) I'm able to fly in a straight line parallel to her mouth. I'm going like this: Bzzzz. (she makes various gestures) And then the cigarette just disappears.

RANDAL: All right. Close your eyes and get into that position again. How does it feel to be this being?

JAN: It feels like I'm a fractionated part of the ceremony that is going on between her and the hawk.

RANDAL: Emotionally how does it feel to be a part of that ceremony?

JAN: It feels good.

RANDAL: You may want to get up for this next one because I would like you to be the big hawk.

JAN: Okay. I wish I could fly.

RANDAL: Well, you can fly.

JAN: All right. (Jan begins to move around making flying motions) I'm flying over this person with the little hawk, just seeing what's going on down there. She's aware that I'm here. I'm going down, getting ready to take a long pass and I fly through her heart. Then I come back up and fly around some more. I'm going all around her body. There are a lot of different movements that are occurring along these lines of energy that are being rearranged. And it's awesome to be able to fly like this. (the class laughs loudly and applauds)

RANDAL: Excellent! Stand there and stay with your experience. Feel your joy. Feel down into your belly. How does your body feel right now?

JAN: Light.

RANDAL: Feel your lightness. Besides light, are there any other adjectives you can give to what it feels like to be this hawk, being a part of this ceremony?

JAN: It feels whole. I feel more aligned in my body and with divinity. I feel like part of the mountain and everything on it.

RANDAL: Now be the mountain.

JAN: It's so expansive.

RANDAL: "I'm so expansive."

JAN: I'm so expansive and my rock formations have changed over eons of time. I feel a lot of good, grounded areas. I go on forever. I start big and parts of me wear down. I'm just all over. I'm also rock so I'm very solid. I'm a big mountain. I'm almost like a mother with my arms enfolding.

RANDAL: Keep your eyes closed and stay in that position. Be the mountain for a while longer. Feel that enfolding, powerful energy and that movement. It's great to experience you as a moving mountain over eons of time.

JAN: I like it. It feels really good. It's good to remember how I've changed through time. I've changed so much.

RANDAL: All right. Are you ready to climb the mountain?

JAN: I woke up before I climbed it.

RANDAL: Well, you completed a ceremony to prepare you to climb the mountain. Be Jan now. The hawk has flown through your body. Are you ready now to climb the mountain?

JAN: Uh huh.

RANDAL: So climb the mountain.

JAN: I'm not clear about why my friend may have been there.

RANDAL: The male friend or the female friend?

JAN: The male.

RANDAL: Okay, let's go with that. Become your male friend and describe yourself.

JAN: Actually I'm the male part that Jan is integrating. I'm part of who she is but she hasn't recognized me yet. I'm going to take her up on the mountain and do something beautiful.

RANDAL: Describe yourself physically.

JAN: I'm a little taller than she is and I have broader shoulders and longer legs, but we both enjoy hiking and climbing. We both really like walking on the earth and being outside. There's a lot of joy in just being outside. I have blue eyes and brown hair.

RANDAL: All right, put Jan in front of you now. What is your name? Do you have a name?

JAN: Part of Jan.

RANDAL: Okay, Mr. Part of Jan. Jan's in front of you. What would you like to say to her?

JAN: Get up off your duff and keep moving. Don't be such a slug. Go into right action.

RANDAL: Okay, switch. Do you want to stand or sit as you talk to this male part of you? (Jan has been standing)

JAN: It doesn't make any difference. (Jan moves to the other side)

RANDAL: Usually I have people in chairs but either way is fine. Do you feel more comfortable standing or sitting?

JAN: Standing.

RANDAL: All right, Jan, talk to your male part and respond to what he just said.

JAN: I'm aware of my tendency to be sluggish. Thanks for your support. I feel that knowing you and having you as a personalized part will help me to move more into right action.

RANDAL: Okay. Switch and be him again. (Jan walks to the other side) Anything else you want to say?

JAN: An acknowledgment of Jan and let's go up the mountain.

RANDAL: So that feels complete. Let's go up the mountain.

JAN: I feel myself getting on my hands and knees and climbing up. It doesn't feel like a struggle, it just feels like being part of the mountain. (Jan makes climbing motions) My body is the center of the mountain. It's a really steep uphill climb and I'm using a lot of strength from my body and legs. It takes really being aware of the energy of the mountain. Some ways up are easier than others. It's hard to do now without an incline, but I can see myself taking big steps and feeling the leg muscles pull. I also can see myself pulling myself up in different places and moving around parts where the rock may be jutting out more. There might be some tree pieces to hold onto and give me some help.

RANDAL: Keep getting into the experience and making those movements. Visualize yourself making that climb now. Vividly use your imagination.

JAN: (laughing) Okay, that's one way to get exercise too.

RANDAL: I know there's a step in front of you right now. (Randal puts a chair in front of Jan)

JAN: (Jan steps up) Okay, then can I step on your shoulders? (class laughs)

RANDAL: If you take your shoes off and you're careful!

JAN: I'm kidding. I can really feel my muscles acting in harmony to bring about the movement.

RANDAL: (Randal stands to the side of the chair, his back toward Jan. He bends his knees and braces himself, putting his right hand behind him for Jan to step onto.) Okay, take another step up. I'll hold the chair for you. (Randal holds the back of the chair with his left hand)

JAN: Well, there's no place to go except here. (Jan steps onto Randal's hand and puts her hands on his shoulders)

RANDAL: See what it's like to go up this far. (Jan pushes herself higher.)

JAN: Okay. (laughter from the group and someone suggests Jan climb onto Randal's shoulders)

JAN: Sit on his shoulders? No, that's okay. I weigh 150 pounds!

RANDAL: Okay, anyone else want to help? (two persons quickly come forward) Michael, all right. And Marleen. (Michael and Marleen stand against Randal on either side, and Jan begins to use them to climb higher) I'm fine. Are you fine Marleen?

MARLEEN: Yes, I'm fine. (lots of laughter from group)

RANDAL: Stay with it, getting closer to the top. Okay, now let's settle down. (they help Jan to stand back on the chair) There we go. Stay with the feeling that you're climbing up the mountain. Make it real for you. Are you still climbing?

JAN: Getting close. I'm about eight feet away.

RANDAL: Do you want to step down now? (Randal helps Jan down onto the floor) Make any more movements you want to make as you climb up to the top of the mountain. You're almost there. (pause) Are you still climbing the mountain?

JAN: No, I stopped to get a little breath. (pause) I'm coming up around the lip on top... Okay.

RANDAL: (pause) Are you now at the top?

JAN: Yes.

RANDAL: How does it feel?

JAN: It feels like being part of the mountain.

RANDAL: How does it feel to be a part of the mountain?

JAN: It feels good. I like it. Everything is part of the same thing. There isn't any separation at all.

RANDAL: Look around you. What do you see?

JAN: Beauty. A lot of sky all around. Some clouds. Some rock formations with different colors and textures in the rocks. And green on one side. Beautiful.

RANDAL: Great. And you are that beautiful everything.

JAN: Part of it.

RANDAL: Yes, and it's part of you. Keep your eyes closed and I'll help you sit down. Focus on your breathing, breathing slowly and deeply. Feel yourself going deeper with every easy breath that you take. I'm going to put my hand on your forehead to help your head to stay in place while I massage the back of your neck. (Randal puts one hand on the top of Jan's head and the other behind her neck) Just feel yourself going deeper. Now I'm going to very gently rotate your head as I continue to rub the back of your neck. (Randal rotates Jan's head slightly in little circles) With each revolution you're going deeper and deeper in relaxation, just turning loose and let- ting go. When I take my hands away now you feel yourself go deeper. (Jan's head slumps slightly forward) That's fine.

Take a deep breath now. Fill up your lungs. As you exhale send a wave of relaxation down your body as I push down on your shoulders. As I rub your shoulders feel yourself going deeper. Way down deeper. Breathe in the life force. Breathe in the prana. As you exhale let out any tensions and go much deeper. Feel yourself sink into the mountain, becoming that mountain and everything around it. Becoming one with the beautiful surroundings. Stay with that feeling of standing on top of the mountain even as a part of you feels that you are the mountain. You're standing on the mountain and you are the mountain. And you are the beautiful world that you see - those wonderful rocks jutting out in different directions and the beautiful trees and plants. You have climbed the mountain and you are on the mountain.

There is a shift that is happening in your life, Jan, that is becoming a natural part of you. You've made it to the top of the mountain and the rest is playing and enjoying and exploring. There are challenges but there is lightness and completion and satisfaction in many different kinds of experiences that you have in your life. You are coming from a place of being on the mountain and enjoying all the things that life has to offer. And being here, experiencing being in your body and feeling your feelings. Sometimes you can feel sadness, sometimes anger, sometimes joy. Sometimes you can feel sexual feelings and sometimes playful feelings. There are many kinds of feelings that you can feel.

These are all examples of parts of you, and you embrace the many parts. You embrace that wonderful little creature that takes away that former substance that is fading out and gone. It's no longer a part of you. You have let go of it. Your lungs are becoming cleaner, clearer, and healthier. You are healthy and strong and getting healthier and stronger every day. And you are the hawk, flying and soaring.

An interesting experience that you're now discovering and rediscovering in your life, is that climbing mountains can be and is an opportunity. You enjoy having more mountains to climb, more challenges that are opportunities for further discovery of yourself. It's as if you are growing into yourself, becoming more yourself.

And I would like to add homeplay, rather than homework. Homeplay to get in the habit of nurturing yourself and appreciating your many fine qualities. Being your own best friend, very loving and accepting of yourself. You deserve it. Does anybody have any appreciation for Jan?

CLASS MEMBER: Jan, I want to tell you that you moved like a dancer, with such power and grace. You're beautiful.

CLASS MEMBER: I see you as so solid and centered, so directed and joyful.

CLASS MEMBER: I see you free like the hawk, able to fly and soar and transcend.

CLASS MEMBER: I see you as a very courageous and able person, and feel you'll be very successful in your life.

CLASS MEMBER: I see you as an artist, really connecting with inspiration and bringing it to the physical plane.

CLASS MEMBER: I thought you were a shy person, and here you did such a marvelous demonstration. You can overcome anything.

CLASS MEMBER: I see you as able to quit smoking.

RANDAL: In fact she's already accomplished that.

CLASS MEMBER: I see you as playful, someone women will want to emulate. I see you as strong, courageous, persistent and alive.

RANDAL: Thank you all. (to Jan) I'm going to count from one to five as you gradually come back. When I reach the count of five you are then fully alert, awake, aware, reborn. Be aware of your hands and of how you are being reborn into a very loving world. A world in which there is a lot of approval and appreciation for the wonderful person that you are. It comes from within and it comes from without. (Randal counts, giving suggestions between numbers) Coming back now. Fully alert. That's good. (after a short pause Jan opens her eyes) How are you doing? Beautiful job.

JAN: Thank you all very much.

RANDAL: You've just had a powerful experience and I want you to stay with it. Take some time during the break and later tonight to just be quiet within yourself, okay?

JAN: Okay. (Randal and Jan hug)

Chapter 21

Barbara's Dream:

Thousands of Butterflies in the Living Room

BARBARA: (telling her dream) I'm walking up the back stairs of my grandmother's house and the stairs all have a fresh new coat of white paint. The railing, the stairs and even the porch floor are all very white. The back door is open. In fact there is no door on the doorway. I'm walking into the kitchen and everything is painted white or has a white finish to it. There are two young girls, both with long hair, who are cleaning. They seem to be hired to clean the kitchen thoroughly, to make the cupboards, the floor, the baseboards, everything spotless. Standing by the sink is my former husband. He's washing something and his back is to me when I walk in.

The two girls see me and say, "Oh, we're so glad you're finally here. We've been waiting for you." I'm kind of surprised because I don't get that kind of greeting very often and I'm pleased that they are so happy to see me. Then they say, "We've been waiting for you because we found an old spray of wild flowers when we were cleaning the cupboards. We didn't know what kind they were but we knew you would know." And I say to them, "Oh yes, I know the names of all the wild flowers. It's a passion that I have." So one of the girls reaches into the cupboard and takes down a bunch of wild flowers of different kinds and colors. She holds it above my head and I'm looking up, pointing to the different flowers and saying, "This is Larkspur and that's Prairie Cone." And as I'm looking up at the Prairie Cone I notice that underneath the petal there is a cocoon.

The moment I see it I become very excited and I turn to the girls and say, "Do you see a cocoon?" They nod but they don't seem very excited about it.

The cocoon starts to become liquid and drops begin to fall. It begins to turn back and forth as it dries. No one is paying any attention. Somehow it seems I've become that cocoon and I begin feeling myself turning back and forth and when I'm all dry I'm all closed up. It's really difficult to move and stretch but I force myself to stretch and I make my wings come out and it hurts. When I have myself completely stretched out I come off that flower and I begin flying around the kitchen. I'm calling, "Look at me! Look at me! I'm a butterfly!" And no one really notices. I fly above my husband's head and toward another doorway. It looks like a living room only it's empty and it's pure white. There are thousands and thousands of butterflies in all different sizes and shapes and colors. They're moving as if they're in a sea of water and there's a huge white butterfly right in the middle. I say to Nathan, "Look! Look at all these butterflies!" And he kind of glances in there and goes back to his sink.

I continue to fly around the kitchen a few times and no one really cares so I fly out the doorway and down the back porch to the yard. I circle around the back yard and see the garden. My grandfather is planting something. He can't see me. I fly down the alley and up to my high school boyfriend's window. It was down the street from my grandmother's. I see him inside and he's sitting at his desk studying... (pause) butterflies. He looks at me and I flutter my wings and fly above the roof of the house. I know that I am a very large blue butterfly. That's all I remember.

RANDAL: How does it feel to be a large blue butterfly? Stand up and get into whatever position you would like. You can move if you want.

BARBARA: (beginning to move around gracefully, her arms fluttering like wings) I have really large wings and it's a soft, fluttery feeling. I'm doing a delicate kind of dance. I feel like a flying flower.

RANDAL: That's beautiful. How does that feel emotionally?

BARBARA: Free.

RANDAL: Do that some more. Just fly and feel yourself fluttering around. (Barbara giggles) Fluttering around the yard and garden, fluttering up above the windowsill.

BARBARA: Little flutters here and there.

RANDAL: That's good. How are you doing?

BARBARA: I don't feel very balanced. And my legs feel really little.

RANDAL: Okay, have a seat here. Butterflies usually don't have to deal with high heels.

BARBARA: (laughing) I felt like I didn't know where the ground was.

RANDAL: Stay with that feeling of freedom and joy, of being so light and beautiful. You can move or not, but vividly become this flying flower. (pause) You can just stay with the feeling or say anything else you would like.

BARBARA: It's a really nice feeling. Nothing holding me back.

RANDAL: Keep feeling that. There's plenty of time here. You've just been born.

BARBARA: That's what it feels like.

RANDAL: You've just come out of a cocoon. What an incredible feeling to be flying for the first time.

BARBARA: I always wanted to fly.

RANDAL: And now you're flying.

BARBARA: It doesn't matter if those people care. They don't understand anyway.

RANDAL: Uh huh. You were concerned earlier but it seems that you've taken a step here. Earlier you wanted them to see and they apparently weren't interested. Now that doesn't seem to be so important.

BARBARA: No, because I can go anywhere now. And there are all those other beautiful butterflies.

RANDAL: Feel that freedom. Say that again, "I can go anywhere."

BARBARA: I can go anywhere and I can land here or there. I can make my own choices about where I go. I can pick the nicest and the sweetest and the loveliest places to land.

RANDAL: So what do you want to do right now? Do you want to land or continue flying?

BARBARA: I think I'd like to land.

RANDAL: All right, so you're this big, beautiful blue butterfly.

BARBARA: Swallowtail. (laughing) I don't think there's anything else like it.

RANDAL: Say "I don't think there's anything else like me."

BARBARA: I don't think there's anything else like me.

RANDAL: How does that feel to be so special?

BARBARA: It feels like nothing I've ever felt before. It makes me feel like laughing inside.

RANDAL: Well, laugh inside. (Barbara laughs) What a wonderful discovery to feel a joy that you've never felt before.

BARBARA: Yeah. Mmm. And I really loved my grandma. I'm glad it was there.

RANDAL: Well, let's make this present tense just as you've been doing all along. Say "I love my grandma." In this reality that you're experiencing is you're grandma alive?

BARBARA: Yeah. Oh, no.

RANDAL: No?

BARBARA: (sadly) No.

RANDAL: You saw your grandfather, though. Is your grandfather alive?

BARBARA: Yeah. She left. She isn't there.

RANDAL: You said it was your grandmother's house, the house that she lived in when she was alive. Your grandfather still lives there, is that right?

BARBARA: Not any more.

RANDAL: Well, I'm talking about in the reality of the dream now.

BARBARA: Yes, he's in the garden.

RANDAL: All right. I'd like you to now be your ex–husband who has been at the sink cleaning something. Describe yourself.

BARBARA: I've got my back turned to everyone. I'm focused only on what I'm doing and I don't notice anything else around me. I don't want anybody to bother me.

RANDAL: All right.

BARBARA: And I'm really large. I'm tall but I'm trying to shrink away.

RANDAL: How does it feel to be this large, tall person trying to shrink away and turning your back to everyone?

BARBARA: I feel like everybody notices me but I don't want them to because they say things I don't like to me. They're very critical.

RANDAL: Who are those people who are saying critical things to you?

BARBARA: The whole world.

RANDAL: So you're turning your back to the world?

BARBARA: Yeah.

RANDAL: If you could say anything you want to the world right now what would you say?

BARBARA: I would say... (pause and then tearfully) I don't deserve that.

RANDAL: Good. Tell them what it is you don't deserve.

BARBARA: I don't deserve for you to be so hard on me and to make life so difficult.

RANDAL: In this case I don't want you to switch chairs. I'm just going to tap you on the shoulder and when I do I'd like you to switch and be the world and respond to what he just said. What is your name?

BARBARA: Nathan.

RANDAL: Okay, be the world. What do you have to say to Nathan?

BARBARA: This is a tough place. (Barbara's voice has taken on a tough edge) You're pretty weak. You can't take the reality. You expect this world to be a bowl of cherries and it's not. It's meant to be difficult because you've got stuff to learn and I'm your teacher.

RANDAL: Now switch and be Nathan. What do you want to say in response to that?

BARBARA: (softer) I know there has to be some good things about this world and I would like to know about those places and those experiences, too. I know about the harshness.

RANDAL: Take a look out the kitchen door to where you can see those thousands of butterflies. How does that feel?

BARBARA: It feels really good. It feels like they're like me. There are things in the world that are beautiful, I just don't know about it. I've not experienced it. There are people who are free. I've just not looked. I've only looked in one direction. I've kept my eyes closed and missed some beautiful things that are there because I didn't want to hurt.

RANDAL: That's what you've been doing, but now you're starting to recognize and see and experience some of these beautiful
things. Look at those butterflies.

BARBARA: Uh huh.

RANDAL: How does it feel now to study those thousands of
butterflies flying all over the place?

BARBARA: (giggling) It feels really...it's beautiful.

RANDAL: Well, you're waking up.

BARBARA: I feel like I want to join them.

RANDAL: Can you join them?

BARBARA: Yeah.

RANDAL: Good. How are you going to join them now?

BARBARA: Well, because I'm a butterfly they'll know. They'll
just let me in. Kind of like driving on the freeway, they just let you
in. I just signal "I'm coming!"

RANDAL: Okay, do it.

BARBARA: One just holds back. We're all swimming in the same
direction. Swimming...it feels like we're swimming now.

RANDAL: Good. You described it before as a sea of butterflies,
like a wave.

BARBARA: Yeah! A wave of butterflies.

RANDAL: Good. You are becoming a butterfly yourself then?

BARBARA: I am one. I just didn't know it.

RANDAL: Ah! Quite a magical world we have here.

BARBARA: It was inside all the time.

RANDAL: So you're being born again also.

BARBARA: It was hard but I did it.

RANDAL: It was hard for Barbara at first, too.

BARBARA: I'd been hiding in the cupboard behind those flowers.

RANDAL: And now what are you doing?

BARBARA: Now I'm flying.

RANDAL: Maybe since you've been hiding so long, that makes
the flight all the more enjoyable.

BARBARA: Yeah, I can fly really high.

RANDAL: What color are you?

BARBARA: Blue...and I have some black and some yellow.

RANDAL: That sounds beautiful.

BARBARA: Yeah. I'm pretty big. I can go really high.

RANDAL: Would you like to take off your shoes and stand up?

BARBARA: Sure.

RANDAL: I'll stand here and help to support you. Get that feeling of really being up there and flying for the first time. That's good. Like flying and swimming at the same time. (Barbara giggles) It looks like you're doing both.

BARBARA: It feels like it. The air is really cool.

RANDAL: What do you feel in your body right now?

BARBARA: Really light. Kind of like the energy...it's tingling.

RANDAL: Where do you feel the tingling?

BARBARA: In my wings.

RANDAL: That's great. Feel that tingling in your wings. Your wings are spreading for the first time. You never knew you were a butterfly.

BARBARA: No. I can feel my whole body.

RANDAL: That's good, feel your body loosening up. Feel that gracefulness and expansion.

BARBARA: It feels like I'm expanding.

RANDAL: Yes, keep expanding.

BARBARA: It's different from up here.

RANDAL: How is it different?

BARBARA: It's an aerial view.

RANDAL: How does it feel to see this aerial view?

BARBARA: Well, everything looks so much smaller.

RANDAL: When you're way up here things way down there can seem a lot smaller.

BARBARA: Uh huh. I can see a lot more choices of places to go.

RANDAL: Would you like to go somewhere?

BARBARA: Uh huh!

RANDAL: Where do you want to go?

BARBARA: Right down there in that garden.

RANDAL: Go to that garden. See how easy it is?

BARBARA: Yeah.

RANDAL: You don't need to wait at stoplights or anything. No lanes.

BARBARA: No, (giggling) just dive right on down to that pink flower right there.

RANDAL: Wonderful. So go ahead and land on that pink flower. You're very light so you can do that, can't you?

BARBARA: Yeah.

RANDAL: How does that feel to be on this beautiful pink flower.

BARBARA: Oh, it smells really good.

RANDAL: Boy, have you evolved. You've come such a long way in a few minutes.

BARBARA: It's really sunny.

RANDAL: The world is a whole different place. There are a lot of beautiful places out here that you didn't even know about.

BARBARA: Yes, it's really warm.

RANDAL: You can go anywhere you want to go or stay right here. You've got all that freedom now. You have wings to fly. (pause) What's happening now?

BARBARA: Oh, that nectar is so sweet.

RANDAL: Great.

BARBARA: The sun is warm.

RANDAL: Do you want to have a seat now? The seat is right behind you.

BARBARA: Okay.

RANDAL: (Randal helps her into the seat) Really relax. As I push down on your shoulders feel yourself go even deeper, but staying light even as I push down. As I let go you'll feel lighter than ever. Loose, limp, and relaxed. As I count from five down to one you go deeper still but the deeper you go the lighter you feel. Five, four, three, two, one. Again I push down on your shoulders. This time you go three times deeper. Take a nice, deep, gentle breath and on the exhale feel yourself go way down. And yet you are as light as a butterfly because you are a butterfly. Taste that nectar like you've never tasted it before. Look out there at those amazing colors in the world, in this garden. Each of these beautiful flowers is tasty and sweet and something that you can totally indulge in.

You can do whatever you want to do, go wherever you want to go. Spread your wings and fly. You continue to discover more every day. After all, you're only a few minutes into this metamorphosis. There are all kinds of wonderful things and experiences to discover. And thousands of butterflies that you can join. Join the sea and move with the sea. You deserve to have all of the wonderful things that life has to offer. There are so many more things for you to discover and you can do it at your own rate, taking your time. Smell and taste the flowers and experience the butterflies and yourself.

Life is about contact and withdrawal. At times you make contact and at other times you go into yourself, for example, to relax or think or sleep. Many times you can reach out and many times you can go inward. Only now, rather than withdrawing from the world, going inward is very nurturing. The world is something you want to often explore and experience. When you reach out with those wings you experience the wonderful world and you are drawn toward the positive.

You were standing by that sink and only seeing the negative and yet you found a way to break through that. You've come to a whole new world, the world of the butterflies, because you are a butterfly. You're spreading your wings for the first time. You've broken out of your cocoon. Your dream is filled with cocoons and butterflies and those that are not yet butterflies are becoming butterflies. All the more parts of yourself yet to be born, to transcend what you knew. You've just had a very brief time to really be a butterfly. What I can tell you is there is so much more. You're learning to enjoy each experience thoroughly.

There are legends about the Buddha doing everyday things but doing them with a certain awareness. Sitting with awareness, walking with awareness, taking a coat off with profound awareness. You're developing a profound and joyous awareness of this big, beautiful world and you have the rest of your life to explore.

If there is anything you'd like to say about your experience or your discoveries you can do that in a moment. I'll count from three to one, and at the count of one I'll tap you on the shoulder, and you'll be able to say anything you'd like to. Three, two, one. (Randal taps Barbara's shoulder)

BARBARA: I'm really grateful.

RANDAL: Really grateful that the world is so beautiful?

BARBARA: Yes, and that I feel free.

RANDAL: Stay with that feeling. Each moment is all we have in our continuous experience but what we have is so much. You were restricting yourself before but now you've got your wings. Feel that gratefulness that you're free, that you're liberated, that you're strong and healthy and vibrant and confidant.

As you explore life there are times when you'll land somewhere and decide you don't want to be there anymore. You want to be somewhere else. Go to that other place and be free. There are many ways to do that. For instance, you can stay in the same physical place but go to a different place of consciousness. Your subconscious mind understands what I'm talking about. There are many ways to explore new places inside and outside, and new ways to frame your experience to create the joy and the freedom of your wings. Feel the tremendous abundance that is life.

In the days ahead, Barbara, you're going to make a lot of discoveries. You'll discover beautiful things around you and beautiful parts within you that you weren't aware of before. So dance and fly and swim with each new day. I encourage you to physically dance and move yourself gracefully and joyously at least once a day for the next several weeks. Feel yourself flying. Make those movements with your arms and with your body. Spread those wings. Make this physical dance into a joyous habit. And meanwhile you are also doing mental, emotional and spiritual dances .

In a minute I'll count from one to five to help you become fully alert and open your eyes. In returning you're going to take all of this with you and so much more. You also have all of your life's experience so you find balance in your life. You find there is so much for you to be open to. You also know that there are good and appropriate ways for you to sometimes withdraw from the negative, but life is very positive most of the time. As you come back to your consciousness it's going to be a beautiful, colorful world and you are a butterfly. You can drink and taste the nectar and smell the flowers and enjoy the sights and sounds around you.

Here we go. (Randal counts, giving suggestions between numbers to become more and more alert) Open your eyes at your convenience. Stay with your inner experience as well. (after a pause Barbara opens her eyes)

BARBARA: Thank you.

RANDAL: You're welcome. Thank you.

BARBARA: (Barbara is laughing) Oh wow! (the audience laughs as Barbara looks out at them) Look at all these people. They're butterflies! Oh my gosh.

RANDAL: (to the class) Look at these beautiful blue eyes of the blue butterfly we have here.

BARBARA: Oh my goodness. I've never seen anything look like this before.

RANDAL: Uh huh. Now that you're a butterfly you'll be seeing a lot more like this too. Take this next thing in. Are you ready?

BARBARA: Uh huh.

RANDAL: Let's show Barbara our appreciation, okay? (Randal and the audience applaud)

BARBARA: Ohhh. Thank you very much.

RANDAL: Now stay with your experience, Barbara. Have some time to yourself during part of the break. You're very soft right now and very open.

RANDAL: (after a break) Some of you were asking me during break, "Was Barbara already in hypnosis or what happened when you did that deepening?" As many of you noticed, as soon as she started telling her dream she went inward with her experience and became very quiet.

BARBARA: As I was telling the dream it was becoming more and more real. It was becoming almost like I was really there and experiencing every single detail. I could feel myself walking up the steps. It was incredible.

RANDAL: That's the subconscious connection. You immediately entered a hypnotic state just by vividly recalling the dream. (to the class) It was a spontaneous induction. Interpretation can keep people in their heads, but as Perls said, "Lose your mind and come to your senses." In this case the hypnosis was particularly dramatic. Toward the end I did a few techniques to take her deeper and encourage her to go further inward. Then I gave her some post-hypnotic suggestions. There was so much joy and discovery going on that just feeding back what she was saying was effective use of suggestion. She was creating a beautiful game and I was going along with it. First I focused my suggestions on what she had been telling me, and then I elaborated and expanded certain ideas into a series of suggestions.

This was an involved, detailed dream that kept developing. Her becoming the butterfly was so profound for her, that we could have stopped there. It isn't necessary to go through a thorough process of becoming all of the characters. I next had Barbara become her ex–husband, the character who was in pain. It was delightful how he spontaneously found his own way to exactly the same kind of metamorphosis. There are various ways in which issues can get resolved, but that is for your client to discover creatively, mobilizing his or her own resources.

Q: Barbara described so much whiteness in the beginning of her dream. The white was all the old world stuff and her new world was full of colors. Now I'm starting to get it, but could you briefly say something about that and why you didn't do anything with the whiteness?

RANDAL: I also felt fascinated as she was walking up the steps that everything was really white. There is a distinctive difference between the white and the colors, but we want to avoid interpretation. The white isn't necessarily a negative or old world thing. It could be a very positive part of herself.

This was a dream that was full of evolution. The butterfly coming out of the cocoon is a classic metaphor. The last thing she remembered in the dream was a feeling of freedom as the butterfly. We could have gone to any number of parts of her dream, but it felt right to start with her becoming the butterfly, the central character of the dream. Then I was drawn to having her face the issue of the negativity of her ex-husband's character. It felt perfect to move from his dramatic transformation to anchoring her process with the hypnotic suggestions, and completing the process there.

Q: At one point after you did some deepening with Barbara you were talking and then you used a counting method before she spoke in response. Why did you count before she spoke?

RANDAL: When I've been talking for a period of time and the person has been passive, it can be distracting or confusing for the person to suddenly be told to speak, especially when in medium to deep hypnosis. I have found that it frequently works well to prepare a person to get ready to talk. As an alternative to counting down I could make an announcement such as, "When I touch you on the shoulder you'll easily be able to speak and tell me your feelings." The counting or announcement also gives more time for the subconscious mind to come up with something to say.

$\mathcal{B}$ ibliography

Here is a small sample of books that are relevant to Hypnotic Dreamwork.

Barnett, E. A., *Analytical Hypnotherapy*, Westwood Publishing, 1989. This well-researched book includes many transcripts of hypnotic regressions, with considerable use of Transactional Analysis and ideomotor methods.

Boyne, Gil, *Transforming Therapy*, Westwood Publishing, 1989. The first book to combine Gestalt and hypnotherapy, by the therapist who integrated these two fields. Emphasizes a powerful collection of hypnotic regression transcripts.

Brown, Lester R., Editor, *State of the World*, W.W. Norton and Company, 1997. Email:wwpub@worldwatch.org. The relevance of these extremely well-researched annual reports from Worldwatch Institute is addressed in the Afterword.

Canfield, Cheryl, *Peace Pilgrim's Wisdom*, Blue Dove Press/Ocean Tree Books, 1996. Deep spiritual insights from a visionary woman for contemplation by therapist and/or client. Good for developing trust in one's own subconscious wisdom and intuition.

Cheek, David B. and LeCron, Leslie M., *Clinical Hypnotherapy*, Harcourt Brace, 1968. This out-of-print classic introduces the subject of ideomotor methods and gives an excellent overview of hypnotherapy.

Cheek, David B., *Hypnosis: The Application of Ideomotor Techniques*, Paramount Publishing, 1994. An interesting many-faceted study of the field of hypnotherapy, including extensive utilization of ideomotor methods.

Churchill, Randal, *Regression Hypnotherapy*, scheduled publication date, Fall 1998. Regression strategies in hypnosis, with a strong emphasis on Gestalt and some in-depth explorations of ideomotor methods.

Cooper, L. F. and Erickson, M. H., *Time Distortion in Hypnosis*, Williams and Wilkins, 1954. After writing a paper on his discovery and including a chapter about it in LeCron's *Experimental Hypnosis*, Dr. Cooper co-authored this detailed book on the subject.

Downing, Jack, *Dreams and Nightmares*, Gestalt Journal Press Edition, 1997. This is the only book of Gestalt dreamwork transcriptions that includes inserted ongoing detailed commentary by the therapist.

Hawken, Paul, *The Ecology of Commerce*, Harper Collins Publishers, 1993. The relevance of Hawkin's momentous book is explained in the Afterword.

Hunter, Marlene E., *Creative Scripts for Hypnotherapy*, Bruner/Mazel,1994. A well organized collection of a wide variety of scripts for hypnotherapists. This handbook can also be effective for self-hypnosis.

Jacobs, Donald T., *Patient Communication for First Responders*, Prentice Hall, 1991. This is an excellent book for developing communication and suggestion skills during hypnosis, including the hypnotic states often resulting from emergencies.

Kroger, William S., *Clinical and Experimental Hypnosis*, J.B. Lippencott, 2nd edition, 1977. This major text covers an exceptionally wide range of material and makes a very effective reference book.

LaBerge, Stephen, *Lucid Dreaming*, Ballantine Books, 1985. A thorough exploration of the subject of lucid dreams.

Mutke, Peter H. C., *Selective Awareness*, Westwood Publishing, 1987. Emphasizes teaching the finger-signal form of ideomotor methods within self-hypnosis.

Perls, Frederick, *Gestalt Therapy Veratim*, Gestalt Journal Press Edition, 1992. Gestalt therapy's colorful primary founder helped put his work at Esalen on the map with this classic. Includes a superb theoretical overview of Gestalt and a large collection of dreamwork transcripts.

Tebbetts, Charles, *Self-Hypnosis and Other Mind-Expanding Techniques*, Westwood Publishing, 1987. A fine introduction to self-hypnosis. In addition, the rules outlined in this best-selling book for structuring auto-suggestions are very relevant for proper use of direct suggestion during hetero-hypnosis.

Afterword

We are living at the most important time in human history. As valuable as it is on a personal level to help empower individuals to make major improvements in their lives through hypnotherapy or any other means, we share an even greater need in the big picture to wake up out of our collective trance and address our intensifying environmental crisis. The effects of our current massive waste and environmental destruction will be felt by all future generations.

The Earth and its atmosphere have begun to make major changes. Momentous shifts have happened on other occasions in the history of our beautiful planet, but our current calamity has already caused a greater rate of species loss than there has been since the early Cenozoic period's extinction of the dinosaurs. This time is also unique in the Earth's 4.5 billion year history because it's being caused by humans. During our lifetimes planetary deterioration has undeniably reached global levels and is accelerating in many ways. While the destruction of our life-giving ozone layer by chlorofluorocarbons is now advancing at a slower pace, global warming is picking up again after being mitigated for a few years by the enormous eruption of Mount Pinatubo. Every living system on Earth is in decline, as Worldwatch Institute repeatedly documents.

We are in an age of remarkable technological advances. Effectiveness and cost improvements in electronics, computers, the internet and the information superhighway are revolutionary. But if we don't make necessary important changes now, the continuing deterioration of our environment will be profoundly costly in the years ahead. With growing overpopulation, hydrocarbon emissions, global warming, desertification, deforestation, soil depletion, ozone destruction, species extinction and so forth, we need to stop assuming that the exponentially-increasing ecological problems will be solved by advancing technology or science or military power or the current pollution-subsidizing so-called free market.

Our time of reckoning has come. Creating a sustainable planet isn't good enough, especially because of the destruction that has already occurred. We owe it to all future generations, and to ourselves, to go beyond just slowing or halting the destruction and begin to restore the Earth. Is it possible for us to turn things around and begin restoring rather than destroying our small planet? The answer is a resounding yes. And despite current jobs versus the environment rhetoric, the very doable solutions for ecological restoration will make the world a much healthier, safer, more prosperous, more secure and comfortable place for us and our children.

We can be the generation to turn around our accelerating pollution, overpopulation and planetary plunder and begin the restoration of Mother Earth. The alternative is to leave the overwhelming legacy of even greater toxic waste, resource depletion, overpopulation, rising oceans and perhaps out-of-control accelerating global warming to the next generation. Imagine over one and a half billion ambitious, hard-working people in a rapidly-industrializing twenty-first century China yearning for the same kind of cars and conveniences of industrialized societies. The ecological mathematics don't even begin to work out. The inevitable breakdowns of current trends will be unimaginably catastrophic in the decades ahead if intelligent shifts in global awareness and policies are not made now and in the years ahead.

This subject has everything to do with this book and, for that matter, any other book being written at this time. This is about the great opportunity of the difference in direction we can now begin to take that will affect all aspects of life. If we care about helping heal individuals, we must also care about making the necessary long overdue changes to allow for the possibility of a healthy, sustainable planet for innumerable generations to come. Inaction at this time will allow forces causing permanent destruction to continue accelerating toward increasingly unmanageable levels.

Thousands of very good ideas from many individuals and dedicated environmental organizations about helping save the environment will not do more than slow the acceleration of the degradation of our planet unless we address certain major issues in the big picture.

For example, the tax systems of governments need to be fundamentally restructured. A revenue-neutral tax shift needs to be established in which income taxes are nearly eliminated and value-added taxes of varying degrees are affixed to products that are environmentally destructive. This is not to punish those who make things which are damaging the environment, but rather to take into account those costs which have been externalized. The many billions of dollars being spent on the 1200 Superfund sites (which have been designated as the most urgent of the estimated 90,000 hazardous dump sites in the United States) does not come close to addressing all of the present and future damage of these sites. It is absurd to have non-consumers of the original toxin-producing products help bear much of the costs of things which had been originally made artificially competitive through the massive subsidy of later charging those costs to others.

Our current alleged "free markets" do not reflect the true cost of goods and services. What we have, in fact, is a socialized market, with the highest welfare subsidies being given to the most destructive producers. Gasoline and oil are cheap in the United States because many costs of the environmental tolls are not factored in. Solar and wind power, fuel efficient products and conservation measures become cheaper and more appropriately competitive when consumers have more money to spend on healthier products while damaging choices are placed in the vicinity of their true costs. Various forms of employment go up when labor is more cost-effective by comparison than environmentally damaging materials. For example, instead of aerial pesticide spraying it can become more reasonable to hire workers to trim brush along highways in rural areas when the environmental costs of spraying, including possible birth defects and other health hazards, are factored into the price.

Like many of us in these important times, I have recognized the relationship of the health of our planet and the health of its people. In 1987 I began having significant insights about major global solutions for a sustainable planet but no book I could find addressed some of the crucial and necessary perspectives. Then in the early nineties some of the books and papers by Lester Brown and others at Worldwatch Institute successfully focused on some of the apparently previously neglected solutions. Worldwatch for many years

has provided excellent leadership in finding comprehensive solutions to our global environmental crisis, including through their annual State of the World reports (see bibliography).

In 1993 Paul Hawken's *The Ecology of Commerce* was published. This is the revolutionary book that truly gives a practical blueprint for much of the restructuring, economic and otherwise, that is urgently required for sustainability and restoration. Extremely insightful, well-researched, comprehensive and eloquent, it is written from the perspective of saving the Earth by saving business and supporting business in helping to lead the way. I can't say enough for the ingenious ideas expressed therein. If the Earth and its people are flourishing in the late twenty-first century and beyond, *The Ecology of Commerce* will be widely recognized at that time as one of the great books in history that changed the world.